I'm
Wild
Again

Helen
Gurley
Brown

I'm
Wild
Again

SNIPPETS FROM MY LIFE

AND A FEW BRAZEN THOUGHTS

St. Martin's Press ⚎ New York

Library of Congress Cataloging-in-Publication Data

Brown, Helen Gurley.
    I'm wild again : snippets from my life and a few brazen thoughts / Helen Gurley Brown.
        p. cm.
    ISBN 0-312-25192-0
    1. Brown, Helen Gurley.   2. Periodical editors—United States—Biography.   I. Title.
    PN4874.B768 A3 2000
    070.4'1'092—dc21
    [B]   99-056096

Design by Pei Loi Koay

First Edition: February 2000

10   9   8   7   6   5   4   3   2   1

For ~

FRANK A. BENNACK, JR.,

the world's best boss,

and

DAVID BROWN,

the world's best husband

. . . .

Contents

Acknowledgments

MORE THAN A FEW PEOPLE helped get this book to the printer, me to the writing. Elizabeth Beier, my intrepid editor at St. Martin's Press, called even on weekends if I needed her. I *needed* her. Naomi Shulman, production editor, and Elisabeth Story, copyeditor extraordinaire, styled, punctuated, and spelled without trampling text . . . hallelujah! Art director Stephen Snider knocked himself senseless to create the jacket. I like it, do you? St. Martin's boss, Vice President and Publisher Sally Richardson, said years ago she'd like to publish my memoir someday, if there was one. There was, she did . . . blessings! My beloved assistant, Susan Schreibman, has been managing "horribles" every day of my life for years to free me for writing and other stuff . . . please don't say I'll *ever* have to do without her!

Most of my time at work these days is spent with International Executive Director Kim St. Clair Bodden who accommodates thirty-nine *Cosmopolitan*s all over the world, makes my days hum and sparkle. If I'd ever wanted a daughter, she'd be *it*. The Hearst executive who launches all those global *Cosmopolitan*s is Hearst International President George Green, another treasured friend and associate. Neptune someday, George? Can't not mention Richard E. Deems, the Hearst executive who bravely trusted me with *Cosmo* all those years ago when I'd never edited even a grocery list . . . thanks, brave Richard the Lionhearted! The Hearst family, one and all, has always stood by me though possibly sometimes in shock.

While naming names, let me just plop in Tony Bennett, Rosie Clooney, and Michael Feinstein, thrilling in concert but who also sang to me like angels Saturday and Sunday mornings for six years during my hour of exercise before tooting off to the typewriter to work on this book; Frank Military of Warner Chappell Music and my friend Guy Flatley supplied the special CDs and tapes of these gifted ones. Guy also compiled a tape of Stephen Sondheim show-knockouts which never fail to convince me you don't have to have been the bard living in sixteenth-century England to write dazzling, fiery, frisky, elegant words that touch the heart (and Stephen's *rhyme!*). Thankfully I mention Donna Karan, Calvin Klein, Rudi Gernreich, and Emilio Pucci, who made the beautiful little dresses, Miriam Ruzow the Gottex swimsuits that sheathed me and convinced me I was sexy, never mind reality. Thanks to Robert Dolce, who booked me two dozen or so times on the *Tonight Show*—didn't hurt my career.

I've talked endlessly about David Brown in this book, so nothing more needed here. There wouldn't *be* a book, or *Cosmo*, or almost *me*, without his brains and pushiness. I'm blessed with the best *boss* in the world, Frank A. Bennack, Jr., who appreciates me *still*. (They don't makes bosses like that . . . thank God they made *one!*) Executive V.P. and Chief Operating Officer Victor Ganzi brilliantly helps Frank. Cathleen Black is the gifted Hearst magazines president who now keeps *Cosmo* hot.

Gratitude—bushels—to the young, not so young, *every*-age-category-and-background females who wrote loving letters throughout the years to say I was their friend. I needed, wanted, treasured *all* of them.

Everybody has a life . . .

good, not so good, inspiring, depressing . . .

and if somebody likes to write as much as I do,

it's hard to keep her from writing about that

life. I haven't been kept from doing so . . .

no way! Hope you'll enjoy reading a fraction

as much as I enjoyed writing. What is

writer's block? Do you think I should send

out for some?

Snippets
from
My Life

Jobs and Men

I won't try to do an hour-by-hour, year-by-year account of my seventeen secretarial jobs or the two copywriting ones, the latter of which led to my writing *Sex and the Single Girl* because I thought I was going to be fired and David came up with the book idea. I'll also spare you a boyfriend recall although there *were* some of those since I started dating at seventeen and didn't marry until thirty-seven. I'll just mention a *few* boy/girl encounters, not necessarily the sweetest ones and, in writing about David in a minute, tell you how I got started as editor of *Cosmopolitan*. Along the boyfriend trail—let's call them male encounters—were these highlights (or lowlights).

Paid for Pleasure

At age nineteen I had one little fling in the escort business. In a magazine article—I think some fairly decent magazine—I read about girls who went out with men and got paid as "dates," not one word about anything beyond dinner, dancing, and just being a delightful companion . . . a regular *date* it would seem. With the article still in mind, I saw an ad in the *Los Angeles Times* for "attractive girls wanted for social evenings" placed by the Dolores Gunn Escort Service and decided this was definitely something to look into. Working at KHJ radio station as a secretary in the manager's office, $18.00 a week, I went over to see Dolores in her seedy mansion somewhere in the Wilshire district of Los Angeles between Vermont and Western Avenues. I didn't actually see Dolores . . . she was behind a screen. Do you think the screen might have tipped me to something like she didn't want to be identifiable in a police lineup? Might have, but didn't. Dolores saw *me* and I passed . . . how bad could you look at nineteen? My fee for the evening would be $5.00—nearly a third of my weekly salary—not bad.

Date picked me up in front of the apartment I shared with Merle and Rosa for a few months while Mary's and Mother's and my little house on West Fifty-ninth Street was getting ready to be moved into. Date was nothing-looking, possibly fifty; we drove around Los Angeles in his Plymouth sedan for a while, finally parked on a quiet street in Santa Monica, kissed some. Where was dinner? Where was dancing? Did I always suspect there wouldn't be any? Probably. I didn't mind the kissing that much, as I remember, though I could be blanking; he didn't get obstreperous or try anything awful.

Presently he asked, "Shall we double the fee—you get ten dollars, Dolores gets her ten dollars, and we go on to the next step?"

Again I wasn't that shocked. "No," I said. "I was just supposed to go on a *date*." Maybe the gods, realizing they were dealing with a low-grade criminal-class amateur, were too bored to unleash their full furies and get me raped, killed, or beaten up. If that had happened, Dolores would have lost her license or whatever escort services carry, of course. Perhaps she actually tried to screen clients as well as escorts and accommodate only noncrazy ones. The evening, as I recall, lasted about two hours . . . however long it takes to drive from downtown L.A. to the Pacific Ocean, stop for a little chat in Santa Monica, drive back again.

On the way home, he said, "Kid, don't mess around. If a man can get it free, he won't have much use for you . . . if you're getting all the milk you want, why buy the cow?" The cow/free milk proposition was popular in those days. Letting me out at my front door, Date gave me $5.00 and, I assume, took care of Dolores. Why wasn't I revolted? I was a little but not utterly. I think even then I was a practicing realist. I knew my date wasn't going to be Tyrone Power. Even at age nineteen and a virgin I realized men "needed things" and there wasn't anything horribly wrong about their needing them even if you couldn't or wouldn't supply. Also from a pretty early age I tried to do whatever you needed to do to survive. At that moment I needed more money. The escort business wasn't going to provide, but I was never a big rebel or complainer. I'd got myself into this silly assignation, was probably lucky to be alive!

Dolores called once more after that; she probably hadn't got a rave review and suggested on my next date I try to be a little more cooperative. We didn't do business after that. God bless that date. From him I learned I wasn't going to make any real money or solve any problems as an escort. I'd have to be good at something else.

Mary and Cleo

One Sunday afternoon in April 1937, playing out in the backyard of their Fifty-ninth Street home in Los Angeles with my cousins Bob and Virginia Gurley, we got the news that Mary had polio. Doctor had thought at first it was simple la grippe, but now a more accurate—and devastating—diagnosis was in. Life would change irrevocably for Mary, Mother, and me. Her legs paralyzed, Mary would spend the next sixty years in a wheelchair, me the same sixty trying to make up a bit with financial support and love for what had happened to her, her life challenge a *little* more major than mine. We had the same parents, I reasoned (Daddy had died five years before in an elevator accident in the Arkansas State Capitol Building, had run for the elevator, jumped on just as the doors were closing—you could do that then—life got snuffed out), were formed from the same gene pool, ate the same food, lived in the same apartment, slept in the same bedroom, breathed the same air, were accessible to the same floating germs out in the street. Polio picked Mary, not me . . . I owed her. I never wished it had *been* me, martyrdom not my thing, but I would never abandon her.

Mary was immediately put in the Orthopedic Hospital, which specialized in polio, Mother and I moved to a little bungalow on South Hope Street across from the hospital. During the many months Mary was in the Orthopedic she had pool treatments, massage therapy, was seen by the best polio doctors in the world, Doctors Brockway and Lohman. Muscle transplants—paralyzed muscles replaced with healthy ones—were performed twice but nothing could reverse the damage, she would remain paralyzed from the waist down all her life. For the next two years I attended John H. Francis Polytechnic High School a few blocks from the hospital where, would you believe, white students mingled with black . . . shocking! One year out of Little Rock, where a black man looking directly in the eyes of a white woman on the street could land in jail, where occasional lynchings still took place on Saturday night, I could have had a problem but prejudice of any kind had never been on the menu in my house and the dusky ones and I, after they got used to how funny I sounded, got along fine. Black boys were fabulous dancers, and the Amazonian black girls, towering over me on the basketball court, actually forgave my getting a ball—finally—into the hoop, but the hoop belonged to the other team. John H. Francis got the best out of me and vice versa.

Mother's time and anxiousness (she knew how to do anxious better than anyone I've ever known) were pretty much channeled into care of her older daughter, now home from the hospital, but I wasn't neglected. Acne was the major problem of her younger child. At that time the medical profession didn't know any more about acne than they did about polio, and mine was virulent. Every Tuesday and Friday after school I saw Dr. Todd, who opened postules and sent me out to face the world with a face that looked as though it had been smeared with strawberry jam. So, what does a sixteen-year-old with an invalid sister, depressed Mommy, terminal acne, and the financial pinchies do to cheer herself up—drugs? drink? temper fits? total withdrawal? Drugs and drink weren't available for teens in those days and wouldn't have appealed anyway; the other two options didn't either. And so a lifelong habit got started: do the best you can with whatever you've got even if most of what you've got isn't remarkable and some of it you wouldn't give a tarantula. My grades were good. Mother and Daddy were smart so I guess I inherited those genes. Acne was the challenge. Shy like my mother—some of my classmates called me "the Bashful Babe"—I willed myself to become more outgoing, even extroverted, divert attention from the skin that was either forming postules or scabbing up from excision. I wrote little skits for myself and performed them before the whole student body in numerous variety shows (show biz!), tried out for the class play but wasn't an actress so that route of expression denied me. Several times I ran for school office and was actually elected: president of the Scholarship Society, president of the Amacitians (girls' club), president of the World Friendship Society. I didn't know Belgrade from marmalade, Outer Mongolia from Mentholatum, but if the club needed leading I was happy to try. At graduation I was one of five honor students—an Ephebian, for God's sake!—photographed for the school paper, made a big fuss over and, of course, I was class valedictorian. Particularly popular with teachers, I was voted biggest apple-polisher in the senior class but also second most popular girl . . . I guess you could be both.

On the dating scene I wasn't a belle but also wasn't a blip. As I wrote in *Sex and the Single Girl*, I felt and feel a girl needs men in her life. My theory from high school on was that until you can collect a prince, you create a court from who's *there*, no matter how disparate the courtiers. My two steadiest beaux, Joey and Lester, I would now say were homosexual but, at the time the "condition" didn't exist and surely wasn't talked about. We danced, picnicked, baked at the beach, drove tons of miles around Bel Air and West Los Angeles on Saturday nights in Joey's father's big old Chrysler, occasionally picked a flowering branch from the grounds of a Bel Air mansion . . . wicked!

The day of the senior prom at Poly High, president of the student body, Hal Holker, didn't have a date, had been just too busy to get on the case and called me that afternoon. It wasn't, he explained later, because he considered me a wallflower and probably not booked but, on the chance I wasn't, thought I'd be perfect. "Gurley could take care of herself . . . good dancer . . . lots of friends . . . wouldn't have to worry about her while doing stuff you have to do as a prom chairman." Dateless, I accepted the offer and we had such a good time he took me out graduation night a week later. Then, if you'll pardon a little bragging (you can check with him if you like), the Number One Man on Campus fell in love with me—acne *had* subsided a bit by them. Some of the best smooching of my life was during those sweet summer months. Still years away from surrendering virginity, I wouldn't take anything for the sexy hours when you struggled your brains out with boy or man, passionate, steamy struggling . . . foreplay that didn't actually lead to *play*. A Little Rock brought-up-girl didn't go All the Way *ever*. Since I could be brought to orgasm by kissing why ask for anything more, and whoever he was put up with it. What the poor creature did when he got home was his affair.

After high school—my prom king was off to Alaska to look for gold—I attended Woodbury Business College to learn how to type and take shorthand, tuition paid by working after school at radio station KHJ for an announcer whose early-morning radio show, *Rose and Shine*, observed birthdays and anniversaries of letter writers. My job was to extrapolate requests from letters so my boss could announce, "If little Willie will go out to the garage and look behind the tool chest, he'll find just what he's been looking for" or "Minnie and Sam Spiegelgrass are celebrating a twenty-third wedding anniversary . . . congratulations, Minnie and Sam." Occasionally I had a twelve-year old boy or girl celebrating their seventeenth year of togetherness . . . mixed extrapolation; rough morning at school before coming to the station must have made me not squeaky careful. Some afternoons when I got to KHJ, somebody there in the morning would report Mr. Wilson having gone mangoes, shrieking to be heard all the way to Cahuenga Avenue that his idiot secretary had screwed up again, distressed parents having called to say Becky Sue couldn't find her birthday doll in the attic because he'd announced it hidden in the basement next to the bicycle rack. For my chores I was paid $6.00 a week, lavishly raised to $7.00 in a few months.

From KHJ I moved on to posh Music Corporation of America in Beverly Hills, continued my thirteen-year odyssey through fifteen more secretarial jobs, sometimes getting fired, sometimes firing myself to try to advance in the world. Finally I was given a chance to write advertising copy but, hey, this is Mary's and Mother's story so let's get back to them.

During my high school years when we lived in the little house near the Orthopedic Hospital, Mary and I were close companions, went shopping, to the movies, sometimes just strolled around. I was proud of getting her wheelchair up and down curbs without bumping. Our next-door neighbor, also a wheelchair-bound polio victim, and her construction worker husband, had somehow got beyond the depression and sads that go with invalidism and were an enormous support to my overwhelmed mother, particularly because they were cheerful. Sue and A. frisked Mary all over town, sometimes took her to the ranch of a family member in Simi Valley where she actually picked oranges.

After my graduation from high school, Cleo, Mary, and I moved to the little house by the railroad tracks on West Fifty-ninth Street where freight trains roared by just beyond the backyard and gophers tunneled up under Mary's and my bedroom, actually pushing floor boards up, the little bastards! We once put a hose down a gopher hole, let it run several hours—talk about big spenders on *our* budget—actually flushed up a gopher! Poor drowned little thing, we didn't try to revive him. Maybe there's a secret cruel streak in all of us but this gopher was eating our carnations and trying to sleep in our bedroom. Mother got a job in the marking room at Sears Roebuck pinning little tickets on merchandise; her marking-room friends were really the only ones she had in Los Angeles. Shy to the point of verbal paralysis, with not one smidge of outer confidence or inner self-esteem, she poured herself into Mary and me and, oh yes, a husband—I should have mentioned him earlier.

After Mary became ill, while I was in high school, Cleo married the sweetheart of her girlhood and he lived with us. She hadn't married gentle, bookish, poetic, much-like-her Leigh in the first place because her family preferred Ira Gurley, dynamic law school graduate, full of charm, hunted and fished with her brothers, sure to Amount to Something and be a family asset. They put the pressure on and she married Ira. From what I glean—I was only ten when Daddy died—he loved my mother but didn't understand her, made her give up her teaching job—which had meant everything to her and they needed the money. In those days, if your wife worked, the neighbors thought you were a lousy provider, Zeus forbid!

So now there was Leigh in our lives, a nice-enough person, good cook (men didn't cook in those days and I hated the food smells that wafted to the living room when a date picked me up), but I found him embarrassing and ineffectual. The only job he ever held was Good Humor salesman; his cart with its icy treasures sat outside our front door every night. Stepfather for five years, Leigh died slowly, agonizingly of stomach cancer. Those visits to him in the Los Angeles county hospital with Cleo were as pain filled as anything you would ever want to know. She loved him, she deserved a little happiness. One would have hoped her childhood was friskier but, as oldest child, she was often nursemaid for the younger eight, heaped with responsibility early, screw having fun. So here she was, widowed again, older daughter an invalid, younger still smeared with strawberry-jam acne, occasionally worried that she was neglecting her younger (not true) for the older.

Cleo also worried about my love affairs that never led to marriage; I worried about a couple of those myself (more in a minute). Mary got a job with C. E. Hooper, the ratings system of the day, telephoning to see what radio program people were listening to. For forty cents an hour she sludged her way through hundreds of numbers copied from the telephone book, put up with hang-ups, no-comprendes, and couldn't-remembers, conscientiously recording data. Sometimes I helped her call for a little while. Socially we branched out to the opera, theater, race track. My beaux were nice to her—one brought her Danny Kaye records—though we could have taken her on outings a little more often. While my sister didn't ever cry or complain *ever*, God knows what demons occupied her. In 1946, when I was twenty-four years old, my mother took Mary from Los Angeles back to live with her folks in Osage, Arkansas. She thought she and Mary would have a better life there among loved ones, or so she said. She really did it because she saw me being a semi-nurse-companion to my sister, too deeply involved in Mary's life (and problems) perhaps to have a life of my own. Cleo's separating me from them was a courageous, unselfish act . . . she could easily have sacrificed me to be a handy, unpaid bound-by-blood helper forever.

At first Mother and Mary lived in Osage, Arkansas—population seventy-five—where several of Mother's brothers and sisters still resided. The year I made my Arrangement with a wealthy New York banker who built a movie studio in California (more later), I brought them back to Los Angeles for a few months, inexpensive rent on an apartment having been arranged for after the banker decamped. They didn't feel comfortable in L.A. and Mother, still wanting to keep me from getting too embroiled in caring for an invalid sister, took herself and Mary back to Osage again.

A few years after that Mary entered a veterans' rehabilitation center in Okmulgee, Oklahoma. They were doing good things for veterans from World War II and Korea but Mary, with legs totally paralyzed, didn't have strength enough to learn to walk again with crutches and braces. She did meet and marry another patient, George Alford, moved to Shawnee, Oklahoma, with him and they lived there for twenty-three years; George died a few years ago. As long as he lived, I was involved with his pain from the grain elevator accident which had left him with crossed nerves not properly straightened out at the time. I schlepped him many places trying to find doctors or treatments that would help. George belonged to my sister, was usually good and helpful with her, so he went with the territory for me.

Mother, who'd lived with a sister in Osage for several years, moved to Mary's house in Shawnee while George was still alive. For forty years, wherever they lived, I visited them twice a year, phoned twice a week, one-hour phone visits on Sunday, shorter ones on Wednesday.

Mary joined A.A. Not hard to understand her need to somehow

get away from the pain, but when drinking didn't get her away from it but brought new grief, she became—after a few lapses—a devout A.A. member, her number listed in the phone book to call if you wanted to investigate A.A. or right that minute were having a dragout time with somebody drunk who needed help.

During my visits to Mary in the fifties, sixties, and seventies, we roamed around town a little. I went to A.A. meetings with her and to the Wesley United Methodist Church, learned new respect for what religious people do to help each other . . . her church friends were terrific. Mary and some other tenderhearted ones founded Soft-paws to help unwanted kitties get adopted—*she* couldn't adopt them *all*—and spayed and neutered. On visits to Shawnee one had to tolerate her own live-in kitty cats—from six to eight depending on how many strays had been recently rescued—nice mixed-breed little kitties except for the two Siamese who worked their glamorous selves into her life, plus two doggies of unprepossessing heritage, stature, and color. I never took much to them. Too emotionally needy, they would sniff at me mercilessly when I was trying sleep on the couch, moan when I ate though they'd just been fed. The kitty/canine crew together didn't make for nice smells despite uncounted cans of room deodorants deployed in winter, doors and windows all open in summer—screw air-conditioning—and I was all for that.

After George died and Mother's arterial sclerosis got progressively worse, a live-in housekeeper joined the household and I began staying at the Holiday Inn at night when I visited accommodated by the Inn's couldn't-do-enough-to-be-wonderful owner, Bobbie Reed. Mary, Mother, and the cats didn't need me after midnight and I would return early next morning after a chug around the hotel pool—an Olympic-size beauty, warm and toasty even in December, with few other swimmers competing for space, except I did tangle with a local high school basketball team one Thanksgiving who were trying to knock each other off each other's shoulders in what could only be considered blood sport and I was a nuisance to them relentlessly lapping away on my side of the pool.

In the last years of her life Mary got pneumonia once a year—polio zaps your lungs—and would be plopped into either the Shawnee Regional or Mission Hill Hospital; I would go see her there. She had good doctors with whom I kept in close touch and they did the best they could for her always, knowing she would be back again in a little while because a mere cold would fill her lungs with fluid; I never felt a squidge of neglect of her in either hospital. In later years when Mary was home but mostly bed ridden, I would sit in a chair by her bed for hours and we would deep-dish soul visit, talking about our mother and father, childhood and childhood friends in Little Rock.

Mary liked me to go through all her catalogs to pick birthday and Christmas presents for myself; I could have exactly what worked and she never ever wanted giving to be unilateral. We listened to music; she had enough tapes and CDs to stock a radio station and a great sound system. John Michael Montgomery and the Gatlin Brothers were favorites, and we watched the Westminster Dog Show, which she would have taped for me. Teresa brought lunch and dinner on a tray . . . tamale pie, stuffed peppers, baked apples . . . yummy! I loved sending or bringing Mary things, and whatever company I worked for had to put up with serious mail room transgressions, particularly the last one where I was an editor and the cosmetic loot came pouring in. I liked better to be there in person to watch the opening, Mary sniffing and trying moisturizers, blushers, foundation, fragrance, mascara, lipstick, candles, signature scarves, airplane cosmetic and shaving kit take-aways. The girl was never jealous. She cared deeply about whether I was happy, never hit me for money, cars, jewelry—except occasionally costume. She was amazing! I don't miss the sixty years of worry and anxiety about her, but I miss *her*. She was a pussycat.

The Year of Being Kept (but Not Very Well)

I was a flop in the escort business. Five years later I was even floppier at being kept. If I'd been good at keptiveness, of course, you and I probably wouldn't be visiting. I would perhaps be a rich Beverly Hills matron living on South Camden or Roxbury Drive and, if you were also a Beverly Hills girl, we might run into each other having our hair done at Privé or lunching at Spago but we wouldn't be visiting as we are now.

He was forty-three, I twenty-four. I thought he was a hundred because he was mostly bald (although the morning we met he wore his hat and I couldn't see his scalp). He limped, but the limp, the baldness, the oldness weren't the problem with our soon-to-begin relationship—I was the problem. Among other failings, I just couldn't tell who was Jewish—an absolute necessity if you were to link up with the card-carrying, unreconstructed anti-Semite—but there were other problems. May I unfold our story? You're always so indulgent!

On a beautiful frosty February morning I went to the Motion Picture Center Studios at 1041 North Formosa in Hollywood to be interviewed for what would be my fifteenth secretarial job. The studio's owner-builder, soon-to-be my lover, showed me around the lot which, in a few years, would be sold to Lucille Ball and Desi Arnaz for Desilu Productions and is now the Warner Hollywood Studio. At that time the facility was spanking new, looked and smelled fresh and friendly. Fragrant wood curls swirled around our ankles as I was shown around the newly completed soundstages, told about the superiority of acoustical tile ceilings and thermal windows—not too boring. Back in his office, across from the biggest soundstage, I learned that my prospective employer was bald when he took his hat off, that the limp had come from an auto accident years before, that he was a member of the Morgan family, the prestigious House of Morgan *banking* Morgans of New York if you please, that, knowledgeable about building, he had decided to move to California and create a new studio. What else would you do but build your own studio if you were he and wanted to get into the movie business? Maybe he was bored with banking, maybe his beautiful wife, Susan Elizabeth, was starstruck—lots of wealthy New York women *are* to this day—and influenced him. Whatever the motivation, he certainly had done *part* of what he planned . . . built this neat little studio with *seven* sound stages, the most of any movie studio in the city.

How anybody as violently anti-Semitic as he could have deliberately embroiled himself in a business that is what—we don't have statistics—90 percent Jewish, give or take a few hairdressers, actors and set designers, is almost unimaginable. His only tenants in the new studio at that moment were the Justman Brothers, certifiably Jewish, who hoped to make movies. If he planned to be spared association with Those People, the man was alarmingly misguided, naïve, or just plain dumb. The subject of anti-Semitism didn't come up at the interview but rose vociferously later. I told him a little about previous jobs, eliminating seven of the fourteen, about my mother and invalid sister who lived in Arkansas and depended on me for support. I explained that we had a little insurance money left after my father's death but Mary had soon got polio (before the Salk vaccine) after Daddy died, there were no March of Dimes, no government funds, or a family to help with her catastrophic illness and we seriously scrimped; Mother took care of Mary in Arkansas, I pitched in. Did his eyes light up at this sad tale? Probably. He asked if I had a steady boyfriend. I said no.

The understanding that we might Become Something to Each Other was present in the interview I would say, me giving off waves of waifdom and vulnerability like a civet cat throwing off musk, him sitting there goldenly like King Midas vaguely promising to make my *future* golden. A financial arrangement for me in return for certain "favors" wasn't specifically outlined at that meeting but words like *stock portfolio, bonds, investments, real estate* were floated about and I would have my secretarial salary to live on. You'd have to say I was not innocently swept into sin but baby-browns wide open, was *encouraged* in; the strain of caring for Mother and Mary *had* become a bit of a drag. Yes, I could try to stop getting fired, get better jobs and raises, become moderately comfortable *some* day (I was solvent now, never owed a penny) but financial ease might take the rest of the century.

After we became lovers, M. told me he could have had any girl in town because of how rich he was. At the time I halfway believed him; freedom from hunger and want, bye-bye pinchies and scrimpies, farewell fiscal fright sounded spiffy to *me*. Well, he probably could have had *several* girls though I doubt Ava Gardner, Gene Tierney, Susan Hayward, or other goddesses of the day. Anyway, regardless of anybody else's availability, where would he find a better keptive? I'm young, cute, intelligent (frequently!), sweet-natured. By supplying the kind of help I so badly needed without any sacrifice whatever on his part, he'd have a grateful little salmon throwing herself up on the shore. Perfect! Was I going to throw up on *him* in bed? No, he wasn't that bad. Not a beauty but not a mongoose, about 5'10", Waspy features, a bit pinched, not *that* old . . . I could handle it.

Soon I was hired for my fifteenth secretarial assignment, given a modest salary of $35.00 a week, ensconced in a spanky new office, and our respective commitments—at least mine to him—began: interview Monday, sex Thursday. Our first carnal encounter took place in his office on a cushy Moroccan leather couch. A few office and motel trysts later, we got me a little flat on South Curson Street in the Wilshire–La Brea district of Los Angeles. I had left an understanding roommate—Barbara wanted security for me also—back on South Cannon Drive in Beverly Hills. Only eighteen months after V-J Day, building wasn't yet booming and apartments were scarce but the father of a secretary-friend at Music Corporation of America had a few rentals and she got me this one; I sent her a handbag.

The apartment was carpeted, furnished, had a wall bed, no place to cook, and nothing to cook on, but who cared—cooking wasn't then or now one of my passions. At the office, though I officially worked as a secretary from 9:00 A.M. to 4:00 P.M., there was precious little work to do; nobody was renting our soundstages or even looking at them. The office was an arid place. Only other occupants than M. and me were M.'s brother-in-law, Phil, married to Susan Elizabeth's sister—weren't we cozy?—and an accountant, no girl play-mates. I read Pearl Buck novels all day and finished off a six-ounce can of Planters peanuts nearly every twenty-four hours, often felt as though I'd been chugging through North China's Dunhuang or Cong Chun. Around 4:00 P.M. each day M. and I would start drinking in his office—him Pinchbottle Scotch, such a cute bottle—me Harvey's Bristol Crème Sherry, four or five glasses. I drank it like Coca-Cola. Can you imagine four or five glasses of Harvey's Bristol Crème Sherry every afternoon on top of the peanuts? If I did that now, I'd weigh eight hundred pounds. Why didn't we start drinking at my apartment? Because his office was bigger and nicer.

After cocktail hour we did go to my flat to make love. The love-making? It wasn't bad, wasn't love, wasn't anything, not even sure you could call it an affair—an affair is sexier. This was two people copulating—he *seemed* to have a good time and men can't fake "seemed to" in this situation, as we know. Moi learned to fake often and well. Though I was never really clutched or guilt-crazy about what I was doing—using this golden opportunity to stash enough money to take care of Mother and Mary and me the rest of our lives—my little body wasn't quite as cooperative as my little brain, refused to have orgasms, never a problem before; though the man didn't revolt me, maybe I wasn't as conscience-dead as I thought. After sex (without birth control—he couldn't make babies), M. went home to Mrs. M. in Holmby Hills each night to fulfill a heavy social agenda. Susan Elizabeth, a beauty, was a little frosty to me but who could blame her? Having previously been a repertory player in New York in a cast that included herself, M., and M.'s previous mistress, also his secretary, why would the woman not get emanations here in California? Susan Elizabeth wasn't a bad person. When her beloved wire-haired terrier ran into some broken glass in the backyard of his posh Holmby Hills pad and had to have an eye reorganized, she took him to a Beverly Hills ophthalmologist for the procedure. I try even now not to think about the ophthalmologist probably getting paid more for this afternoon's work—usually with humans— than my yearly salary. When mentioning his wife to me, M. always referred to her as Ms. M. I guess in his circle there had to be a sense of appropriateness when discussing your wife with your mistress, though I know married men who come right out and shamelessly call a wife Clarissa, Agnes, or whatever her name is in conversation with a girlfriend. Why did M. have a mistress? He never said. In later years when I asked a friend—not a boyfriend—with a pretty and adoring wife why *he* had a mistress, he said, "I can tell you in two words . . . it's civilized!" There you are.

What's developing for little me on the money front? Virtually nothing! My secretarial salary—I wished there had been more work—paid the rent. In two months of employment I had not been presented a share of stock or one little Treasury bond. One day I found $750.00 in a file drawer in a brown envelope, stashed before my time, dutifully told M. about it, and he said go spend it, buy some clothes. Yippee! Can you imagine $750.00 in 1947 dollars to squander on clothes? To give credit where due—if meager—he was clothes-generous from the beginning. I would be sent off to Saks or Bullock's with a handful of cash—no credit cards then—to buy cashmere sweater sets, skirts, summer dresses, a few nightgowns and peignoirs. No Giorgio Armanis or Versaces at the time—Susan Elizabeth was undoubtedly into Balenciagas and Mainbochers—but I didn't know or need designer clothes, barely had anyplace to wear the things I bought except to the office, the nighties after 5:30 P.M. for an hour or two. Jewelry? One little high-school-girl-type wristwatch with beige cord band came through—nothing else. Fur coat? It's summer in California . . . lynx or mink were not discussed. A car was supposed to be mine, and two years after V-J Day a few new ones were finally coming out of Detroit. M. acquired two Chevys, one for the young man who got cars and other Impossibles for him, another for his brother and sister-in-law; I didn't make the cut. I was given Appletrees, a seven-year-old wood-sided Buick station wagon with a roof the rain came through that had belonged to his estate on Long Island. Wonder if there is still an Appletrees estate.

Okay, I guess you could say I'm living comfortably, not getting rich or even prosperous, sugarplums still dancing in my head. From his lifestyle, servants, bank connections in New York, phone calls from Important People, I can clearly glean the man is *rich*, surely my ship is in the harbor waiting to come in. I'm lonesome a lot. M. and I didn't have dates, not even lunch dates, never dined together. My two best friends, Barbara and Berna, were Jewish—more in a moment—and could no longer be openly in my life, though we saw each other. M. did once say—magnanimously—he'd heard "the women aren't as bad as the men," but that didn't mean I should see any of them. For sure I couldn't date. Offices had always supplied playmates of both sexes; this one had nobody in it but me, M., the brother-in-law, and, for God's sake, the accountant. No substantial married friends were in my life to whisk me to the ballet or even dinner. What to do? After M. left the apartment around six-thirty every night, I would squash up a batch of Philadelphia Cream Cheese (three packages), mash in several cloves of garlic, wolf the globby treat down with a major sack of potato chips, gargle Listerine before going to work next day. I needed companions but who needed a stove? Television hadn't yet arrived. I read.

One afternoon after acquiring Appletrees I got daring (or desperate?) and picked up a young man at a stop signal on the corner of Beverly and Santa Monica Boulevard hitching a ride to the Beverly Hills Hotel where he was a tennis pro. We had dinner . . . nothing naughty happened . . . a little hugging and kissing. Next morning, being honorable, I told M. about the encounter, leaving out the hugging and kissing. Was I nuts? Possibly. I think I thought he was clairvoyant and would find out anyway. The report went down like chopped stone dragon. I promised never to do *that* again and didn't. Just once I allowed a previous lover to visit me on South Curson Street.

This had been a serious love affair, lasting three years, him a successful, sexy (Jewish, of course) agent at Music Corporation of America, me secretary to the head of the radio department. Girl employees weren't supposed to fraternize with executives. If you did, girls went, men stayed. I was also dating my boss, married, and I think the firing came not from office protocol but because I was sexually involved with the boss's associate, not him. Losing my job wasn't the worst problem of agent's and my relationship; his not wanting to marry me was. I kept leaving and getting reeled back in;

this time we hadn't seen each other for several months. Lovemaking that night was never headier but he hadn't come over—surprise!— with a marriage proposal; I didn't suppose he had. I told him about my arrangement. His reaction? Enthusiasm! Does an agent sense a killer deal when he's right there in the room with it? H. suggested we start seeing each other again, maybe even live in the same build- ing, work out our schedules. Did I know how to pick men or *what*! My keeper might be a little dull and stingy, offer no social benefits, but was almost princely compared to *this* snakey person. *Occasion- ally* I could use my brain; I turned down the proposition, stopped hankering totally for the other kind. Years later Mr. Devastatingly Snakey actually became David's agent . . . it's called You Never Know.

M. was a passionate anti-Semite and I want to tell you about that for a minute. He couldn't understand my not understanding his po- sition, was incredulous at my "ignorance." I really *wanted* to under- stand . . . what had Jews done wrong, aside from being Jewish, of course, to make him so angry? We never got it sorted out. He couldn't come up with anything sensible they'd done wrong or else, because everything he said was so silly, I blanked it out. I couldn't tell who *was* Jewish, possibly a good idea if I wanted to avoid any more of the "enemy" getting into my life, I thought. At Music Cor- poration of America where I held my third and later sixth secretarial jobs, I was asked one day by one of the men, "Do you realize you are the only shiksa in this place?" No, I didn't realize . . . what was a shiksa? As I mentioned, in Little Rock, where I grew up, religious discrimination didn't exist or none that I knew about. Maybe Jew- denigrating was buried deep down under Main Street . . . we were pretty busy with Apartheid. The most prosperous—and philan- thropic—Little Rock families—the Blasses, Pfeifers, Roses, Thal- heimers—*were* Jewish, and once a part-time cleaning woman said to me as I was scatting out the door, "Oh, you're going over to see that little Jew girl," but discussing who was or wasn't Jewish and discrim- ination itself I *think* were unknown to my mother and father.

Ex-roommate Barbara, Jewish, whom I wasn't supposed to see but did anyway without telling M., tried to help with Jew identification so I wouldn't hopelessly annoy my keeper and screw up the get-rich plan but Barbara couldn't say *either* how their noses, eyes, complex- ions were different any more than I could figure it out myself. After M. suggested and succeeded in getting me loose from any of my

Jewish friends which I took the pains to find out about (Barbara *told* me who they were) we pretty much stayed away from the subject.

Was I abandoning principle with my attempted Jew discernment, forsaking not only friends but ethics? I was being fearfully tacky, yes, but I didn't then or even now feel too bad about my pursuit. I wasn't trying to learn who "they" were so that I could hate anybody *ever* because of his ethnicity or religion. This was just me trying for a little enlightenment for a Special Situation, *temporary* eschewal of a particular group until the arrival of Financial Security. As I said earlier, who could have used a coach in Jewishness was *him*. How somebody who hated Jews as much as he did could build a movie studio without knowing that's who he'd be dealing with had to be seriously *dumb*.

Okay, not being able to tell who was Jewish wasn't my *major* problem. Not acquiring wealth *was*. In the beginning at least I don't think M. meant *not* to help me financially. Soon after my arrival we drove up to the top of Mulholland Drive to see a little lot that he owned across the street from Ginger Rogers's house. He actually said the lot could be mine and he would build me a little house . . . he was in the building business; lights went on like Las Vegas and Chinatown's New Year's Eve. The lot never got transferred, house was never built. Perhaps the Big Provider sensed (with reason?) that I wasn't nuts-crazy about him, that kind of thing can be a keeper turnoff. I needed somebody to tell me how to *treat* a man in this situation, how to flatter and cuddle and coo, I should have done it better.

Even now I think of a thousand things I could have, should have done to get protein into my diet instead of bear claws, to acquire treasuries instead of sweater sets. A portfolio to me was a rust-colored expandable cardboard folder you kept papers in, the only market I knew was the Los Angeles Farmers' at Third and La Brea whereas M.'s previous secretary, Marcella, was right there at the bank in New York with him and Knew Things (like the bond market and commodities). Marcella took away $100,000 when he moved to California he told me . . . great jumping lizards! Like Marcella, I should have brought the financial pages to his office every morning, early on asked him to explain the Dow Jones, price-earnings ratios, and venture capital (others have been trying with only moderate success ever since). I could have encouraged him to buy me just a few shares of Coca-Cola and Monsanto, tracked their progress each day, flown into his office, eyes all alight, to announce, "Look what's happening to my American Pipe and Foundry, should I buy more shares?" I needed a coach.

Of course, possibly he *was* basically cheap, learned early in the friendship he wouldn't have to spend up a storm to "keep" me. Once or twice when I actually had the gumption to ask about the stock portfolio and the house and lot and whatever happened to them, the man accused me of being interested only in his money, can you imagine! We didn't have that discussion often; I needed the job even with its pitiful rewards.

After three months at the Motion Picture Center Studios with no action for its owner—few tenants and God knows M. didn't know how to get a movie made—he sold the studio and we took unprepossessing offices on Westwood Boulevard, called ourselves the Viking Investment Company. The afternoon the studio changed hands lawyers met all day, M. came to my apartment as usual at 4:30 P.M., we made love after which I fell soundly asleep. He finally woke me up and asked, "How can you sleep when I've just lost three million dollars!" (The equivalent of eighty or a hundred now.) Good question. We are surely talking here about lack of compassion and empathy, even comprehension of what three million dollars *was*, but I was so disappointed about not getting the things I'd been promised I couldn't feel or care about his loss.

Soon after moving to Westwood we got me a rather sweet little apartment near the office on Montana Avenue west of Sepulveda. I should stop referring to things as little. Compared to my previous shoebox, new flat was a villa . . . two (small) bedrooms, living room, dining room alcove, kitchen, tiny front porch, really quite sweet. Since there wasn't yet much new apartment building and all apartments were in demand and pricey, M. gave owners enough money up front—I don't know how much—for me to move in. You had to do that then. Because of the "up front," rent itself was reasonable; I paid it myself, of course. We bought me a stove, refrigerator, some (el cheapo) furniture—two chairs, couch, bed, no carpeting, nothing for the dining room so I put up a card table and borrowed two chairs from the office. Berna's decorator friend Sam made living room draperies for me for twenty-five dollars.

M. soon announced that my mother and sister could now join me from Arkansas, something he'd promised early in the day and seemed to be trying to make good on . . . he always "liked" my family if not anybody else in my life. Still no keeping money and I soon found out what the "generous" apartment acquisition was about; he was leaving California. He and Susan Elizabeth were going to Europe for a few months, the movie business—surprise!—had not been rewarding and he would be looking at something in Brussels or Dusseldorf. Perhaps when he came back, we could resume our relationship but, for now, why didn't I look for a job? I don't remember gulping in pain at the notice, applied for unemployment insurance the minute he left, first time ever and the last, not working was not my style.

Before first unemployment check arrived, I got secretarial job number sixteen at the Sam Jaffee talent agency, brought Mother and Mary and their three kitty cats to Los Angeles on the Super Chief—I had just enough money to do that. Alas, none of the felines or people were real happy in their new home. Beloved Muffie had the gall to die on us almost immediately on arrival and, though they had lived in Los Angeles previously, the girls soon began to feel *they* weren't meant for big-city life either. Soon after Muffie went to the big catnip patch in the sky, Brother (I guess you run out of imaginative names eventually) joined her. Those ungrateful felines . . . after what I'd done to get them there! Mother and Mary were in deep mourning for the kitties, carried on as though kitty deaths were life's only important mater . . . "such fine healthy cats when we brought them here."

Six months after joining me in California, Mother and Mary returned to northwest Arkansas to start life anew or resume their old one, to acquire siblings for their surviving cat, Minnie. Though I didn't realize it at the time, as I mentioned, by withdrawing herself and Mary from my daily life, Mother was actually freeing me to have a life of my own. When M. and his wife returned from Europe three months later, I saw him twice. Over. We didn't remain friends. He and Susan Elizabeth adopted three little girls. How did you turn out, girls? I've always wanted to know. In five months I lost my sixteenth secretarial job at the Sam Jaffee agency, immediately got my seventeenth at Foote, Cone & Belding Advertising where I would stay for ten years, five as secretary (I got to be *efficient!*), five as a copywriter. How lucky can I be to have been so inept a kept girl—*forced* to make it on my own (is this what's called "no free lunch?"). Sometimes I wish M. were around to see how well I turned out. I know he would be absolutely floored!

Appletrees

Before we go on with boyfriends and such, may I tell you for one minute about the car that survived from the "keeping"—a really special car I was very fond of—something *good* from the keeping experience. Appletrees, my first car—I've only ever had four—was a 1940 8-cylinder forest green Buick station wagon with real wood sides . . . even in 1947, when I took possession, a classic. It's fun to have a car nobody else has. In the four years Appletrees and I were together in Los Angeles, I only saw two or three Buick station wagons from the same year and none with my car's personality or name painted on the side. Wagons with metal sides arrived a few years later. Men in the station where I got gas and parking lot attendants greeted Appletrees warmly like you would a beloved retired race horse, though Appletrees was anything but racy—we could get up to sixty with a real push. "How's Appletrees today?" they'd ask. Other drivers stopped at a light would roll down their windows and ask about Apple's heritage.

Mechanically I never had any trouble, though Apple had already racked up 100,000 miles when we met. Her only real flaw was a leaking roof. Sometimes I would drive around Los Angeles with an umbrella up inside the car. A new roof? Who had money for nonessentials? Station wagon owners like to pile lots of things inside the back . . . almost like having a closet. I stored tennis balls, books and magazines, small pieces of furniture, a change of clothes, empty bottles to be returned for deposit. After two bottles rolled out on the pavement under the port cochere of the Beverly Hills Hotel, I gave up the empty bottle returns, talking about feeling *tacky*! When it was time to sell Appletrees in 1951 and move up to a 1950 used Chevy, lots of people responded to the ad despite Apple being so old. Two housepainters made the winning bid. I liked to think about Apple being useful, hauling brushes, tarpaulins, and buckets of paint to eager customers. I never saw her again. I feel she should be in the Smithsonian.

Just My Bill

This was a major (nine-year) boyfriend so perhaps he deserves a little synopsis . . . it's Don Juan time.

We were the same age, Midwest background, both in advertising, Wasps, mad for Jackie Gleason, David Rose—record collectibles of the day—lots in common. Not a golden boy but a beigy-creamy one. . . . yummy good-looking . . . sandy brown hair . . . six feet tall . . . easy grace, an *Esquire* page on a junior executive salary . . . loafers without socks on weekends, tie knotted around his waist for a belt (yes, he studied Fred Astaire). W. G. was twenty-eight, me twenty-seven when we met, thirty-seven and thirty-six when we parted . . . is that nine years or *what*!

On each date he would ask about two or three times during the evening, "Who do you love?" I would answer, "John Foster Dulles." Him: "Too international, who do you love?" Me: "Che Guevera." Him: "Too revolutionary, who do you love?," etc. The game allowed him to show his considerable knowledge of world events and politicians. I would study *Time* or the *Los Angeles Times* before we met to collect names; Gregory Peck or Frank Sinatra was too plebian.

We went to spiffy restaurants, he was never cheap, spent the night at his or my flat. Breakfast in mine—he had no kitchen—consisted of gimlets (beaucoup), scrambled eggs, chicken livers, toasted buttered bear claws . . . tears come to my eyes . . . have I *had* a bear claw in forty years, let alone buttered? The man was criminally unfaithful. *All* women had to be aware of him as in classic Don Juan—he dated my girlfriends. I won't say he charmed effortlessly. Sinking into that many women had to take concentration and skill, but charm (like a snake) he did. Need one mention he was bow-wow in bed—tender, passionate, caring. Nobody ever had to tell or show anybody what to do; making you happy was as indigenous to him as bone marrow.

We had two glamour trips—Hawaii and Mexico. He paid, bless his heart. Shopping together in those cities he bought presents for other ladies. "The jade cigarette holder is for *who*?" "Aunt Leonora." He didn't *have* an Aunt Leonora. Brooks Brothers were shirts favored for his ladies. Mine would be marked "pink" on the box, the blue, yellow and green went elsewhere. He broke my heart. I let him, of course, as captured girls do. I was always trying to get away so as not to be so unhappy (one's confidence *is* shattered when you aren't the only one in bed) but he would reel me back in, world-class angler with a frisky marlin. Sometimes I stayed away as long as six months. Scoop . . . back in the net again. I didn't really have to *know* how unfaithful he was, but a womanizer often insists that you do, not by what he says but by leaving clues. Once in his apartment alone, I went through all his drawers, as he knew I would, found letters from a New York girlfriend, "Darling . . . that was so incredible, I think the happiest week of my life . . . I miss you dreadfully!" They had named her breasts (Liebchen and Schatzi . . . I swear!). Yes, a storm-out from his apartment ensued on that one . . . temporary, of course. Six months after I actually *left* the old angler, somebody lovely and decent arrived . . . my incredible David.

A shrink told me I could love a *good* man and he was right, I have been in love with David for forty years. He gave me himself, gave me *Cosmo,* gave and still gives me an incredible life. Marilyn and Alan Bergman's lyric for "On my Way to You," recorded by Barbra Streisand, says it perfectly. "If I could change a single day, what went amiss or went astray, I may have never found my way to you." This kooky person I loved and was tortured by and one or two others, though not so much, were stops on my way to David. Through the years my old tormentor has written notes, supposedly funny, usually not hitting the mark. On heavy bond paper, in his elegant scrawl with a serious ballpoint, "Darling . . . Penthouse Paul was at Fisherman's Wharf last night asking about you" (referring to a rather slick beau I had before him). When the *Wall Street Journal* did an unfriendly article about me when I was leaving *Cosmo,* he wrote a fuck-them condolence letter. Thoughtful. He is married for the fourth time (never to *me,* of course); I hear she is nice. I recently sent him, at his request, six *Cosmo* T-shirts for his ladies. I hope she *got* one of them.

Jack Dempsey

Okay, one more boyfriend story? We were a very odd couple so that's why I'm including us. Mousy advertising copywriter, age thirty-one (me), ex–heavyweight boxing champion of the world, age sixty-two (him). We met when Foote, Cone & Belding hired the ex-fighter to endorse Bulldog Beer, a new product of our client, the Hughes Brewing Company. Jack was a riot . . . couldn't pronounce beer so he said "burrrr" . . . "Get yourself a bottle of good old Bulldog Burrrr." Everybody in the Southwest was mimicking him and we sold a lot of beer. My boss, Don Belding, uncharitably said the champ was interested in me, his ex-secretary, solely because of my connection with the agency, that Dempsey needed the beer money. Maybe he did but I think he liked me. We dated—that's what people called it then—for a year. I was given two nice presents—silk lounging robe and pajamas from a ritzy Beverly Hills store and cheesecake from his restaurant in New York.

At Mocombo, Chasen's, Grace Hayes Lodge in the Valley, photographers scrambled around him . . . I was sometimes scooched to the side; Winchell reported us as "Jack Dempsey and brunette." I told myself I didn't mind. I'm sure I would have liked to be in some of the pictures. He took me to the fights at the Hollywood Legion Stadium and a stadium in downtown Los Angeles. That was fun. Some fights he refereed—maybe he did need the money—but not on our dates. We made love in my little apartment on 405 North, Bonnie Brae Street . . . a super stud, yes. "Straighten me out, darling," he would cry at the appropriate moment; presumably I did. A buddy/driver waited downstairs to drive him home. I don't think he drove. Later Jack married a dress-store owner—she could have all the silk pajamas she wanted; I believe they were happy.

The Year of Getting Married

Twice married and divorced, David had no wish or need to have a third wife. "Why can't we go on the way we are?" he would say when I brought up the subject of marriage, about thirteen months after we started seeing each other in June 1958. "We're happy, I'm faithful—why would you want to get *married*?" "Why would *you* want to get married?" I would respond "I *haven't* been married two times like you or even once and I want to be." It had been a frisky year; I was crazy about him. After his second divorce, a mutual friend, Ruth Schandorf, also a friend of wife number two, had "saved" David for me until she thought he was "ready for a nice sensible girl," but first he had to go through his starlet phase. When Ruth thought he was through it—the mothers, divorced or widowed, of his nineteen-year-old dates kept asking David, "Haven't you ever thought of an older woman?"—she had a little dinner party so we could meet each other and our dating life began.

I think the decision to try out the friendship was probably made by him when he walked me to my car, a sweet little 190 SL Mercedes Benz sports car for which I had paid all cash and had told him about.

To buy the Benz I'd recently traded in my 1950 Chevrolet coupe named Catherine Howard—a handful just like the Queen—purchased after I sold Appletrees—I told you about Apple. Only a few weeks before meeting David I had cried nonstop coming and going to Tijuana to the bullfights with girlfriends Charlotte and Angela, guilty sick at the car extravagance, but I soon realized, on meeting David, the car had been a *brilliant* purchase. Never having been married to or involved with a woman who bought her own bobby pins, let alone paid cash for a car, this acquisition had to seriously impress my new friend; we began seeing each other.

My cute little single girl flat, done up in shocking loden green and white, was in downtown Los Angeles on Bonnie Brae Street; David lived in a crumbling mansion on the edge of a cliff in Pacific Palisades. Almost immediately I realized he couldn't comfortably keep driving all the way from Pacific Palisades to pick me up in downtown Los Angeles on Bonnie Brae Street for dates, so I moved closer to him to Dorothy Street in Brentwood in the neighborhood where years later Nicole Simpson was killed. We drove by that apartment the other night and the building looked dingy and scruffy. "I'm surprised you ever caved in and married me, David," I said. "Look where I lived! The neighborhood isn't bad but this building is a wreck!" "It looked better when you lived in it," he said gallantly. I cooked for the man in my little flat—that wasn't the frisky part of our dating; I'll get to that—finally asked my frequent guest if it didn't ever occur to him to bring a bottle of something as in wine or vodka when he came to dinner. He caught right on.

The frisky part of dating was Hollywood itself. As executive vice president creative operations at Twentieth Century Fox, David was on the movie glitz scene and took me places like Buddy and Anita Adler's welcome-home party for Ingrid Bergman at the Beverly Hills Hotel after she'd been ostracized for having an affair with Roberto Rosselini, this night wall-to-wall movie stars. When Ingrid stood briefly beside me fanning herself—"You'd think this hotel would know about air-conditioning," she hissed—we chatted for a moment; she was big, beautiful, earthy. David took me to Writers Guild dinners, Academy Awards—I always bought new dresses—screenings of movies in his private projection room at the studio; I got to ask pals and show off.

One night after fifteen months of dating, I'm at his house for dinner and the housekeeper brings in fabric samples. Ms. Neal: I think this tweed for the den, don't you, Mr. Brown, the blue for your bedroom. David is carefully examining corduroy and damask. I soon realize nobody is thinking of me as possible future house occupant or they'd have been consulting with *me* about samples. "I love you and I'll miss you," I told my beloved that night. "Don't call me unless it's to tell me you want to get married." Tough talk and you have to mean it; one little slippy-slide and you're back in his coat pocket again. The man will always call up to say, "I've got to see you . . . we've got to talk this over," and you must say, "We did talk it over. If you aren't calling to set a date to get married, I'm still not here!" Many girls marry men whose very own idea it was to marry—bless them—but mine wasn't one of those men. If you have somebody you think you would *like* to marry but he hasn't got around to considering the idea favorably, this is what you have to do. You get the hook in. Darling, charming, delicious, sexy you has to have sunk into him so seriously, the hook buried so deep he can't get it out without severe pain, i.e., can't live without you. You then close in and deliver your ultimatum. I had to deliver mine twice.

Though David did call pretty soon after the fabric-sample evening and we did set a date, the Man Couldn't Go Through with It and I had to leave a second time; he came back and married me. That was forty years ago and we have never been close to a breakup. David may have considered it once or twice. He hates my temper tantrums—he's one of those people who doesn't *have* tantrums, he gives them—also my cheapness (I'm *not* cheap, I'm thrifty!). We fought so hard recently about two friends (invited) adding on two *other* friends (not invited) and David picking up a restaurant tab of $825 that when we got home he told me I could never enter his den again. Well, I knew from the hour I met him if I ever lost him, I would never find anybody as good so, of course, I went right back into his den, uninvited, a few hours later and told him he had to keep me. So far he has.

When we married, David had no money, *none*. He paid $300 a month rental on his crumbling Spanish palazzo, drove a tattered Jaguar that loved to stop on Sunset Boulevard and try, often successfully, to blow its top. I had $8,000 in the Security First National Bank, painstakingly saved through secretarial work and one copywriting year. Just weeks before David and I met, as I mentioned, I had uncharacteristically plunged for the barely used 190 Mercedes Benz sports car for $5,000 but still had $8,000; penniless David had a great job and prospects. At the time he was paying an accounting firm in Beverly Hills 5 percent of his income. I quickly got rid of their platinum blond employee who came to his house once a month to go over his checks, took on the check reconciling myself. I don't do that now—not good at it—but my limited talent never landed us in the slammer.

Sale of *Sex and the Single Girl* to Warners for a movie brought our first money, $200,000; other money-producing activities kicked in after that. I can't believe we have any money *now*, between indigent David who never knew how to husband funds and anal me who didn't know how to let go of any to invest except in the Brentwood Savings Bank for baby percent interest but, after the *S.& S.G.* money came along, David turned out to be a shrewd investor. I would say neither of us ever worked for money except me to pay the rent all those single years. We're wealthy now and, have a good (understatement) life.

We are a good *team*, he is a good man. When people ask the secret of a long-lasting, even happy, marriage, I always say, "Marry a decent person. The world is out there handing you enough grief. You don't want to go home at night to a *rat*." I don't go home to one, and David gave me a big-time career—the book and *Cosmo*. I turn my check and other checks right over to him but I think he likes my person as well. When I was turning blue one morning in an open Land Rover in Botswana out looking for leopards, he peeled his heavy sweater off and tucked me in without a whimper, having told me six times earlier to dress warmly but I went for chic. He does stuff like that.

Didn't anybody ever want to marry me before David (who really didn't want to?) Yes, three and a half people proposed. The half was the beau who already had a wife but said that would be no problem if I'd start staying home and be faithful to him *now* to show my good intentions. Was something the matter with that proposition? I thought so at the time and declined. Are three and a half proposals for such a long singlehood enough? I don't know, you'll have to decide. I mentioned two men I wanted to marry who didn't want to marry me—the killer womanizer and the MCA agent who said his reluctance to wed wasn't because he'd have to take care of my mother and sister—financially, he could handle that. (I would think so . . . Frank Sinatra, Dean Martin, Jerry Lewis, among others, were his clients). He never discussed this problem with me but I think part of his resistance to wedlock came from being an Orthodox Jew, stocking-to-skin close to a mother and two sisters he probably couldn't see me fitting in with—I was also fourteen years younger. I think he also found me a little emotionally unstable—imagine! When the subject of marriage came up, he said we'd be divorced in two years, an undoubtedly accurate prediction. My life has turned out so well we have to bless those two ungallants who said no, don't we? Thank God I never got the hook very far into either of *them*. It was the agent—*really* ungallant—who said he wouldn't mind sharing me with a temporary "keeper" under whose aegis I was going to get financially secure. Agent married an MCA receptionist, became David's agent years later as I mentioned, called *me* every Friday afternoon from California for forty straight years just to check in; sometimes we had nothing whatever to discuss but the weather!

So the hook went *deeply* into and landed the best man there could be in the world for me. He's calling right now on his private telephone in my office to ask, "What's for dinner?" I won't tell him—Mrs. Paul's Frozen Fish Cakes, Stouffer's Spinach Souffle, Stouffer's Macaroni and Cheese, Welsh Rarebit—I'll just say "You'll like it." These specialties have been selected by David from a wider variety submitted by someone who doesn't like to cook but *does* (with a little frozen-food help) every night and weekends when we're home. I'm too cheap to have a live-in cook, and I certainly don't want to restaurant-dine every night . . . you can't take off your panty hose and relax. I never got into the habit of ordering in, possibly because you have to shell out cold cash when the food shows up but you're also sweating out arrival of food and people at apartment at same time—I've never done it even *once*. David gets to eat spiffy at lunch in his beloved New York restaurants. At night he can just do other stuff than eat. He's very cooperative.

Leaving Cosmo . . . but Not Really

What did it feel like being told I wouldn't be editor-in-chief of *Cosmo* anymore, that a new editor had been selected? What do you *think* it felt like? Gruesome! They had to tell *me* it was over . . . I would never have got around to telling *them*. Although many things *don't* change in the human condition and a younger reader might continue to take advice from a *smart* older person, I knew, at seventy-four, I was getting way too far out on the ledge (to put it mildly) to continue to be guru of an eighteen to thirty-four year-old reader. The Hearst executives, being of sound mind, knew nobody could be lion queen forever and had sensibly thought about succession. Didn't I think Bonnie Fuller, then editor of their recently launched *Marie Claire,* should be the one? What could I say but yes, of course. Bonnie wasn't sure she *wanted* the job, said she might prefer to stay on at *Marie Claire* and see what she could make it become, like profitable . . . it wasn't yet. I had to help persuade her.

My boss, Frank A. Bennack, Jr., president and CEO at Hearst, came to my office with his nice little package: two-year contract at my present salary, Bonnie would become deputy editor until she learned *Cosmo* in, out, up, down, sideways and, when I felt she was ready, not a minute sooner, she would become editor. No hurry, they said, take the whole two years if that's what I felt was needed . . . how fair could they be? When I stepped down—that's what they call it—I would go to a new job as editor-in-chief of *Cosmo International*—there were then twenty-nine international editions. When presented with what was pretty much fait accompli—refusing wouldn't have allowed me to edit *Cosmo* another thirty-two years— I wasn't agasp with joy or soggy with grief, though I did tend to go over The Happening with David until he finally said, "Helen, if you'll cut a tape, I promise to listen to it faithfully every night right after Larry King."

A story that appeared soon in the *Wall Street Journal* devastated me. Management had asked me not to talk to the *Journal* and I hadn't, but a number of ex-Hearst employees and a few presently employed who were also asked not to talk, did and gave nasty (not accurate) statements (I had thought everybody *loved* me!). The article said Hearst was picking a new editor because the magazine had to be brought up to date. At that *moment,* out of 11,475 magazines published, *Cosmo* was still number six in the newsstand sales as we had been all the years of my tenure. We were the number-one seller, for the sixteenth straight year, at college campus bookstores. How much updating did we need? The *Journal* writer got one of my two or three furious letters in a lifetime—I don't believe in writing or reading them; they were never shown me at *Cosmo*—but I made an exception in his case. The *Journal* didn't apologize or run a more accurate story after the official announcement of my departure. Banks of flowers arrived from happy wishers. I kind of liked having all those flowers *now* instead of when I was dead, though there was a tinge of melancholy to the whole tribute. One word kept playing endlessly in my mind . . . over . . . it was *over*. *Cosmo* had been my life for thirty-two years; there was *nothing* I'd been saving up to do. I'd written seven books, been around the world a couple of times. Ownership of a country house I could now devote more time to still didn't appeal; *other* people's country houses were to visit.

The new life began. Bonnie soon arrived at the *Cosmo* offices and continued to edit *Marie Claire* from another location. We dutifully worked together, but I knew a two-year break-in was too long to ask her to be a trainee. She was already a serious pro, a successful editor (*Marie Claire* wasn't yet in the black but getting there). Her previous magazine, *YM*, had done well, and she didn't need to sit at mommy's knee and train for that long.

Exactly a year after I heard The News, I left my job. It was decided that February 1997, my last issue, would be a whammo-good-bye-Helen issue and we would mercilessly pound advertisers to come in. We did and they did—our biggest issue in ad pages ever and fun to put together. Bonnie became U.S. editor, added beauty and fashion pages, made the magazine sexier, younger, less concerned with writing . . . sales went right up! Yes, you could kill her but, on the other hand, if management was going to be so generous with me right to the end of time—the way they are with their "retired" editors and particularly *me* since I'd performed so well for them—I'd better be glad *Cosmo* was doing well.

I became, still am, editor-in-chief of the international editions of *Cosmo*. This involves opening new editions all over the world, attending the launch, helping the already-existing ones put out a better product. At the time I started my new job we had twenty-nine international editions—I had usually been present at the launches. Since then, we've launched ten new ones: Indonesia, Thailand, the Philippines, Poland, Hungary, Croatia, Lithuania, Beijing, Finland, and Romania. The launches—sometimes in a place I've never been—are ego-satisfiers. Television and press make a big fuss, hospitality is lavish.

Every month I now critique roughly twenty *Cosmo* international editions, particularly the newer ones, and tell editors where they are going right or wrong.

Where are the blockbuster man/woman photographs? The major career article? We need more text to help with her life, cut back the tchotchke layouts, etc. There is a Cosmo *format and it works all over the world. Your management didn't hire you to reinvent the wheel,* etc.

One third of the editions have a licensing agreement with Hearst, the rest are partners. Critiquing is being a nanny rather than an editor but there is a pretty good reason to do it. Sales can climb in nearly all those countries, whereas the competition among women's magazines in the United States makes sales climbing seriously tough. A wonderful associate, Kim St. Claire Bodden, oversees the day-to-day operation of all *Cosmo* and other Hearst magazine international editions. By the year 2000, Hearst expects the revenue from international editions to be 50 percent of its magazine revenue, so I have a mission. Right now *all* the international editions of *Cosmopolitan* are in the black.

My bosses decorated a scrumptious new little office for my new life in the main Hearst building. Decorator Edith Berke and I thought lush, not sensible, for the décor. Walls are covered in dusty rose pure French silk, couches, draperies, and window shades are a wild cabbage rose print, pillows abound like a Persian harem. A teddy bear in Chanel pearls rests on the couch. So do needlepoint pillows that say "I Love Champagne, Caviar and Cash" and "Good Girls Go to Heaven, Bad Girls Go Everywhere." An antique armoire takes up a wall, cane chairs are upholstered in red silk plaid, a leopard wall-to-wall carpet keeps my stocking feet toasty. In my john hangs a custom-created Kliban kitty in hair curlers, an evening-gowned Erte lady with Russian wolfhound who watches out for her. Outside my office Butch, Deidre, and Catherine—all very fat pigeons—make love on the windowsill . . . they are *shameless.* Other times one of them goes down the other's throat to get fed . . . just pulls the food right up. The girl pigeon is probably the food provider, don't you think? The Hearst maintenance boss keeps threatening to evacuate the pigeons—nesting and scumming up the wall adjacent to my office. I tell him do that and I will report him to the ASPCA. My office looks out on a lovely garden, flower-splashed in summer, silvery in winter . . . I have survived.

Beloved assistant Susan Schreibman and driver Michael Lopez came with me (he with the new Mercedes 500 SL the company gave me). A book I wrote after leaving my editing job, *The Writer's Rules—The Power of Positive Prose—How to Write It and Get It Published,* was published last year by William Morrow. People always thought sex made *Cosmo* successful. The good writing is what did it. Book contains *Cosmo*'s edit and writing rules that could work for anybody who would like to get into print. Bonnie was always polite to me. What the poor girl went through hearing about wonderful me when she took the job must have been nearly unendurable. She kept three and a half people from my staff—happens with new bosses. Hearst did pick the right editor. Despite *Cosmo*'s good health when she came in—her sales zoomed—she presently moved to Condé Nast to edit *Glamour*. Bonnie has basically turned *Glamour* into *Cosmo*. Their sales are up but haven't reached ours. Kate White came over to us from *Redbook* and *her* sales have exceeded Bonnie's—over 2 million copies are sold each month at the newsstand plus the subs. Kate is a splendid editor. Her *Cosmo* is far sexier than mine and is going like a baby steam engine. One of my young editors, Atoosa Rubenstein, has created *Cosmo Girl*, a magazine for teenagers that's also selling well. We don't know why Bonnie moved so quickly. She was surely paid well, appreciated where she was. Maybe she wants some day to be editor of *Vogue*. Condé Nast is where it could happen. I may or may not stay tuned.

The Night I Got Busted in San Antonio

We had gone to San Antonio for the wedding of one of my boss's (Frank A. Bennack, Jr.) daughters. Frank has five daughters. They marry and I like to show up for the wedding. Frank, CEO of the Hearst Corporation, a darling, and his wife, Luella, also a sweetie, grew up and lived in San Antonio where he was publisher of the Hearst newspaper, the *San Antonio Light*, before being tapped for the CEO job in New York; their daughter Shelly was to be married in the chapel of the military base where Luella and Frank were married.

Okay, it's 11:00 P.M. David and I have arrived at the San Antonio International Airport after a giantburger fight on the plane. David: "Helen, the trouble with you is that you can't *change*!" Me: "F———you!" I'm off to the ladies room to have a good cry. I rarely cry but this day and previous week have been squashers. I'm in the ladies' room—about fifteen minutes—until asked to come out. I know that desperation feeling. You're *outside* while a gentleman *inside* removes a six-week growth of beard or a female tries out six shades of lipstick and new eye gloss preparing for her date on arrival. Back in the seat

I explain to my beloved that I *can* change, am perfectly *willing* to change, but if we use the new design for *Cosmo,* created by a hotshot freelance designer, we will have to cut half the copy. *Cosmo* is a magazine that helps young women realize hopes and dreams, solve problems—have I told you that before? We can't do that as effectively with half the words. Prize-winning graphics, make-your-eyebrows-soar photography are okay but—repeat—basic *Cosmo* will be gone-zo with only half its words. David understands what I am saying, is very sweet with me the rest of the flight, but the trip and the week have been hectic.

On arrival, the airport is crowded, possibly two dozen planes have plopped down about the same minute. Our luggage arrives . . . great! Between us we have a suitcase, garment bag, smaller suitcase, large Vuitton pouch stuffed with books and manuscripts for David (who is leaving for Los Angeles from San Antonio, then London and Moscow for a movie location and needs stuff), a suitcase and garment bag for me. We get our seven bags off the conveyor; there are no carts or baggage handlers and no way can we carry luggage anywhere ourselves. I leave David with bags, go out to curb to flag a prowling cab—no prowlers. Return to David. In two trips, we manage to move luggage out to the curb but still no prowling taxis. Next step: in two *more* trips we move luggage to the *island* a few yards further out from curb—you know the configuration. I leave David with luggage, including Vuitton tote containing my purse, go prowling to the end of the island to look for cab. Voila, a cab stand with a cab *in* it. I couldn't see the stand when I'd gone outside the building the first time. I engage the cab, tell driver to wait just a minute, I'll go get my husband and the luggage who aren't that far away. Don't do that, says driver. We'll go pick him up. Fine. I get in cab but when we get near David, driver says he can't make a left turn, we'll drive around the airport and come back for him. I am not happy. Cab was only a few yards from David when driver made the announcement. We start driving. As meter reaches $3.00 I am really pissed, jump out of cab, slam the door, and start walking to where I hope I have left husband. March, march, slog, slog, slog: I'm in the tall grass, a little dampish, sinking in an inch or two, not sure where I'm headed—the highway is alongside me—but assume I'll get back to David sometime during the night. If I'd stayed in the cab, I know meter would have reached $8.00 because we'd have to go all the way outside the airport and come back to fetch a passenger inside, this before we even *start* for the city.

About eight minutes into my tramp, I hear a siren screaming, lights are flashing, a police car pulls up. Officer gets out and asks for my identification. I haven't any, I explain; purse with identification is with my husband back at the airport. Another police car arrives, woman officer this time. She gets out, frisks me. I am trying to explain my predicament, husband back at airport probably worried sick, could they please take me back there. Not interested. They are asking two thousand questions about where do I live, where do I work, what is my income. I am asking *them* what have I done, why are they doing this? Aha, I have stiffed the driver—jumped out of cab with $3.00 on the meter. I suggest that I will be happy to spend the night in the San Antonio jail and remain there *forever* before I pay that fare.

One of the policemen has been using his walkie/talkie and, through a colleague, located David back on the island at the airport. My policeman has told his colleague, "We have a demented woman here." Colleague tells this to David who says, "That's my wife!" Woman police officer tells me to get in her car, we drive back to David. I've reestimated: Fare would have been at least $10.00 if I'd stayed in the cab before we fetched husband and luggage and headed for San Antonio; the *passenger* would have been stiffed. David awaits with our possessions, I *think* happy to see me, if embarrassed. Policewoman finds us a cab, tucks everybody in, we're off. New driver very friendly, says we mustn't hold our experience at the airport against the city. San Antonio is a real great place and we must enjoy ourselves. We promise to. "It was just a slow night for that driver," our new friend explains. We hold no grudges, it is a lovely city. Now, of course, I have a police record in Texas. When I get home I call the manager of the *San Antonio Light* and ask if maybe he could get my police record removed. He'll try. He may still be working on the case—I haven't heard.

Television Moments

Television has been good to me, helped me sell books, magazines, tapes. Sometimes I have been good to *it*. Speaking frankly (some say *too!*) the host and I have kept people awake. I was the tenth-most frequent guest on the *Tonight Show* ever, not often with Johnny Carson but with whatever guest host wanted me—Joan Rivers, David Brenner, Jay Leno, Burt Reynolds, etc. The show paid my round-trip way to California. Merv Griffin, a widely syndicated show in the sixties and seventies, I could do as often as I wanted, standing invitation. Phil Donahue had me for five one-hour shows . . . a pussycat. Geraldo Rivera wasn't a pussycat but a friendly tiger . . . I often guested. Oprah and I first visited when she was a pushy little-girl-upstart causing gasps with her candid questions, wild commentary. Has anything changed? Oprah and I were together the morning Anwar Sadat was assassinated but just pushed right on. She's helped me celebrate anniversaries, sell millions of *Cosmo*s since. I raised Regis Philbin from a puppy, having first been with him in San Diego on the NBC station KOGO when he was twenty-nine years old. Through the years I saw him through various co-hosts up to and including the delicious Kathie Lee. Promoting a book, *Sex and the Office*, I met Larry King in 1963 when he had a radio show at a beachfront café in Miami; he is a uniquely great interviewer . . . studies the material, asks everything that will let you show off and push what you're pushing. David and I have been to two of his weddings. I was his guest for an hour last year. First *Today Show* was with Barbara Walters, then Tom Brokaw and Jane Pauley; later I visited them on their shows. Barbara and I have become good friends. Katie Couric, a star and a sweetie, did two segments with me last year. Diane Sawyer was already a golden girl when we chatted on *CBS Morning News*. Two biggies—20/20 and *60 Minutes*—helped me sell a ton of magazines. Every Friday morning for two and a half years I gave advice on *Good Morning America* and later guested with Joan Lunden.

Through the years TV crews were frequently at *Cosmo* to find out exactly what we did to make the magazine so successful, sometimes just to ask my opinion about sexual harassment or the Jackie Onassis magic. When I was promoting a book, I did local television in Detroit, Chicago, St. Louis, Los Angeles, Memphis, Denver, wherever. When we launch an international edition of *Cosmo*—thirty-nine so far—Argentina, Australia, Brazil, Taiwan, Hong Kong, South Africa, Japan, Russia, the Czech Republic, Portugal, Spain, Germany, etc. etc., I go there to explain and promote, do television, talk to the press. Yes, they have interpreters.

Has anyone given me a bad time? On one of his early shows, Mike Wallace and an actor from a show called *Route 66* put me away with snippy questions about women who worked outside the home instead of caring for infant children . . . not the subject I was supposed to talk about at all. I was too dumb to get out of the way but learned not to let anybody ever do that to me again and they really haven't. Mike has interviewed me since and we're friends. Not *too* many people have been bad to me . . . I'm too adorable and basically know what I'm talking about, at least what's true for *me*. I get to say what I want even if the host is sputtering with rage.

For three seasons I had my own syndicated shows, *Outrageous Opinions* and *View from Cosmo*, but I'm a better guest than host. People who produce and helm TV shows have to work; guests only need to show up and talk. I've rarely spent fifteen minutes preparing material ahead of time though sometimes the show will preinterview by phone. Probably the best interview I ever did was an hour with Charlie Rose on PBS just after the announcement that a new editor-in-chief would be coming to *Cosmo*. Somehow I was calm and quiet and said everything exactly the way I wanted it to be said. Six or seven Saturday mornings were rewarding with Richard Heffner on *The Open Mind*, PBS's longest-running show. No commercials to interrupt when you're on a roll. One of the best things about television is having your hair and makeup done—they don't want scruffy-looking guests. I try to amortize their investment by going someplace spiffy afterwards or at least later that night. You don't want to waste all those great before and afters.

I'm grateful to my toes to those television hosts and producers who let me talk, sell product, and become famous . . . yes, television is how it happens. I'm not a *big* celebrity . . . just well known enough so that people sometimes come up and say hello and tell me they like me . . . I like that. Don't think I'll ever want to have a Web site. I prefer a real live human being person to look at while I babble.

New York and the Street Where I Live

I don't trust people to love me back the way I love them, but my city does. I give it unconditional love and it loves me back the same way. I never think I am loving too much as in vulnerable . . . that the city might someday hurt me as lovers do. I know it won't find somebody better to fool around with—we'll be together all my life, though the city will not be lonesome after I'm gone.

David and I moved to New York from Los Angeles in 1963 after Twentieth Century Fox closed the studio and sold off the back lot because of colossal losses from *Cleopatra*. You might say the studio closing and David's subsequent unemployment were his own fault.

When Spyros Skouras, Twentieth Century Fox chief at the time, asked David for suggestions for a property that might possibly become a blockbuster, badly needed by the company at the time, David remembered Twentieth having made a brilliant *Cleopatra* some forty-five years earlier starring Theda Bara and suggested to Spyros this might be the subject of a sensational new production. You're on! As David wrote in his book, *Let Me Entertain You*:

> Never was so much money given to so few for so little. Forests must have been cut down to make paper for the scripts that were written and rewritten. When Leon Shamroy, the cinematographer of *Cleopatra*, saw the forum set in Rome, his first words were "There are not enough lights in Europe to light this." At one point, photography had to be deferred from autumn until spring when the days grew longer. Everyone remained on salary that winter and the winter that followed. Actors and crew alike spent eight months at high salaries and prodigal expense accounts doing nothing. Elizabeth Taylor's and Richard Burton's coliseum-size love affair spanning days when they hardly got out of bed to come to the set were the least of the cost escalation.

My husband said, "Nobody could imagine the project would burn out four heads of production, one of whom died, bring down the president of the parent corporation (Spyros), close the studio, and get me fired. The cash drain of the picture would leave no alternative for Twentieth Century but to sell its entire 252-acre studio lot, one of the richest parcels of urban real estate in the world, for a piddling fifty-five million dollars, perhaps two percent of what it is worth today." Poor things. They also couldn't imagine the picture would ultimately *make* money, even though when completed the studio would be missing, sold to pay for the movie, and so would my husband's job. So here we are in New York, David out of the movie business for the time being, now executive vice president of New American Library, a medium-size publishing company whose principal asset was Ian Fleming and his James Bond hero. My first New York year I spent completing a second book, *Sex and the Office*, sometimes not leaving the apartment more than once a week but gradually exploring my new city . . . loving it. New York, I soon recognized, loves women, whereas Los Angeles loves girls. I'd been a girl in L.A., now it was time to be a grown-up lady in New York.

Two years after our arrival came the chance to re-create *Cosmo-politan*—I'll tell you about that in a moment. By then David had rejoined Twentieth Century Fox as creative head for its new boss, Darryl F. Zanuck, working with production chief Richard Zanuck, but he got to stay in New York. I'm pretty much on my own as an editor, with no experience whatever! David offered unstinting pillow talk assistance, read manuscripts when I brought them home, was available for a quick ride around Central Park in a taxi if I needed to go over something during the day. In addition to already liking New York, I am now loving it because of my new career. Little girls from Little Rock, Los Angeles, Keokuk, Indianapolis, and other less worldly places do well here. Whatever you've got, New York will get it out of you, make you polish, hone, scrabble, win like you couldn't any other place. As I said, this wonderment all began to happen to me after I'd been transplanted from Los Angeles for two years. For a Los Angeles country girl, with or without a career, getting acquainted with New York is a supreme adventure. In some ways the city looks as foreign as Bangkok . . . haughty Park Avenue apartment buildings; the just-try-to-impress-us lobbies of the Waldorf, Plaza, and Regency; Eighth Avenue's Korean markets bursting with flowers (also crummy strip joints). Madison Avenue has to be the best window-shopping stroll in the world, a Persian bazaar, rich people even buy things there. The New York Stock Exchange is among New York's finest zoos . . . mad crush of good-looking and *not*-so, young and *not*-so men who make killer decisions every minute. Skyscrapers—isn't that a cute and accurate word for them—scrape the skies, medieval churches guard the streets and remind you that lots of New York's architecture and many of its people originated in Europe. Many talented writers and photographers have written about and photographed this glorious city so I'll stop.

I love every part of it—like a mother who loves all her children, even the scruffy ones—but for me maybe the magic is best gleaned from the windows and terraces of David's and my apartment. We live on the twenty-second floor of a lovely old landmark building on Central Park West. Our flat consists of four floors including one that used to be maids' rooms under the kitchen where we store wine, my summer and winter clothes when not in use, and David's radio room for his ham radio equipment ("W 2 I O Y—Indiana Ocean Yankee—calling C.Q. Calling C.Q." These people don't have conversations, they just signal each other). The apartment's top floor is one huge room like an artist's studio in Paris; giant glass windows provide views everywhere but into the fireplace. Mike Nichols owned the apartment for ten years and did wonderful things to it architecturally, including knocking out walls for windows—you can't do that anymore. Mike has great taste and along with the apartment we bought all his furniture including a Steinway baby grand. I think he would have liked to take the piano but possibly couldn't face getting it down to the ground from the twenty-second floor—not the kind of thing that fits into a freight elevator. I grabbed the baby hoping Stephen Sondheim (I am a Stephen Sondheim groupie) would come over and play some evening. He did come to a party but wouldn't play. Piano lessons didn't take for me as a little girl but I may try again.

Having lived contentedly on the East Side of New York in a boxy little apartment at Sixty-fifth and Park Avenue for thirteen years, I had to be dragged to the West Side. Even my beloved psychiatrist, Herb Walker, said, "I don't see you and David over there." The East at that time was the desirable side of town, West considered tacky regardless of any architectural wonders that might be over here; perception has changed since then. David, as unsnobby as it gets, wanted the apartment badly but was patient with me, then one day the real estate agent called to say a Middle Eastern man in a long black limousine had been driving around the neighborhood all day and had visited "our apartment" four times. David said we must make up our minds. We did—it was a go. We've always suspected the Saudi prince was hired by the agent from Central Casting to run around New York and close apartments but whoever he was I'm glad he did what he did.

The apartment I love goes with the city I love. May I tell you about it? Our big terrace—there are three terraces—is lushly planted, has its own bumble bees, looks across Central Park to the East Side, all the way up to the George Washington Bridge and southern tip of Westchester County on the north, and Central Park South to the south. Hard to get ourselves to come indoors. From May to October, we're hanging over the rail viewing the view but we also see it (them) inside the apartment from several rooms. May I tell you what we see? In summer Central Park is a green cacophony of trees so fluffy you can't see the trunks from up here. Within 843 acres of total park, 26,000 trees faithfully report the seasons—all fluffed up and chattering to each other in summer, ready to change costumes and dance in autumn, whispering encouragement to each other in frozen winter. A small glassy lake in the middle of the trees is rowed around on by baby rowboats in summer, skated on in winter. Another much smaller lake sparkles in front of neat little Belvedere Castle that houses the U.S. Weather Bureau; its castle flies a small American flag. Several times a year a stage is set up in that area for performers and their equipment for free concerts in the park. People sit in the Great Meadow, listen to Garth Brooks, Simon and Garfunkel, Diana Ross, Shakespeare, and visit with the Pope; for the Pope's visit sharpshooters came up on our roof for their own surveillance. The Meadow got all scruffed up when Disney premiered *Pocahontas* there—100,000 people scruffed up the Meadow that night but it's been resodded and is gumdrop green again.

Sometimes our view includes fireworks—prezzie from the city a few times a year. A big tranquil reservoir where Jackie used to run every day is on view to the north. In summer we see masses of people walking back and forth through the park, sometimes stopping to sun, but, viewed twenty-three floors up, they're just part of the scenery. To the east, way over there facing Fifth Avenue, hulks the Metropolitan Museum, not imposing from the back or from this distance but, knowing what's inside (do Bill Gates, Jr., and Warren Buffet look like anything from the back *or* the front but knowing what's *inside*) . . . awesome! I know just which part of the bulkiness is the Temple of Dendur. To the south we're able to see Central Park South, a spiffy street holding the Plaza Hotel, Essex House, Hampshire House, and the New York Athletic Club, where I have often played, danced, sometimes worked—still do. I smile at them. General Motors is the big-daddy building further east, further south are the Chrysler Building, Empire State, once the world's tallest, still mighty tall, which whimsically lights itself up green and red for Christmas, red, white and blue for the Fourth, once all blue for Frank Sinatra's birthday.

At night the gray, beige and black stone and concrete behemoths of Fifth Avenue and Madison Avenue, in our view to the east, put on their diamond, emerald, sapphire, ruby necklaces and brooches . . . all tarted up with glitter for the night; the park is strewn with hundreds of lamps that shine friendly light puddles on the ground. Sometimes I imagine what is going on in the apartment buildings across the park . . . marriage proposals, making of love, unpacking from the safari, welcoming kids home from college, paying the help . . . all these people have "help." I never think what friends in those apartments—

the Steinbergs, Stems, Schwarzmans, Woody and Soon Yi, Mike Bloomberg—might be doing, only imagine an Auntie Mame party or scene from a Rogers and Astaire 1930s movie.

At dawn the buildings (I think they all know each other and visit at night) turn chocolately pink. A pink angel-shaped cloud may show up and point itself toward downtown, one of the loveliest times to visit the city and the park. Looking at all this . . . trees, meadow, reservoir, baby lakes, water tower, Metropolitan Museum, aristocrat apartment houses of Fifth Avenue, further into the spires and turrets of Madison Avenue, south to the glamorous skyline of Central Park South, I'm nearly always seized with a baby joy. David and I occasionally talk about living in Paris or London or, more sensibly, since I'm so cold-natured, Tucson or Mustique, at a time when our work needn't keep us here but we'll never do it. No divorce for us nor from the beloved city. I was made a New York Landmark by the New York Landmarks Commission along with Walter Cronkite, Brooke Astor, Brendan Gill, and some other nifty people. The New York Public Library and Grand Central Terminal are also landmarks and they aren't leaving town. Neither am I.

Walking in New York

Bennett Cerf, founder of Random House and longtime panelist on *What's My Line* (I was a frequent guest), taught me how to walk in New York. If you have a lot of blocks to cover that involve north or south *and* east and west—like you have to get from Seventy-ninth Street and Madison Avenue to Seventy-second and Second Avenue—go with the signals, never ever stand on a corner waiting for the light to change. This means you don't go straight in one direction along one street as far as you need to, as in walking to the end of Seventy-ninth before cutting over to Second, then walk straight down second but, instead, you zig and zag. You may get to a corner and the light is green but don't necessarily cross the street *with* the light. Instead, round the corner to right or left and keep walking to corner of next block so when you get there you have a choice of which way to go depending on the signal. For something so simple I'm not explaining this well. I know when you start doing it, you'll understand. You do not *ever* wait for a signal to turn green if you can avoid it. You zig and you zag with whatever is possible at the time. I've saved a million hours.

Sex / Affection

Women in Pants

Talk about antique ideas . . . I don't think pants are sexy for women. Not that women in pants by the millions don't have sexual assignations, but pants don't strike me as something to wear if you are hoping to encourage sex. He can't get up them, under them, through them, or *into* them, if you'll pardon the expression, without unzipping and dragging the garment down over your hips . . . a *chore*. If you put up even a tiny fuss, which is part of the game, he has to have hands to crack hickory nuts or detonate a dynamite charge to get them off you. You can get the pants off yourself, of course—it happens—but we're talking seduction here, not let-me-do-that-let's-get-on-with-this directions. Dresses, on the other hand, are meant to be crept up inside of until hands touch underwear . . . a sweet, friendly, almost innocent pursuit, much sweeter than him *or* you boldly unzipping the fly of your slacks. Okay, you aren't wearing what could be called underwear under your dress, you are wearing what could be called "panty hose," a garment some passion-pursuers consider as passion-encouraging as a plaster cast. Doesn't have to be. Although panty hose are a challenge, a Real Man can get your dress scooched up over your hips and the panty hose away from your waist enough for him to touch real girl underneath. Oh, I'm sick of explaining this to you. I'm just saying somebody in a dress is giving off sexier vibes than somebody in pants, even those disguised by Armani or Calvin Klein. Yes, slender eighteen year-old nymph is delicious in anything, but as one gets a little further over the garden wall (forty? fifty?) dresses are just friendlier, prettier, more feminine.

Girl Blessings

I wouldn't want to be a man the next time I come back—men can't fake orgasms. They can in a very limited way if they are with some idiot person who doesn't know anything, but it isn't easy. Men are supposed to be showy. If they say it happened, something has to come *out*. The man can say, "It's all *Inside* you, my dear," but it would *Still* come out when you go to the john. No, it's a distinct disadvantage for a man—he has to come *through* . . . *we* can fake our brains out and get nothing but credit.

Hugging's Better Than Kissing to Express Intimacy

In olden days even a tiny kiss among friends was considered slushy, so you didn't. Now that everybody is kissing *everybody* on both cheeks (headwaiter, salesclerk, person you met last week and can't remember his name), a real hug says much better than cheek-kissing, "I like you, I'm glad we're in each other's lives." It's fun to hug men except they're so much taller, but they usually don't mind bending down.

Sexy Thai Women

A reporter who interviewed me for the *Asia Times* in Bangkok was married to a Thai girl, and I gleaned he had intimate knowledge of several others. "The most sexual creatures in the world," he told me. "What do they do that makes them so sexy?" I asked. "It's their touch," he said. "Gentle, beautiful." "What *else*," I encouraged. "It's how you make *them* feel," he said. "You make them so happy."

Ah yes, the old you-make-me-so-happy response. I resisted telling my new friend the happy responders aren't all right there in Thailand. In other countries, even right here in the United States, young women are being made happy by loving partners and don't hesitate to say so. Maybe "You make me so happy" has more credibility coming out of a rosebud mouth in a childlike face. An American journalist, also in Bangkok, told me the Thai women indeed *seem* childlike . . . sweet, passive . . . but put them behind the wheel of a Mercedes and they're killers. Out comes the aggression. Instead of "You make me so happy," it's more like "Cut me off one more time like that and I'll blast your balls off." I like those Thai women better now.

The Touch System

Men who touch you—on the sleeve, shoulder, anyplace "safe"—are the best. The touchers. These are warm, confident men. Scared-of-touch, scared-of-*feelings* men . . . nontouchers . . . these are the dangerous ones. How anybody could object to a man coming up behind her at her desk and massaging her neck I can't imagine. I would *pay* him.

Giving Permission

Breathes there a woman with brain (or bod) so dead she thinks she is doing a man a favor to "let him do things to her," as in fondle, probe, enter, feels that *she* has committed the ultimate human sacrifice to do certain things . . . I believe it's called fellatio, though we don't call it much of anything while it's happening . . . to *him*? I'm afraid there *is* such a woman, perhaps many, who still believe the old "giving in to his sexual inclinations is a big fucking [if you'll pardon the expression] capitulation." What is she, a *flower*? A teenager, being force-fed cod liver oil? A female buried alive in the Jane Austen era? I don't *know*. Is *he* a globby, grabby, despoiler of virgins? No, she dutifully stopped being a virgin several years ago. As I write about her I can hardly believe the reluctantly tolerant woman still exists but men—who tend to tell me things—have reported the condition . . . "she *lets* me but she's doing me a favor." Weird. Done right, what he's doing to our heroine should be for her as good as it gets. Whatever she does to *him*, the tomcat is smart enough to purr up a storm and know he isn't doing *her* a favor . . . he *knows* about good as it gets.

Driving and Sex

I believe good drivers—focused, don't show off but never get stuck behind a truck making a delivery, a bus letting off passengers, or a car double-parking—are good in bed. These people—we're talking men—I never think about whether women are good in bed—just very smoothly, efficiently get the girl or the car to do what they want and what the *girl* wants . . . no bumpiness, swerving, dawdling. A friend says good dancers are good in bed. Maybe, except some of the best dancers I know are gay and what good would that do *me*? I'm sure you have your who's-good-in-bed theories. He can get asparagus to grow in rotten soil? Always knows when to get back on the tour bus before it leaves without him for Salerno? I think my theory holds up better than these.

Lovemaking for Grown-up Girls

When a woman is, say, up to thirty, all she has to do is show up for the lovemaking, cooperate, and be adored. He is so turned on by her youthful person just being there, he will, sometime during the evening, even selflessly do things for and to *her*, daffy-happy for the privilege. In there somewhere it changes. When she is fifty, sixty, maybe only forty, the most successful lovemaking is her doing things to *him*. He still brings her to orgasm—pleased with the feel of her pliant body—but concentration switches over to his penis . . . to the stroking, loving, sucking, handling and, most of all, admiring thereof. Not a bad exchange. We still get sex when his brain and body might—and what do we mean "might"—prefer a younger, less puckered-up body but hands belonging to that body wouldn't do the things we can and will do so adroitly. I'm not unhappy with the arrangement.

Postponed Orgasm

There is nothing like holding off and not having an orgasm one week, two, more—whatever works for you—to have the greatest orgasm of your life when it happens. This takes discipline. You have not to masturbate no matter how inclined you are. You could get betrayed in your plan by having the event happen in your sleep but if you're over nineteen, that isn't too great a possibility. A really longed-for, ready-for-it, haven't-in-a-while orgasm doesn't have anything much better than it.

How Big *Is* He?

The vertical indentation in a man's ear that dips down into the fleshy part of the lobe is an indication of how big his erect penis will be. Shallow ear-indentation correspond to small penises; deeper (like the shape of Italy) go with larger. I haven't been able to corroborate this theory recently but in my single days found it infallible. Elliot Paul, author of *The Last Time I Saw Paris*, told it to me. Check it out.

Penis Envy

Who would want a penis or anything that goes with penis ownership? The owners have to fish it *out* every time they go to the bathroom, when finished, shake it free of droplets, tuck it back *in* shorts and pants . . . tiresome. Sex, poor darlings . . . like someone who *always* gets stuck with the tab, an entertainer who is invariably asked to play or sing at civilian parties, whoever has a penis is expected to get it up and get it *in* . . . ditch digging! He with his penis is permanently *on*, so to speak (or, up, in this case). He can't fake and he can't lie. I would never want to have one.

Men in Love

Men are so goofy and sweet and touching, when they're in love you could squeeze them to pieces. They're little-boy tender and do sweet things . . . build a greenhouse for her cymidium orchids, find the out-of-print Edith Warton she's hyperventilating for, make cocoa and toasted cheese puffs for her Sunday breakfast. I'm not talking about an intimidated man trying to placate a harridan, a mama's boy who has gone oedipal with his mate, not even about a loyal, supportive man who recognizes fair-is-fair, she's a good wife and mother, he will do good for her. I'm talking about an in-love male person who is simply sappy to make her happy.

When I was writing this book, my Royal 440 manual typewriter keys were buried in sludge—I hadn't taken time to clean them in fifteen years—so one Friday night I impulsively sponged them down with a ton of Carbona cleaning fluid, somehow jammed the keys so not one word could be typed, and I couldn't get the keys unstuck. Devastation! I had planned two full days of typing-writing and now I had nothing to do it on. David came home from Los Angeles that night, assimilated my grief, didn't take time to loosen his tie, and barely dropped his luggage when he said, "Don't you remember you've got a spare typewriter down in the annex [that little room under the kitchen where we store wine, summer and winter clothes]? You bought it from Hearst for $25.00 when they were dumping old equipment. I'll go down and get it." He descended steep stairs from kitchen to annex, hoisted typewriter back up to my bedroom desk. "Try it out," he said. Typewriter worked. Saturday, Sunday workload saved, this before he even announced, "I had the hot fudge sundae on American Airlines, don't hate me, what's for dinner?" his usual greeting. He bailed me from the typewriter crisis because he loves me . . . understands his workaholic wife, wants me not to be unhappy, to smile. He was proud of himself all weekend. "Did I find you another typewriter, or *what*!" Tender. Goofy. I sometimes think they are better than we are in love, though I guess there are goods and bads in both sexes.

Married Men

One of my close friends and I were talking about a fortyish, attractive, achieving—more in philanthropy than commerce—woman who had an affair with a high-ranking official in the Nixon administration. Nola is horrified. How could the woman *do* that with a married man? Though I adore her, Nola doesn't live in the real world. Married to a prince at age twenty, she and Marshall are still married, though divorced once and remarried; they have two children, two grandbabies . . . life is good. Nola was never old enough or needy enough to "pick" on a married man and maybe she never would have anyway. It's always kind of refreshing—if irritating—to hear her views on single women not eschewing married men—whores! Some of us are a little more sympathetic to the single one and don't expect her to do a lot of eschewing. I am tiresome on the subject but may I tell you my thoughts again?

From the married man a single woman may get sex, even *great* sex, worship, wooing, help with her career, and other perks, usually not financial because that puts a whole different spin on the friendship, makes her too dependent. Expensive dinners and lunches, a trip or two, maybe an Armani suit if the man is rich are fine. He, of course enjoys great sex, corroboration of his *manhood*, one thousand-watt attention from an interesting, pretty woman who doesn't put his children and her parents first. My take is that a girl shouldn't be expected to help a wife protect her turf, it's up the wife. I protect mine with everything but a Thompson submachine gun; I know whose responsibility keeping the man faithful is, though sexual faithfulness may not be the *most* important part of the marriage to many women—and that's *their* business. A good marriage—or at least better than the alternative—is comprised of *lots* of stuff.

To carry on just a *little* more, there are too many single women *over* the age of forty in our midst these days . . . have you noticed? . . . divorced, widowed, usually married at one time, to match up with the too-few single men who, when they pick a bride, usually choose one much younger than they (how about press lord Rupert Murdoch, sixty-eight, and Wendi Deng, thirty-one??) I am of the persuasion that a woman needs a man in her life for purposes of sex and relating to the opposite gender. A woman, *particularly* if she isn't nubile, may need to borrow one who isn't getting quite what he needs at home, she so very grateful and he grateful as well. My friend Toby has had a married man in her life for two years for purposes of sex and even romance. They both travel in their work, he a lawyer with international clients. Any city they are in at the same time, including their home base New York, is the backdrop for a big-time assignation. Toby doesn't need money, job help, or glamour, but the man makes up for not being "hers" with devotion—flowers for no reason, sometimes a *good* present. Widowed, great-looking at fifty-three, Toby tells me, "He keeps me from having that desperate, hungry look you see on single older women who are looking, looking, looking. I'm taken care of in the sex department, and don't give off desperation vibes. I've been smart enough not to fall in love. Naturally I keep dating every single man I can get my hands on but how many are there? His wife has their three houses, the money, is Ms. Somebody. I'm not stealing much from her that she wants. Naturally this arrangement can't go on forever but with the statistical shortage of men in my age group, to me I'm only doing what seems sensible." This shortage won't show up in the U.S. Census report, incidentally, which lumps gay, drug-addicted, imprisoned, or otherwise unavailable men in the same single category.

P.S. If you'd been a single woman in the mid-nineteenth century in a frontier town in the United States, you'd have been stampeded with mate offers. Not nearly enough females to help man the covered wagon, stake out new territory, fight off Indians . . . you deal with the statistics they hand out with *your* birthdate.

Adultery Check, Oh My!

Why *are* we (not me) so horrified that people cheat? I guess I don't know. Carrying on as though somebody sleeping with somebody, not your legal mate, is just this side of bombing churches or blowing up buses seems a little extreme to me. How can people, sensible about so *much*, think all *other* people must/can/should tamp down sex feelings for any but a marriage partner, all you need is a little get-away-from-me power? Doesn't anybody *get* it . . . adultery is about sex. Sex is about it *feels* good . . . *very* good; I have been saying for a long time that sex is one of the three best things we have, and I don't know what are the other two (warm cookies? Petting a baby shih tzu?). Are you supposed to feel this intense pleasure only with the person you are married to the rest of your life? Supposedly, but we aren't dealing with "supposedly," we are dealing with *bodies*, one part of which—the genitals—frequently gets in touch with *another* part—the brain—and tells it to move in the direction of climbing into bed with somebody a little more stimulating than Gladdy or Oliver to whom body parts' owner has been married possibly twenty years.

Although sex isn't the only component part of an affair—all that rapt listening by a new person can kick in—these strong physical feelings do sometimes ignite adultery, surprise, surprise! Repeat: sex is a *physical* feeling, to be intellectualized (as in it isn't *there*, I don't feel a *thing*) in order to accommodate a moral imperative at one's *peril*. You can suffocate the sexual inclinations, sure, but the loss can cause twitches, tension, and depression or, in trying to suffocate the feelings, you drive off a cliff some night coming home from a party. Reality check: in suggesting that people give up sex ever again with a New Person, we're not talking about eschewing pepperoni pizza, white chocolate truffles, sloe gin fizzes, or your favorite Ingmar Bergman reruns the rest of your life. We're talking about New Sex, aside from whose physical yumminess is dynamite, there is also the dynamite intimacy, the "we've got something special going here . . .

so much to *tell* each other." Nothing headier than orgasm joined with flowering friendship. Am I pushing adulterous sex? No, just explaining what makes it happen, why it's hard to kill it dead, as if you didn't know.

Each of us has a contract with ourselves and a mate about sexual fidelity whether we talk it over or not. I have been able to stay faithful all these years because (a) I like my partner and (b) I got the "play" out of my system in seventeen single years. No longer a virgin at twenty, married at thirty-seven, I had a few seasons to experience (though the world didn't think single girls *had* sex at that time, let alone enjoyed themselves) the thrill of a new partner or two . . . we aren't counting, are we? *Everyone* except partners of an arranged marriage has a few single years to frolic and play if so desired, and more and more have a few between divorce and remarriage if life goes that way, but few have endless summers for sexual dalliance. If someone feels he or she can/must/should/*will* remain faithful, bravo, but for the world to expect fidelity as the norm and get all puffy when it isn't seems a little looney to me. I feel straying isn't anybody else's but the participants' business *ever*, and that surely includes public figures.

Though I fitted other worries into my day, what grieved me almost as much as the Clinton calamity (the discovery and exploitation by media and Republicans, not the deed) were high-ranking men and women in the U.S. military, lieutenant colonels on down, who wound up jobless for having Given In. Sexual harassment wasn't involved in these cases; these were grown-ups consensually having sex. All that silliness that adultery in leaders somehow endangers the country, are we nuts? Other countries think so. They don't expect their prime ministers and presidents to be puritans or feel having mistresses and girlfriends interferes with the ability to lead. Closer to home, extramarital sex also has little to do with the effectiveness of a Fortune 500 board chairman, union leader, school principal, or veterinarian if they're good at the job. Perhaps you subscribe to the lust-in-the-heart-is-okay-as-long-as-you-don't-give-in idea. Fine, go ahead and lust only in *your* heart and don't give in if that's the way you want to play it. Actually, it may not be all that difficult in your case! Possibly nobody asked you (to lust). If nobody asks, you don't have all that gut-tearing decision making to do. I *hope* the lack of an offer isn't what's keeping you so "pure."

Homosexuality—Female

Some people, frequently gay themselves, say we could *all* be homosexual . . . all are *inherently* homosexual if we'd just let ourselves go. This group thinks sexual preference is carefully taught. As we are taught not to have anything to do sexually with a family member, we also are taught not to fancy our own sex, that without those inhibiting instructions we would just go willy-nilly for girls if we're girls, boys if we're boys. I don't think so. I started being crazy about little boys when I was six. In first grade (I didn't go to kindergarten so I couldn't start sooner) I was getting crushes on male classmates. Nobody *told* me to go for baby boys, not girls. Girls were your *buddies*—*are* your buddies, frequently your *intimates* . . . it just isn't physical. I remember my best friend, Betty Engstron, and me, ages seven and eight, sitting on her living room floor on Spruce Street examining our own genitals, though it would be forty years before anybody civilian called them that—at the time it was just "down there." We then smelled our fingers but only our own, not each other's. If one were going to be attracted to one's own sex, wouldn't that have been an occasion to get started? Never entered *my* little head to go near her nor anybody else my same sex ever since.

Around the same time my sister Mary and I used to look at the medical equipment offered in the Sears Roebuck's catalog—enemas, high colonics, bedpans—and, I believe, get mildly titillated but not about each *other*, just tiny twigs of sexuality getting started. In Pulaski Heights Grammar School and Pulaski Heights Junior High School in Little Rock, one's interest in boys fully developed and never flagged. In eighth grade there was a handsome girl—tall, strong-featured, a young Greek warrior—who was noticeably interested in my pretty friend Elizabeth Jessup, though Elizabeth didn't pay much attention. Handsome girl later had a sex-change operation, not, I'm sure, because her facial and body structure said masculine but because her insides *told* her to. Programmed *in*. Ingrained.

No other girl has ever made a pass at me, though twice I think somebody got close. One was an older famous writer who had just me to her apartment for dinner when I was twenty. The cousin of a friend, she was maybe fifty. I later found out she *was* (gay) but she must surely have gleaned that I *wasn't* and didn't make a move. I'm sure I bored the socks off her with nothing sexual to offer, and she sure didn't get much of anything *else* from my twenty-year-old brain.

Later, one of my neighbors was *too* helpful . . . making hors d'oeuvres for my party, helping out like a slave, trying, I think, to let me know how much she cared for me . . . you get feelings about it when somebody is sexually turned on, man or woman, but that never got to the first pass. I like to think I haven't missed anything or not much anyway in life. I missed the experience of being with another woman sexually, but it didn't appeal.

Bisexuality? Always looks to me as though the bisexual person prefers his or her own sex but is willing—let's don't miss anything here!—to try both sexes. Many so-called bisexual people marry the opposite sex, wanting children and/or not wanting to suffer the public gasps at same-sex marriage. We, the public, are getting a little less silly in this regard and gays a little more brave. So, who can explain it, who can tell you why . . . we haven't actually figured out the root of homosexuality, have we? Why some of us are gay and some aren't. Ingrained is all I can come up with.

Cheer for the Hopelessly in Love Who Think They Are Going to Die

Cheer up! You can feel just as rotten about somebody else as you do now about this one. You don't find this cheering? Of *course* you do. If you know that someday you can suffer as badly with a new person as you are now suffering with this one, that means present torturer *isn't* the sun, moon, and Wolferman's buttery little crumpets you'd thought—there's *life* out there! Of course, you're going to have to get rid of him or her to find the new torturer, not easy because this one undoubtedly has assets like the end of the world in bed; you may even *love* him or her. Also you've bailed previously . . . left, come back, left again, come back, a tub of *tallow* with all that loving, leaving, reuniting, hurting worse, on and on. Promise: one time the leaving will be the last one and you can get on with suffering over somebody new. You're not cheered *yet*? How about this? Not only can you fall in love with another bad person and hurt over him or her as much as you do this one, you can fall in love with somebody who isn't a shit at all. I did that. The important thing is to stop "knowing" that this present miserable large-looming creature is the only one, there can be no other. There *can* be. Repeat: the proof that you're wrong will be when you hurt nonstop about a new one— shall we get going?—or maybe even connect with a sweetie. But isn't there such a thing as loving only one person good or bad, really loving them in a lifetime? Maybe if you meet in high school, marry soon after, and can tolerate endless boredom, pique, and aggravation—plus you think falling in love again is immoral or too much trouble. If you *think* there is only one true love and you've found it—maybe even years *after* high school—fine. Many of us don't belong to the once-in-a-lifetime crowd. We think you're missing a *lot*.

Marriage: Hollywood Royalty Style

Hiring, firing, job advancement, alimony, child custody, car and house-leasing . . . now all equal opportunity . . . bravo! Another equal op, more and more invoked by women who have amassed lots of money of their own: the prenup. Anyone gasping about Barbra Streisand's prenup, if she has one and we don't actually know whether she has, with husband James Brolin, and suggesting she was "buying" the man, must still think men walk nearer the curb to protect a woman from horses and carriages running amok in the street, that fat makes a man jolly and healthy. Far from buying him, Ms. Streisand was probably protecting her ass.

Prenup details are not usually made public unless by the divorcing wives of Donald Trump or Donald himself, and there was the well-publicized case of Lee Radziwill leaving her about-to-be husband, Newton Cope, as they were actually walking up the aisle and she learned of his unsatisfactory financial arrangement for her: we don't know the numbers.

What caused twitters about the Brolin agreement, should there have been one, were the numbers reported in various publications "based on sources close to Streisand." Reportedly, in the event of a divorce before their tenth anniversary, she will pay him one million dollars plus $300,000 for every year the marriage lasts. Should the marriage last ten years, that could run the tab up another three million. After that, the price of a divorce for her, according to the printed rumors, would be ten million. Considering how much money she probably has—an estimated 100 million—this amount doesn't seem excessive. What about other sums she might have to shell out in case of divorce and, listen, we hope it doesn't *happen*. Usually a spouse keeps the assets he or she brings to marriage. If these assets increased during marriage, the spouse who didn't bring them can sometimes *still* claim a portion of the profits if he or she can prove he or she contributed (sound investing, shrewd advice) to the escalation of assets. If Barbra's estate is the estimated 100 million, one can imagine it would increase substantially through the years. Maybe her husband could convince the court that he helped make it grow and get half or a third of the increase in case of divorce; a prenup giving him cash on the line at divorce time might encourage him *not* to *try* to participate in the asset growth, and such a stipulation might have been written in. During marriage, if one spouse earns more than the other, after living expenses are deducted, the money belongs to both. One assumes, though he is doing pretty well, Barbra's income (concert, movie, and record deals) would top his by many millions. Perhaps something was included in the agreement saying that he doesn't *get* half of what they accumulate together since her accumulation would be so much greater, never mind *Pensacola: Wings of Gold* doing well and a seven-year deal with AAMCO. We're just conjecturing here. I know you don't like to be unsentimental at times like these, but Brolin was a catch. Maybe we could say the money she promises in case of divorce is a signing bonus with terms of disengagement, a standard part of many employment contracts these days, not that discharging marital duties is exactly like helming General Electric. Could we talk for a minute about another kind of prenup delineated by the Menninger Foundation a few years ago? According to the famous psychiatric facility in Topeka, all marryers have three contracts: One: the formal agreement, documented by a marriage license (they don't mention a prenup). Two: an informal agreement—couple decides where they will live, country or city, apartment or house; whether or when to start a family; whose parents will be visited oftener at Christmas. Pool salaries? Funds acquired together will go into T-bonds, real estate, starting a business, etc., etc. Three: the Secret Contract, never discussed by the couple, possibly not even acknowledged by either party to *himself*, but subliminally known: the psychological composition of the other which dovetails with and even enhances his own. Example: wife, a world-class ditz, presumes the falling yen is a tree losing its leaves; Baby Bells go on tricycles; if the IMF bails out people, maybe they could help Uncle Fred. Husband, a ranking intellectual, far from finding her ditziness embarrassing, finds it comforting. The dumber she is— she's also pretty—the smarter, more superior he . . . great emotional fit. Another Secret Contract: husband attractive, charming alcoholic, wife plain, teetotalling, moral fiber tightly woven. As long as husband continues to drink, she, his jailer, is superior and safe, he is hers forever. Should he quit drinking, not be a weakling anymore, he might find a more attractive mate. Abrogated Secret Contracts can cause major mischief. None of us know the Brolins' secret contract, they surely have one. I'm just pointing out the not-too-sentimental reasons a man and woman may find one another palatable that have nothing to do with money or even love but could lead somebody toward a generous prenup. Their secret emotional needs fit.

There's one more deal that marrying couples cut—again not openly discussed. I call it The Package—we all come with one. What is in a courting person's package is very important if he or she is the one trying to sign up the other party. Wooing partner throws in everything he or she can cram in . . . may even come up with extra stuff (borrow your boss's ranch house in Jackson Hole for a nice little getaway for you and your lover, reveal that you have paid cash for a Mercedes Benz sports car as I did, be adorable with his kids, etc.). If he is the one who desires marriage more than his girlfriend, he may promise to take her on virtually every glamorous business assignment no matter where in the world after they marry. He didn't offer that with his first wife. A package comprises only good stuff. In Barbra's package: Rich—very. Famous—big (many people *like* a glitzy mate). Talented—awesome. Smart—furiously. Sexy—yes. Connected—she can get everybody from Michael Eisner to Sumner Redstone on the phone, thrilled to hear from her, should her mate's career need a little help, never mind his new contractual commitments. Brolin's package: Handsome—very. Successful—yes, though not in her echelon. Sexy—divinely. Financially secure—yes, but not Warren Buffet. Eligible—*mamma mia!* A few hundred thousand (sane) women—divorcees, single, widows—would be happy to say yes if asked. There's a shortage out there, if you didn't know, of attractive, solvent men *his* age who will marry somebody less than fifteen years their junior. Brolin is fifty-eight, Barbra fifty-six. An important part of this man's package is that he is *age* appropriate. So, I'm just callously pointing out what a nice fit they are, what she brings in her package to him, he to her and why she might be talking Money Out There Sometime because of their secret contracts (which we don't know) and the content of his package, which we do. Oh yes, they both seem to be in love but, as I said earlier, her prenup, with sums to be dispensed at time of possible divorce, if accurately reported, is anything but out of line. I think he is divinely lucky, probably so is she. I wish her every good thing, this genius diva who has brought me and millions of other besotted fans enough pleasure to make us start burbling and gurgling at the first spin of a B.S.C.D.

What They Do for Love

Maybe it's more a male than female thing, the cuckooness of lust. Do you know that a gentleman bison loses up to two hundred pounds in his furor to get a lady bison to accept him sexually? She's in heat but hasn't decided whether he's the one. He hangs around, paws the earth, stomps occasionally, bellows, furiously fights off the competition, gets skinnier and skinnier (if you can call the remaining nine hundred pounds skinny) trying to accommodate his lust. Of course, she's playing games, enticing and leading him on. Maybe you could say lust cuckooness is also a female thing.

Emotions

Insecurity—a Girl's Good Friend

Okay, it's final! Insecurity keeps your fires lit, maybe even makes you more alive while kicking hell—I am resisting using a really *bad* word here—out of you! Insecurity keeps you striving your life long to be better so you'll be good *enough*. Sometimes—in little dabs—briefly, fleetingly—you feel you've actually *hatched* . . . you are now a real-live chicken but you don't feel hatched very often.

I'm afraid we continue in life to be who we *were*. I started as insecure as a jelly doughnut—is that how we *all* start?—but I didn't ever get to be a nice pulled-together sponge cake (we're switching pastries here). My father, Ira Gurley, died when I was ten and left enough insurance money to care for our little threesome—Mother, sister Mary, me—for a little while, but when Mary got polio or polio got Mary (before the Salk vaccine prevented such catastrophic illness) the money flew. There was no March of Dimes or government funding to help people like us; hospitals and treatment took virtually all the insurance money. My sister would be left an invalid the rest of her life with muscles paralyzed from the waist down. My mother would be frightened, anxious, semi-melancholic a lot of the time the rest of *her* life. Cleo was a little melancholy anyway by nature, but her older daughter's health wipeout solidified the condition. So, with depressed Mommy, wheelchair-bound sister, no money, no relatives (all hillbillies up in the Ozark Mountains) or anybody else to help out, and acne like they don't *make* anymore, I was feeling less secure than most teenagers, many of whom are *socially* insecure. In high school I began the fight that fear makes you fight, using my okay little brain and pushiness plus hard work to make a few decent things happen. I don't know what my IQ is, but I think just average.

I once took a test in *Coronet* magazine and came out at 115—would that be about right? I was class valedictorian in high school and president of the Scholarship Society but that's high school, now comes grown-up time.

We couldn't afford to send me to college so I hit the deck running. Other people face problems other ways, of course . . . a dive into drugs, alcohol, prostitution . . . they didn't even occur to me or I didn't occur to *them*. I wasn't pretty enough to hook. Drugs and alcohol weren't very available then and I wouldn't have liked them if they were. The insecurity was in there deep and permanent, even to this minute, to keep me trying, doing the best I *could* and can. I had seventeen secretarial jobs from age eighteen, writing advertising copy in my midthirties—that paid better and was more fun than secretarial work—married David at age thirty-seven. Along came *Sex and the Single Girl*. In trouble in my advertising job (too few assignments for too many copywriters), I thought I was going to be fired, so I asked David to think of a book I could write—he knew how to do that for people. "Why don't you write about being single," he said. "You were like no other single girl I knew . . . you were never home." I was home. I had the phone in the refrigerator. If I'd heard it ring—no answering machines in those days—I'd have caved in and answered and he'd know I wasn't Miss Popular, out on the town. From the book came *Cosmo*, a solid hit . . . you have to hear how we got *Cosmo* started in a moment. My darling husband, the movie producer, has *himself* done well and made us financially secure. So does *that* get you off the hook—money, success, the Academy Award, the Thalberg Award, the newsstand-sale award? Of course not! You still try harder in order to be good enough or stay wherever you get.

My husband—also having been hit early and hard with Needing to Make up for Things—is pounding around Moscow in winter in his eightieth year producing a movie called *The Saint* starring Val Kilmer and Elizabeth Shue. It did well. I'm thinking what to do after I *someday* leave *Cosmo*. I've left as editor-in-chief, as I mentioned, and now work on and open up new international editions. Not as much fun as putting out a single product every month but the work ethic, somewhat making up for the insecurity, doesn't leave you.

Further insecurity-routing. I exercise twice a day, forty-five minutes each time . . . *nothing* gets in the way. After a hysterectomy—major surgery—I was back on the floor in a week, though exercise was strictly forbidden for six. When I could get to a pool, I did laps despite being told I'd open the sutures. Exercise simply makes you feel Good Enough. You are fighting back against the goblins, the furies, the scummies, plus it lets you eat without ballooning. In order to have pasta, meat loaf, hot dogs, hamburgers, pizza (four persuasions) chased by a rainbow of Häagen-Dazs sorbet and ice cream at the daily buffet of the Holland America Rotterdam, I did sixty laps every morning in their miniscule swimming pool five decks below main deck. A little murky and scary down there—I figured sharks and piranha were swimming right next to me separated by a steel wall though, of course, the ship would have shooed them away. Nobody but a nut case would go down there and spend as much time as it took me to do the laps—I'm not a good swimmer—and in such a tiny pool I did them katty-corner to lengthen the distance before turning around. Why go through all that? I already told you. So my body will be strong and hard and not get sick—and not be fat. So far it hasn't. Insecurity drives me—often in the right direction.

Chutzpah—Leaving Home with Some

Part of success, I think, comes from knowing when to push, how hard, and when to stop because you're going too far. You can't get by in life without *any* chutzpah and I think you learn that early. I don't mean kindergarten or puppyhood . . . all kids push parents and loved ones . . . but later out in the world. I did a baby push at eighteen, not too successfully but a beginning. When I was attending Woodbury Business College, learning to type and take shorthand as quickly as possible to get a job, I used to shop in downtown Los Angeles on Saturdays, not to buy—who had money?—but just to hang out with the scarves, dresses, and handbags. Next door to the Broadway Department Store—my favorite—on Fourth and Main Streets was a small hotel where I would plop in, sit in the lobby to rest. One of the bellmen was nice to me—not coming on—me a scrawny, acne-infested little person and obviously not a hooker he could negotiate with as a middle man, but frequently we would chat.

"Do you have any celebrities in this hotel?" I asked one day, mad about celebrities like everybody else. "Yes, we got a woman commentator," he said. This was 1940 and we're talking radio, not television. A woman commentator wasn't a movie star like Bette Davis or Carole Lombard—the term even sounded a little weird, nevertheless . . . "Do you think she would let me interview her for my school paper?" I asked. "She just might," said bellman-friend and called her room. If I had never heard of *her*, she never heard of Woodbury Business College, but she agreed to be interviewed and came downstairs. From here on it was mushy ice . . . I borrowed some paper from my hotel friend and what we have here is chutzpah in its embryo state. I was shy as a garter snake, didn't *work* on the school paper, didn't even know if we *had* one—a business school?—and had no idea what kind of questions to ask. I squizzled through a few—How did you get started? Where did you grow up?—she was a good talker. I typed up my interview and—surprise—there actually *was* a school paper. They turned the interview right down—poor sacrificed commentator never got to see her words in print—but at least the paper got back to me and, planted in my baby brain, was the knowledge that sometimes if you *ask*, no matter how nervy, appropriate or not, you may *get* it.

Fade to the present moment. I have invited sixteen people to dinner, my first dinner party in three years, so why start with easy? I asked Peter Jennings; Barbara Walters; Rupert Murdoch; Ron Perelman, principal owner and CEO of Revlon, big advertiser at the time; Felix Rohatyn, senior partner of Lazard Freres who had saved New York from bankruptcy, now U.S. ambassador to France; Roone Arledge, head of news and sports at ABC; Frank A. Bennack, Jr., president and CEO of the Hearst Corporation and my boss. Not a bad little list. In doing chutzpah, you know instinctively whom/what to ask—not Woody Allen and Steven Spielberg, friends and neighbors but they wouldn't come (actually both did a couple of years later) but the probables or *possibles*. I'm doing fine . . . they all said yes, gratifyingly. Day before the party Perelman cancels—has to go to Washington. I ask Jody, with whom I've been dealing, to give Ron a message. If he doesn't show up for dinner, I will never *ever* speak to him again and I mean it! Very imperious. How big a deal would that have been for Ron? Doesn't seem real big but somehow it (the old chutzpah!) worked. He showed. Several days before *that* I'm in Prague launching *Cosmo* in the Czech Republic, message comes to office that Peter Jennings will not be attending party. Two different secretaries have booked him two different places the same night and my party didn't make the cut, he'll be at the house of an old college chum who is getting married. "Charlotte," I demand, "send him to the college chum's house *first*, but deliver him unto me for dinner even if it's late." I am bossy *again*! Peter missed cocktails, showed up for dinner, and stayed late.

People think chutzpah is in the genes. It isn't . . . it's in the needing and longing and being willing to fall on your face. It isn't fun . . . who wants all that rejection, but life is sweeter if you make yourself do uncomfortable things. You learn how far to go not to have people think you a nutcase but far *enough*. Giving a dinner party isn't that much of a challenge? For *you* it isn't. For me it's gum surgery!

Working and Suffering at the Same Time . . . Compatible

All the personal crises, traumas, headaches, heartaches, dreads in the world needn't, shouldn't slow you down at work. Unless you're needed at the hospital, courthouse, funeral parlor, police station, you work and suffer simultaneously. My brother-in-law, George Alford, of Shawnee, Oklahoma, lived for twenty-eight years with chronic pain, sometimes severe, caused by a grain-elevator accident which crushed nerves that never realigned properly. From the mid-sixties to early eighties when he died, I was making arrangements for entry into yet one more pain clinic, one more consultation, neurosurgery with yet another neurosurgeon in still another city. I brought him to California for acupuncture when acupuncture still wasn't legal in the U.S. Movie producer Robert Evans got his friend, Las Vegas lawyer Sidney Korshak, to fix me up. At one point we put George in Oral Roberts University in Tulsa because they had some courses dealing with the masking of pain. Didn't help. At another time I signed George up with the head of psychiatry at the University of Oklahoma to figure out what was mental, what was real (pain is tricky). My brother-in-law also visited local Shawnee doctors, managing to get hooked on drugs.

The biggest treatment plunge was bringing him to New York University Hospital for some fairly delicate surgery involving the untangling of nerves. After the surgery, my sister, invalided from polio and in a wheelchair herself since age nineteen, was really pissed with me because they'd got awfully close to severing something important which could have left her husband incontinent. She couldn't get to the doctors but she could get to *me*, frequently at the office. Oh yes . . . suffering at work, which is where we started; it wasn't wonderful getting those phone calls from hell from my sister ("Stupid doctors, careless medical institutions, why in God's name did they do the surgery if it was that dangerous?") particularly when I'd been doing everything I knew how to do for about fifteen years for her suffering husband and each new round of treatments failed. Still we kept getting out *Cosmo.* When Mary's call would come during a meeting, I could feel George's pain, like a long-tentacled squid, reaching all the way from North Pesotum Street in Shawnee to the halls of *Cosmo* at 224 West Fifty-seventh Street in New York.

Here I should mention that although nothing ever worked, I had to keep trying for George because I adored my sister and he was reasonably good to her. A couple of years after George died, I remember getting a sister-call one evening when *Cosmo*'s managing editor, Guy Flatley, and executive editor, Bobbie Ashley, and I were together. More pain. Mary said she was sitting in her wheelchair in the middle of her living room in Shawnee completely alone, nobody to call up or turn to. New housekeeper hadn't worked out, had just left and we had to start over. She had to start over. She pulled somebody in who lasted a few months. You do family pain and your own pain and somehow you get to the printer. Obviously you don't suffer only before 9:00 A.M. or after 5:00 P.M.—after 7:30 P.M. in my case—because pain doesn't arrive just before or after work. Job crises with David have caused some of my intensest pain and at all hours! Before I was married, pain, to me, was a man cheating but I've switched over.

Feeling sad to the bone because he's hurting and you can't help is the worst pain. After David and Richard Zanuck were thrown out of Twentieth Century Fox—Richard had been studio head, David executive V.P.—David was so angry, so unhappy, it got into my very bone marrow and didn't conveniently go away while I was at the office. I ached for my husband, the more so because there wasn't a bloody thing I could do to help. No wife with a job-driven husband—are there other kinds?—could possibly think of his job crises as low on the agenda of what to take seriously and suffer over all moments of the day. David's took me apart. I remember telling *Cosmo*'s beauty editor, Mallen de Santis, of my pain one day—this after Dick and David became independent producers and Warner Brothers, the studio they hooked up with, had turned down six projects in a row.

Black out there, I told Mallen, but David had given me my career (*Sex and the Single Girl* and *Cosmo*), incredible blessings starting in my fortieth year, and if he never got a picture green-lighted, I would support him. I needn't have been so noble. *Jaws, The Sting, The Verdict, Driving Miss Daisy, A Few Good Men, Deep Impact, Angela's Ashes,* the Thalberg Award came later. Of course there was the night at the Cannes Film Festival David and Richard had a monumental fight that had them severing their twenty-eight-year friendship and twelve-year partnership, and maybe that hurt worse than all the other David work-pain although this one attacked away from home and office for a change and got fixed (they're closer than ever). My employees—*Cosmo* editors, art directors, assistants—suffered every kind of trauma at work: husband buying a girlfriend jewelry on wife's salary; death of a spouse (you can see which crises I rank first); a deranged mother who used to wander New York streets slightly drunk, picking fights with strangers until the cops picked her up, took her to jail, called George, and he'd go get her out. Kids' crushed bones, unmarried daughter impregnated by a drug dealer, don't even mention the love tragedies of my lovely *Cosmo*-girl office mates, all endured while working their day job. The magazine came out, sales climbed (usually), advertising soared (frequently). Personal pain never slowed or closed us down. Work actually seems to cut the pain a little, certainly distracts, sometimes for hours.

Conflict . . . the Worst

A real mucky problem isn't any fun but at least it's graspable—you may even develop a plan to knock its teeth in. Much worse than straightforward trouble with a beginning, a middle, and possibly even an end is conflict—not knowing which way to go. Placate J, you'll lose W, cater to B, you'll horrify S. Turn this way, you're schnock-ered, the other way, you're scrunched, do nothing and you're mired. Conflict is a zapper. Trouble you can occasionally get *out* of. Conflict you eventually do, too, but it's tougher than plain old trouble.

Revenge

No one should be without vengeance if he or she deserves it . . . I just don't think you have to wreak it yourself. Assholes haven't been assy just with *you*; they spread it around, eventually do themselves in. I have never known vengeance not to work that way . . . not just with jerks but with really venal people who have caused a lot of pain. Sure, getting even might take a little less long if you get right on the case yourself, but this requires energy and time you may need for other things, like making a living. You've heard that living *well* is the best revenge? Okay, but that requires amassing endless stuff, paying vulgar restaurant bills, and you may not be a tipper. Writing a rotten book about them is satisfyingly vengeful but that is *really* going to remove you from whatever else you were planning to do with your life and there's that tiresome business of trying to find a publisher. I think it's best to let your tormentor get his from the S.E.C., a swindled client, a shaky business venture that took his last peso while *you* get on with your life. If a man-creep-lover has betrayed you, some other lady will take care of him—he wasn't skunky just with *you*. It may take time for the bad guys to actually lose, and you don't have to help them do it. The blueprint for your revenge is built right into their DNA which makes them creepy in the first place.

Doesn't Take Himself Too Seriously . . . This Is a Compliment?

You hear these words said admiringly, affectionately of a tycoon, entertainer, civilian, meaning, I suppose, the person is down-home just like you and me, not given to big-shot-itis. He may not be given to big-shot-itis (i.e., doesn't brag or puff up in public), but if *you* don't take yourself seriously, for God's sake, who will? It's even money those people seeming to be casual about themselves are a mass of self-concern when you aren't there. They may get off a sardonic laugh on themselves occasionally, graciously tell a hostess, "I thought it was fine your grandniece wanted to tell me about her plans for postgraduate work while I was talking to the mayor," and little charming stuff like that but don't ever doubt this gracious person is a *mass* of seriousness about his own self. Figures. Healthwise you're supposed to be able to get out of a chair without a hoist, not have flabby gums, flaky skin . . . this conditioning requires serious-taking of oneself as in diet, brushing, moisturizing. Along with taking body parts seriously, when you ask for a raise, try to collect from a friend who owes you money, tell your upstairs neighbor to quiet down after midnight, you might not get too far doing your Robin Williams imitation. I think not taking yourself seriously simply means don't go public, you only agonize with husband or wife, best friend, shrink. Serious-taking of oneself is best confined to this group.

Pain Collecting

Some of us collect psychic pain the way squirrels collect acorns, teenagers T-shirts, I know it's out there and, by God, I'll find it. Once collected, you'd as soon give it back? I'm not sure. Pain is what you do. Like foster parents who can take in one more child, bless them, you can fit in one more pain-causer though it's crowded in there already. Capacity to suffer is very expandable for us psychic masochists. When one pain-causer actually disappears (you got the money you needed or the invitation or the job) you hardly notice because you're out there trolling again. Fortunately the supply is endless. If nothing else is cropping up you can always eat yourself into blimpdom and weep.

Other People's Pain

It's hard to feel somebody else's pain even if you've had the same kind yourself once or twice so you *know* it. Just as well we can't double over and writhe around for them—we've got enough pain of our own which we *can* feel all the way to China without needing to feel anybody else's. Nevertheless, I made an exception last week and at least *rationalized* I was feeling somebody else's pain enough to let him off the hook about something I was mad at him about.

Ron Perelman was across the room at the Four Seasons and I just decided during lunch *not* to stay mad at him for canceling all *Cosmo*'s Revlon advertising two years ago (too boring to go into—not our fault and Ron says it's never coming back). You know, I said to myself, he has a lot of problems. He's not very tall (5'7"? 5'9"?—his office won't tell me), not Tom Cruise in the handsome department, has a bald spot on the back of his head. I'll bet Ronald *hates* those things about himself, I said to myself . . . plus he's inching towards sixty. Sure, smart beyond smart, rich beyond rich, but I'll just bet he doesn't like the way he looks! That gets him off the hook in terms of our not getting Revlon advertising. I was looking for a way because anger is so debilitating. Of course I don't care so much about the advertising now that I've left *Cosmo* but I'm glad I forgave him. We're actually kind of friends and he sends me Revlon Red lipstick, my favorite coral-red. Actually, I think he's getting better-looking all the time.

So Screw Pain

My shrink and friend, Janet Kennedy, lost a strand of ten-milligram real pearls this week and was cheated out of $11,000 on some antique furniture she sold. Not a specialist in drug therapy, she suggested to a client she consult a *psychiatrist* who *was* a specialist and get an opinion. Client did that and never came back to Janet. Janet broke her ankle recently because no one warned her not to look down at floor with her new bifocals; she looked, tripped, and broke.

"How do you *stand* it?" I asked my friend. "I know you are a shrink and more emotionally stable than most of us . . . goes with the territory . . . but you have so *much* gruesomeness to bear right now." "I have a secret weapon," she said. "What, *what*?" "I have no choice," said my doctor. Well, looking at it that way surely saves a lot of agony, I guess, plus indecision. You have no choice so you just start up and go *through* it.

Forgive Us Our Debts

The Lord's Prayer is one of my nightly go-to-sleep mantras, but when we get to "forgive us our debts as we forgive our debtors," I have trouble because I don't think I *have* any debts . . . I've paid off everything. The Presbyterian Church's version—"forgive us our trespasses as we forgive those who trespass against us"—is murky to me . . . what's a *trespass*? Whatever trespassing is, I don't think I'm doing it. A little while ago I decided to substitute faults for debts. "Forgive us our faults as we forgive the faults of others!" Improvement? I think so. We all have faults. Next line, "Lead us not into temptation but deliver us from evil." I've always wondered what they were thinking about in olden days when they wrote that. Don't mess with

Sarah's husband or Aaron's teenage nephew perhaps? Don't even *think* about appropriating Absolom's lion-head shield for your collection or luring Balthazar's calves over to your place and mingling with your own . . . possibly. For me, temptation is just one thing: don't scoop all the petit fours off the plate at a tony restaurant into your purse and, if scooped, don't eat them all at once when you get home. Try to make yourself throw them in the john. I never met a cookie I didn't eat now or later, and what I've just suggested would be *serious* temptation resisting for me.

Okay, in the prayer I've asked to have my faults forgiven instead of my trespasses or debts, but now I've got a *different* problem: I don't have any faults, at least to me they aren't. Whatever other people might think faulty is something I probably can't do without. Does the killer thrift hurt anybody except a few greedy hairdressers and freeloading friends? Not really. Is recycling baggies, using the back of paper only used on one side, waiting for buses instead of running for taxis, and never *ever* not using senior citizens' fare criminal? I can't see it. Planning what I'm going to do the next fifteen minutes, fifteen days, fifteen years instead of listening to somebody drone may seem a little cavalier, but he doesn't *know* . . . he's lucky I'm *there*. The workaholism—I'd rather work than go out and play with you—some might think selfish but is so deeply ingrained and, more important, income-producing, I'm not giving it up. So how can you be comfortable with a revised Lord's Prayer "Forgive us our faults" if you don't have any? I've worked it out. "Forgive us our faults as we forgive the faults of others and seek to know which of ours are indigenous (hard to rout . . . shaky nervous system, need too much sleep, etc.), which have been collected like barnacles through the years and can be scraped away with guts and perseverance." I haven't promised I *will* scrape them away, only that they will be identified. I think that's a good revision. The original prayer-framers aren't going to care and I'm not actually praying to anybody anyway, just using this nice prayer and its soothing, beautiful writing to shut off the day.

Parents

Could They Actually Know Something?

Parents have enormous power over us when we're little and want to keep the power no matter how old we get. "Your hair would look better short," she says. "Why don't you get a haircut?" "I don't see this company going anywhere," says Dad. "You should get back to those bio-engineering people who called you last year." Still, they've lived a long time and might actually *know* something. I *never* listened to my mother *ever* in my youth but now find myself wearing only pink or white next to my face, "Yellow makes your skin muddy," and eating two eggs for breakfast every morning, "Would it *hurt* you to get something in your stomach?" I thought my mother knew *nothing*. I wish I had been a little nicer to her and done some of the things she said sooner.

Don't Tell Me about It

The incredible casualness of children. When I was eight, nine, ten years old, my mother told me often that her car, a sweet little grey Chevy, was her horse in the city, took the place of Topsy in the country. As a teacher in a small country school in Osage, Arkansas, she had ridden Topsy to "work," three miles away from home, every day, now the Chevy was her conveyor. Fine. Did I ever ask her if she saddled the horse herself—not a mean feat for somebody 5'1", weighing ninety-five pounds, or did one of her brothers help? What did Topsy do all day while waiting for her owner's return, just stand around? Did the horsie get anything to eat? Were the children interested in the steed or disinterested because probably they had one of their own?

If somebody I just met or knew already told me she/he had ridden a horse to school every day, I'm *pretty* certain I would have asked a question or two, out of politeness, yes, but also out of interest—a little revelation like that isn't without interrogating possibilities. My mother was never asked *once* anything by me about the school transportation.

Cleo also told me a hundred times—two hundred?—through the years that her body was torn up giving birth to both Mary and me. Country doctors didn't know from Caesarians then, just "let her rip"; she still had pain. Did I ever bring *up* the subject of her residual pain, ask if she was sure there wasn't something still to be done? No. I knew my father, Ira, had taken her to the Mayo Clinic in Rochester, Minnesota, for repair work because Mary and I went along, surgery not real successful. For me that seemed to take care of the subject.

A mother's comfort or lack of was not riveting talk material or even endurable for a child. As a grown-up, I took care of my mother financially, wrote her an almost daily letter when she and Mary lived in Arkansas, me in Los Angeles or New York, *loved* her—she was a good mother, as I have already written, but I was never much interested in *her* life as a kid when *I* was a kid or even in things that happened to her later. Kid casualness. I wonder if my callowness, not so off-the-wall unusual for a youngster to exhibit with a parent, and even later casualness when I wasn't so young, *never* asking her to talk about her life, turning away a bit when she did, kept me from rushing to want to have young persons in my own life (i.e. babies). Who *needed* a child's boredom, his or her eye-glazing when one was talking about oneself even if the child caved in and started paying a *little* more attention when he got to be about 39. Along with other possible motives not to want children (you have to *sacrifice* for the little creatures once they get here!), I think knowing how I was with *my* mother in terms of never asking a question about her life or listening much when she talked *may* have been a turn-off toward wanting somebody like me in my *own* life!

Mother and Daddy and Your Birth Sign

Your astrological sign depends totally on when your mother and father made love, doesn't it? Nine months from that night or day, if something "took," you will come down the chute, that day will be your birthday. Yes, I suppose they *could* have said, "Wouldn't it be wonderful to have a May baby . . . we'll be in our new house by then and your mother can come help" or "August would be good for a baby . . . things are slow at your plant." Maybe a couple starts consulting the calendar like Copernicus his maps to see when they ought to be "at it" for the convenient May or August arrival, but I doubt it. I doubt even more they are calendar-consulting to produce an entertaining and versatile little Gemini or compassionate Pisces. The conversation the night you were conceived was probably more about ski vacation, his attraction to and denial of attraction to the new office redhead, the dismal state of the market at closing that day than a May or August arrival *or* "I'm glad we decided on Virgo or Cancer." Maybe they had been trying to have a baby—any baby— and been skipping the birth control but I doubt anybody said or even thought, "Let's forget the birth control *now* and go for a fiery baby Aries or a sensual Taurus." Your arrival day and astrological sign could also have to do with her forgetting her diaphragm that passionate night or his screwing up with a condom. Even if they were planning, as we said, for an artistic Libra or loving Leo, development of a fetus takes incipient mothers different amounts of time from the moment of conception until birth date. Your late or early arrival by a few days or even hours could have plopped you into Sagittarius instead of Capricorn. You might think about all this next time you feel all perky and preordained with the tenacity of a Taurus or intensity of Scorpio. But maybe you don't care whether they planned you as a Virgo or a Cancer, you *are* that sign, a perfect exemplar of each. Have it your way. I am an Aquarius, a sign categorized as "friendly, willing, reformer, healer, idealistic, intellectual, wise, faithful"—absolutely accurate except for the last six! I've also read that "Aquarians may excel in photography, radiography, electronics—anything connected with the electrical and radio industries—aviation and everything technical." I can't use an electric can opener *or* type on an electric typewriter. I tend to be with Kaye Ballard, the nightclub entertainer, who says, "How can you believe in a science predicated on Hitler and Shirley Temple being born in the same month?"

Friends

Comforting a Friend

When somebody is in trouble . . . the worse the trouble the more this is true . . . they don't want to hear that somebody else had the same problem. It is simply not comforting to know that your cousin Rhonda had a messy income tax audit or you, too, were recently confronted by an angry ex-roommate who said you stole her binoculars. When Walter Cronkite was recovering from knee-replacement surgery, he had a note pinned to his shirt that said, "I already know about my knee and I don't want to hear about yours." Listen hard and say "You poor baby"—and mean it—endlessly, at several different sessions if necessary. Later if/when asked for advice, you can dredge up what some of the others did or even invoke your own experience.

Late People

Woody Allen says half of success is just showing up. Is the other half showing up on *time*? Probably not, but promptness surely is nice for the ones being shown up for. What kind of excuse is "I got stuck in traffic" (there is *always* traffic, start earlier) or "Jo Jo called. . . . got trapped just as I was leaving." Tell Jo Jo you'll call back later. A pox on the one who fits in one more thing before leaving for *your* date, your time obviously less precious than his so you can deep breathe until the breathless one shows up twenty minutes late, the car washed, dog shampooed, ham casserole assembled, Jo Jo gossiped with. Unlike mammoth IQ, classic beauty, or athletic skill which one may not have been allotted, being on time is the courtesy of winners, something you can control. Have you ever known an always-late person who wasn't creepy? Me either.

Forgiving Friends

It takes twice as much energy to stay mad as to forgive, so I usually cave. Two years would be forever for me to stay mad. Revenge is maybe even better than forgiving but I have trouble with revenge and usually let *life* take care of the enemy. Diane Von Furstenberg went for the revenge a few years ago after I had betrayed her. I wrote in my book *The Late Show* something racy about Diane's love life she had told me in private. I told myself there was a chance she would actually *like* my reporting. A chance *indeed!* She was livid.

I apologized for about two years and she *seemed* to forgive me. We had a nice lunch one day, chatted like old friends, but when I couldn't get another friend to return my phone calls, finally reached her, and asked about the blackout, she said Diane had told her I had said she, Maudie, the non-phone-call returner, never left her house these days but stayed in bed all day smoking pot. I'd actually told Diane about her staying in bed but not about the pot because I didn't *know* about it. . . . that was said by Diane to *me* but whoever said it, you wouldn't tell the person it was said about them, would you, if it's something they won't *like?* I nabbed Diane one day in the Four Seasons when she was having lunch with *Harper's Bazaar* editor Liz Tilberis and asked why she had told Maudie those things, one of which I surely hadn't said, one I had, and Diane simply said, "Now we're even." Maybe revenge is *better* than forgiving, though it's hard to get. Of course Diane won't be revenged when she reads this *second* thing I haven't run by her and she'll have to use up all that energy being mad again. I, on the other hand, am quite relaxed. I have forgiven *her* for that terrible report she gave Maudie.

Friend Indicator

I don't think anyone is a really *good* friend unless she complains once in a while about her husband, do you agree, or at least tells you *something* unpleasant in life that pisses her off. Someone asked me the other day if Evelyn Lauder and I were good friends. I said oh *yes*, I've known Evelyn for twenty-five years, a *super* person, and then I remembered I'd never head a cross word from Evelyn about Leonard, her mother-in-law, Estee, her son, William, her brother-in-law, Ronald, her sister-in-law, Jo Carol. How good friends *are* we? Of course, maybe all those people in her life are perfect and there's nothing bad to report, or she's heard that I tend to tell other people what's been told me so it's better to keep quiet. I don't mean you have to be really hateful when loved ones are mentioned . . . just acknowledge that yours are flawed like *mine*. I'm going to hear it from *somebody* anyway so it might as well be *you*, who know best of all.

Who Are the Good Guys/Bad Guys?

It's very simple: Good guys make you feel good . . . they *like* you, care whether you're comfortable and happy. Bad guys make you feel bad. Alas, the good guys may be bad to *society* . . . a little crooked, deadbeat alimony-paying, celebrity-f———g, mildly crass but if they do nice things for *me*, I can't help liking them. Conversely, the bad ones to *me*, may be strawberry shortcake to *you* . . . religious leaders, writers of bestsellers, talk-show hosts who wow the world, but if they make *me* feel bad when we're together, I can't praise or like them as well as *your* villains who are good to *me*. Is this all a little vague? You can't *not* know what I'm talking about. Let's hope his brother-in-law isn't on a meat hook in the kitchen or her father indigent in Ohio, but don't *you* like the person who helps you with impossible-to-get stuff . . . job interview, booking on a sold-out flight, 40 percent off wholesale, lights up and listens when *you're* in the room like Katie Couric with her most prized guest? Don't ask me to check his or her moral credentials if he or she's in my corner.

The Rudest

The rudest celebrity I ever met was Rex Harrison, whom I worshipped and would rather have had my eyelashes tweezed out one at a time rather than offend, but I did. Linda and Richard Zanuck, David's partner at Twentieth Century Fox, David, and I were visiting Rex at his home in St. Clous just outside Paris when he was working in *Staircase* for the studio. Dick, head of production, and David, executive V.P. creative head, were paying Rex a courtesy call to straighten out a few production points. *Doctor Dolittle*, another Twentieth Century movie in which Rex starred, was ready for release. I wanted to make a nice impression on starry Rex and told him I'd just heard the Sammy Davis, Jr., album of music from *Doctor Dolittle*, it was thrilling, and that having such a major entertainer sing the songs would constitute major promotion for the film. Rex went mad. He turned raw liver color and started screaming, *screaming!* How could somebody else sing *his* songs? How could any other performer *care* as he did? How could Twentieth have made this monstrous, humiliating mistake? Who did Sammy Davis presume to be and what could be done immediately to stop distribution of the album? This wasn't just a case of shoot the messenger, but was torture and destroy the insensitive ninny admiring another singer singing *his* songs! Sexy Rexy stormed, fumed; Dick Zanuck thought he was going to *hit* me. We all went on to dinner at Laperouse in a private room. Rex's wife, Rachel Roberts, and I sang bawdy songs at high decibel level. I wanted to show Rex talented people could sing songs other than the artists who introduced them. Rachel did bird calls. I think the room is still echoing her crested Australian cockatoo and North American hermit thrush. She was a good woman.

I can't remember any other celebrity being heartless. Barbra Streisand was mad at me when *Cosmo* ran an excerpt from an unauthorized biography of her but, as I explained to her press agent, Lee Solters, if she had ever given *Cosmo* an interview, as requested fifty or sixty times, we wouldn't have had to resort to the excerpt. Barbra later forgave me and we became friends. Burt Reynolds was pissed—who could blame him—when *Cosmo*'s art director lost the nude picture he and his associates had painstakingly picked from hundreds of transparencies . . . *lost* it! But he didn't stay angry. I am so namby-pamby around celebrities and hold them in such awe (as I did as a preteenager in Little Rock, saving pictures of Carole Lombard, Joan Crawford, Jean Harlow, Maurice Chevalier) I would presume never to get on somebody famous's bad side. Aside from that excerpt saying Barbra and Jon Peters, whom she had just met, were in a hot tub together on their first date, I don't think *Cosmo* has ever printed anything rotten about a celebrity. Rex forgave me also and we visited him backstage when he appeared in *Aren't We All* on Broadway. I gave Burt Reynolds back every single transparency from that famous nude photo shoot with Francesco Scavullo, there must have been fifty of the actor totally starkers. I'd said I would and did, now I wish I hadn't. I would never have sold one of his photos or given it to the *Enquirer* but having one to look at occasionally would have been pleasant . . . this is one good-looking naked person.

Communication

There is a kind of phone communication as infallible as body language that tells instantly whether the news about to be delivered is good or bad. "Ms. Brown?" Voice inflection instantly says he can't do what you want. Sure enough, "Mr. Brokaw will be in Phoenix that day." "Helen?" You know from inflection it's no again. "I'd love to but I'm having an impacted wisdom tooth out." "Honey?" Even an endearment may not produce sweet tidings and you can tell from that one word. Exactly. "Honey, Carol and Lou aren't buying the tickets, *we* are" (for the evening they invited *us* to). Salutation itself has nothing to do with the negative or positive message to come . . . the inflection communicates everything. Knowing a flash before the bad news doesn't negate it or *fix* anything, just gives you a tad longer to assimilate the pain and get beyond . . . don't have to wait for the boring explanation of why they *can't*.

Getting Them to Tell You Stuff

There is almost nothing I can't get a person I don't even know to tell me by just asking. How much money do you make? How much money did your husband leave you? What did the Jaguar cost? *Especially* what did the Jaguar cost? People love to reveal what they paid for a treasure and are dying to be asked. Maybe later they will be sorry they blabbed but going in they either don't have the gumption to say it's none of your business or they are actually longing to tell *somebody* like people do Oprah, Sally Jesse, Rosie, and Geraldo, and you wonder if they've lost their minds. "Do you ever cheat on Eleanor?" "Have you ever wanted to kill your kids?" "What's the worst thing you ever did?" *I* ask these things. Maybe people comply because you are showing an interest in the real *them*. I can't remember anybody *ever* saying it's none of your business when I asked something pretty nosey except Edgar Bronfman, Sr. Seated next to him at a dinner party, I merely asked, "What did you do today?" One of my really innocent questions, and he said, "Kiss my ass." He actually *said* that! It must have been a horrible day.

Son of Jackie and JFK

I *think* JFK Jr. and I were friends, though lots of people probably felt he was their friend because he was friendly. When *George* magazine was young, one day at lunch at San Domenico—one of his favorites, I understand—a captain whispered to me that JFK Jr. was in the room, over there by the banquette. Not lacking in chutzpah, as we know, I left my companion and scooched over to his table to introduce myself. Whether the woman with him was Carolyn Bessette I don't know. I don't *think* she had long blonde hair, but who was looking at her *or* listening to the introduction? "Oh yes," he said, very friendly upon being approached, "I've always wanted to meet you. People tell me I have to have a column like the one you write in *Cosmo* every month. . . . Is that a good idea?" "It's a wonderful idea," I said. "People will gobble every word. *Do* it!"

He did create an editor's page for *George*, though he didn't always write about himself or his life. After lunch I went back to the office and "critiqued" two issues of *George*—put little yellow markers in the pages, commented on articles and art. "How about more of this, less of that, etc." Pretentious? Absolutely. Did anybody *ask* me to critique *George*? No, but I had a successful magazine and felt I knew things a young editor might take advantage of to gain sales. He responded graciously, even enthusiastically, said he would try some things. I didn't do any more issues, I wouldn't want anybody critiquing *my* magazine. Soon after that I saw him at the Tommy Hilfiger luncheon at which Hilfiger's fragrance, Tommy, licensed by the Estee Lauder Company, was being introduced. "Aha," I said, "I see you've got it! This is what a magazine editor does!" Yes, he said, he got it. *George* did receive an Estee Lauder schedule, one of the first companies to advertise in the magazine.

This past year we were both guests at the Trophées des Arts dinner—an organization that promotes French culture—at the Pierre. We were seated at the same table, neither of us accompanied by a spouse; he may have been there because *George* is owned by a French publisher, Hachette Filipacchi. When John's seatmate, Catherine Deneuve's daughter, left the table, I plopped over to chat. Pussycat time. I had planned to ask him about his magazine and his life, he wanted to talk about *mine*. Alas, I never saw him again, though I have a nice photograph from that evening. *George* never soared skyward with sales or advertising but at least its president/editor had the courage to do something nobody *handed* him, to launch and keep his magazine alive, to be seriously involved.

I only talked to Jackie twice. The first time at a party we chatted about Egypt—she knew a lot more than I; next at a New York Library Literary Lions dinner where I spent more time with her companion, Maurice Templesman, than with her. Like others, I have always felt Jackie had to be an incredible person to have raised, in addition to everything *else* good she did, this terrific son.

Bought and Paid For

In my job as magazine editor, I have been in a position sometimes to be seduced by presents into friendship . . . not that you can't turn them away, I just didn't. Starting my second year at *Cosmo,* the owner of a ritzy skincare salon in New York gave me real pearls, eighteen-carat-gold earrings, a man's antique pocket watch, champagne flutes, Limoges plates. Motive: to have her salon and her work featured in *Cosmo.* I couldn't, didn't. The magazine cared lots about skin and wrote about it, but in connection with a particular New York salon or *any* salon we couldn't. Only 8 percent of our readers lived in New York, and M.'s products had no national distribution, so neither her products nor hands-on expertise could help a girl in St. Louis. Why didn't I send back the presents? Pure greed, but the gifts arrived at Christmas with lots of other loot—magazine editors do deliriously well at Christmas (I *miss* that perk!). Through all the years, M. never bore down hard with her requests. She would all but dragoon me to come in for facials—not a bad offer—but I was busy. I paid back finally in the mildest—*very* mild—way. When M. opened a salon for men, I sent a man to write about his cucumber-mask, blackhead-excision experience . . . more an entertainment piece for our female readers than a lure for male customers. I also found M. a good P.R. firm—what she needed in the first place. The gifts, aside from an occasional bottle of cologne stopped, but not the friendship. She's eighty-five. She's special.

Another friend seduced me with hostessing *and* presents! J. and her husband, foreign diplomats and he later ambassador to the U.S. from an exotic South Asia country, were thought well of by the Bush administration but felt they needed help in influencing general U.S. opinion favorably, so why not call on journalist friends? Why not. She kept trying to give parties for David and me in Washington. "Invite all your friends," she would suggest. We explained we didn't *have* well-connected ones in the capital, at least nobody important to whom we could say "Get your ass over to this party," but J. would set dates, invite people we didn't know, say the party was in our honor, and suggest we show *up*. We did. The parties would turn out to be fun and she was another present-giver—silk saris from her country, eighteen-karat-gold bracelets again (I feel like a chorus girl), these thin and hammered, a set of eight, Dom Perignon, crystal flutes. I never ran articles about their country in *Cosmo*—not a smidge—nor stories about the ambassador—a prince, but not a suitable subject for us. When J.'s husband stopped being ambassador, the big-budget prezzies stopped, but not the friendship or smaller presents. J. accompanied me to the hospital when I had a hysterectomy, cheered me with Zabar's Scottish smoked salmon, Greenberg cookies, and her own soothing presence after cosmetic surgery . . . who needs saris and bracelets? In friendship seduction, you do it your way, right? And don't go all pompous on me about "buying friendship." We all use our own legal tender. The day I pursue with big-deal presents will be a snowy day in Fiji, but I give career and personal advice (I'm supposed to be good at it), write over-the top enthusiastic letters when somebody has performed or written well, try to listen hard core (like I was never before fascinated by what someone is telling me this much in this lifetime), try to be fun (frequently miss!). I love generous people and try to encourage them because I think giving somewhat lavishly makes *them* happy, so why deny somebody this pleasure!

Craziness—Ours

We are all victims of our own craziness, right? Whitaker Chambers, the Communist sympathizer–turned–conservative in the late forties, said, "We are strung on the crosses of ourselves." Other people are flawed, yes, and give us a bad time but not any badder than we give ourselves . . . you'd think one of us could get it right. I worry incessantly, am drained and preoccupied so much by it that when the thing I am worrying about is either (a) over—I got through it or (b) never happened, I didn't need to be worried about it in the first place, we can now get on to (c) a feeling of wild release—is that what you call an epiphany? I am addicted to my worry, unhappy as it makes me at the time, for the dubious pleasure of having it turn out not to be what it was cracked up to be! Of course I'm also "addicted" to a mild permanent feeling of Not Quite Living up to What's Expected of Me by bosses, the public, people who look at me on streets and in buses and don't think I'm pretty enough to get a second look. I frequently feel I've somehow let them all down. I don't think I've disappointed loved ones and friends . . . you can almost completely control what you do with them and do it right, but life itself I frequently feel is asking more than I can deliver, more than I can get up for it, as in erection, though I try. Am I idiotic to live with this small permanent melancholy after all the good stuff life has given me? Absolutely, but it's there in my DNA.

Now I'd like to get back to their craziness which is much worse than mine, at least more debilitating. I manage quite nicely with the baby melancholia always in me a little. There's my friend Sherry who can't get straight what is important. She thinks what is important is that Archie is taking Mavis to lunch at Le Cirque instead of Sherry, who needs him badly. What would be good for Sherry to recognize is that Archie doesn't want to see her or take her to lunch no matter how much she would like him to do that. No grasp of reality is Sherry's craziness. She gets nothing but hurt, sadness after sadness when one more desired one or thing doesn't come through while I'm out there having epiphanies (I think that's what I'm having). Maybe you can't compare crazinesses but I think Sherry's is crazier than mine.

Work

Motherhood and Career

Since I haven't done it, I don't know how I would know but, from what I glean, you can have a big career, husband, and children but you can't have a big, *big* career without the children not turning out quite the way you wanted. Frequently they don't turn out the way you wanted anyway, but to do the stuff you have to do to grow them spiffy and happy, you may need to spend more time with them than affordable if you are meeting, conferencing, speaking, strategizing, junketing . . . those hours tote *up* while the kids are back-burnering. I surely couldn't have done what I do with children, though other magazine editors do.

I talked this career/kids issue over with Ellen Levine, whammo editor of *Good Housekeeping*, whose husband is a whammo gynecologist, delivers many babies of the famous and other kinds and they have two (older) ones of their own, and asked what she thought possible in the world of big achievement for mothers. Ellen said she was able to be ambitious because she had had her babies early and the boys were ten and twelve before she got heavily into a career, also they could always afford good help. Ellen mentioned Queen Elizabeth and Christie Whitman, governor of New Jersey, as two who had family funds to allow for plenty of child care so careers could take off. In the queen's case, not sure the helpers produced totally functioning kids—at least they didn't learn how to pick good mates the *first* time. Mom's career turned out okay. Christine seems to be doing fine.

If good help is the answer, I'm wishing you well.

Getting There

You don't have to have a dream. You do what's there in front of you—the chores, assignments, drudgery. You don't do the friendly stuff first, the ugly stuff last, you do it the other way—the uglier the faster—or you might never get *to* ugly at *all*. With ugly out of the way, you can do friendly. Self-discipline I think it's called (I also hear it called "postponing pleasure,"), is available to everybody, not just the smart and gifted. Self-discipline may be about all that *is* available to us unsmart and ungifted, though at least we are smart enough to *go* for it. As you keep doing what you do—getting your daily work done—somewhere along the line you find what you are better at than other things and it becomes your career. You may then become *really* better at it than other people and the career takes off.

Being successful doesn't mean perfectly awful things don't continue to happen in your life . . . this is news? No, this is *life* . . . still getting handed shit by the fates when you have been such a good person and done your very best. Success makes the shit a little easier to cope with because A. money is probably not such a problem as it once was if you've been hacking away and B. maybe you now have a little clout so you can call up people whose help you need. So, I didn't have a dream. I didn't go to college. I just did the boring awful stuff first every day for years—still do—until at age forty-three I got to be a magazine editor. It isn't physical energy and brain energy that drive you . . . it's needing, longing, wanting, but no specific dream like some day I'll be a great writer or president or ballerina. Doesn't even have to be some day I'll *show* them, the bastards . . . you may not have the guts for that dynamic boast or at least those words are never specifically in your mind . . . what you do is just deal with a not-wonderful bunch of stuff in your life, at all times inching toward victory! Eventually you actually *do* show them.

Work Is Play, Play Is Work . . . I've Got It All Screwed Up! (Mumblings of a Workaholic)

Spending Sunday morning with my manuscripts, memos, mail-answering, notes to housekeeper, instructions for Susie, working on this book, brings pleasure. Talking with other talkers at a reception, cocktail party, luncheon, any social splash in my careful makeup that doesn't make me beautiful *enough*, straining to be smart and funny while listening heavy-duty is work, not fun.

I don't know when I began not to like parties, and it doesn't matter. I think about age thirteen when I was a new baby wallflower . . . not a pariah but just a little waifish . . . anxious. You sit in your cherry-red crushed velvet evening dress a loving mommy has virtually stitched you into on your way out the door and wait for somebody to ask you to dance in it. Nobody does. Party suffering. My dresses these days are terrific, but dresses don't get big cocktail parties or receptions off the hook. You pray these three men you've interrupted—"What are you all doing talking to each *other!*"—will stay five minutes. They don't. You've screwed up their meeting. You wish you could ditch the worthy but dull girl who's trapped you; she sticks like peanut butter. This is *fun*? Reprise: fun is not parties, (except for nice little dinner parties and an occasional book soiree). *Work* is fun. You know you are good at it . . . maybe the best or close to of anybody in your field. You attack, finish, feel peaceful . . . bring me *more!*

A shrink once suggested my workaholism was created by shame . . . shame of not feeling pretty enough, sparkly enough, pedigreed enough early in life. There was the virulent acne, living by the railroad tracks (literally!) in south L.A. Trains roared by as a date and I sat in the car at evening's end . . . you could get roared right out of your seat! A sister in a wheelchair needed to be introduced when dates picked me up. Could a man get interested in a person attached to a person in a wheelchair? Let's be brutal here. Ferociously shy mother, stepfather who manned a Good Humor truck parked right outside the door . . . not confidence producers. I fought back. Working hard, getting paid, sometimes being recognized and applauded for work does make you feel less ashamed.

So I got rid of the old shame-causers, new list is shorter: ashamed of being *old*, not old*er*, old! Alas, workaholism doesn't make you one scrap younger (or less ashamed) and, while working like that, you get even older. Never mind. Ashamed that rewards of my work aren't as glossy nor fame-causing as they once were? Yes. For five years the *World Almanac* listed me as one of the twenty-five most influential women in America . . . that was nice!

Well, diminishing rewards or no, I am working as hard as ever because I don't think I'll ever get the hang of play—just a few skirmishes when young and then work and its compensations set in. The *Cosmo* international editions keep me thumping. I have this book you're now reading to finish, signed contract for another one. What will I do when these projects are finished? Alphabetize the CDs and laser discs, climb on a ladder with Carbona in one hand, toothbrush in the other and attack the dining room and hall chandeliers? Sure, but these chores can only take a morning. Read the Bible? I've tried several times and found it tedious except for the Psalms. Still, a girl has to deal with the Possible. Maybe Deuteronomy, Corinthians II, Leviticus, and their ilk will challenge enough to shut me up about where is my next work assignment coming from. I hope so.

Improve It *Later*

Darling friend Faith Stewart Gordon gets a book contract to write about her life and ownership of the Russian Tea Room, New York's once most-visited restaurant, lots of frisky things to write about. We talk July 10. Faith is elated but anxious. This book most important thing imaginable, but how can she possibly write that fast? "Easy," I tell her. "You do the book first thing every day—seven days a week if you need to—nothing gets between you and starting in on your book every morning." I went on. "Yes, I know you'll skip some lunch dates, I know your phone will be turned off during working hours, you may even go to bed early in order to rise up fresh, but along with my command to concentrate on the book every day comes the demand that you do it *before anything else in the morning*." Incredible how delicious, even joyful, straightening up a room, fluffing pillows, rearranging pencils and clips on your desk, writing a couple of thank-you notes long *long* overdue can be. You sink into those sweet chores like an opium addict reaching for his pipe in the den. Why would you find these chores so delicious? Because you can see progress right that minute. Writing may require all day to get five pages . . . sweat, sweat, sweat. I tell all new writers to get it down on paper, get through your first draft, don't stop and improve your brains out as you go along. An amateur writer friend told me recently, proudly, she spent an entire afternoon improving her first paragraph . . . very important, she said . . . sets tone for the whole article. What is also set is her *back*, with her delivery date by only the muses know how much. Get it *all* down, go back and improve later. That's the fun part. Apparently Faith listened. Her book, *The Russian Tea Room—A Love Story*, was delivered to and published by Scribner as a Lisa Drew book last October. It's terrific!

How to Be a Good Employee

Why would you want to be that? Two reasons: 1. A job, not necessarily this one but this plus others, will eventually give you the recognition, money, self-esteem that make life wonderful. 2. "Good employees" have more fun while waiting for the money, recognition, self-esteem. In a book published a few years ago, *Having It All* (by Simon & Schuster/Linden Press), I wrote about being a "good employee" and will borrow a few of those ideas. Did I always pay attention to what I'm now recommending? Not always. I began work life as an eighteen-year-old fluff-brain but, after growing up a bit, getting smarter in my jobs, I did better and got happier. You may not want to do the things I'm recommending, may wish to work *less* hard, have what is called "a life," nor may you be in an office where I always was—you're opening a bookstore, restaurant, giving karate lessons. Some people don't need "happy" rules anyway. Terrific technology skills make them so valuable—not enough of you to go around—*scruffy* behavior will be tolerated; feeling blessed you're there, company will be trying to make *you* happy. If you're in a somewhat more traditional situation in a company or corporation, here are a few thoughts you might want to consider toward being "happy." Let's start with your first or early jobs, then *build*.

1. GET YOUR NOSE OUT OF THE AIR ABOUT DRUDGE WORK

Most young people have to drudge and drone for a while . . . word process somebody else's output, run personal errands for a busy boss on *your* lunch hour, arrive at the office two hours early to let a television crew inside, redo the address book. Nobody's idea of a career, but you have just trustingly to know this present job is part of your odyssey to the light (though you may be pretty young to know it at the time). My fifth secretarial job consisted of typing names on badges for security-risk employees in a defense plant . . . was *that* creative?! Brave little worker stuck it out until job six—a *trifle* better—showed up. You are learning to be a pro, okay?

2. BEING A GOOD (HAPPY) EMPLOYEE MEANS NOT BEING STINGY WITH YOUR PERSON

Could you come in on Saturday? Could you take anything home? Can your boss think of anything that would be helpful to *him* or *her* personally (those denigrated "personal chores!") or the project? . . . You don't care if it's menial, you just want to help! Turn in work nobody asked for—it may not be accepted, but there's almost no way people can't be impressed that you *did* it. God knows you aren't taking the work home for *them*, it's for *you*. You want to get on with your life and make real money, and the way to do *that* is to extend yourself. That goes for helping the other girls, too, including that bitch Angela, who would have done us a favor *not* to have pulled through her bout with mononucleosis.

Not helping simply means you are dumb. Your head is wrong. Nice girls finish *first*. Do get credit if you can—no use coming in on Saturday to straighten the files if no one ever knows you were *there*. Just don't be too stingy with your "free labor" for bosses or co-workers.

3. ACCEPT AND ASK FOR EXTRA WORK BUT DON'T BE A PEST

You may not be ready to represent the firm at the sales seminar in Denver, prepare an executive vice president's remarks for the annual report, make recommendations about company cost-cutting. Don't let them overlook anything you are ready to do, but don't pester for the inappropriate. When I was a secretary at the William Morris Agency, a call went out for actresses to try out for the lead on the Corliss Archer radio show. An actress! Lights! Fame! So I tortured myself for two straight days, threw up both nights and, finally could *not* get up the nerve to ask anybody about an audition. What I saved myself from was total, ignominious humiliation! I could barely deliver *phone* messages, let alone a dramatic line. I think the only way you can become an enormous success is by not doing anything *false* to your character, anything that doesn't "feel right," like pushing friends, bosses, strangers to give you the big chance too soon. Of course, it is absolutely okay to use family or other connections to *get* a job (there is no use being stuffy), possibly some place above the bottom—then you'll have to fake it for a while as you learn the job you aren't yet actually qualified for. You may be fine and can skip early slavery jobs altogether—I just never had the connections to *get* a job by pull. To be a good (happy) employee, I think you work at the job you're *in*. Do more than your share in that job. Study. Inch along. Pile up "goodness" if not in this present job, then in the next one.

4. SHOW UP ON TIME

Almost no more important rule for a baby worker, a teenager, or mature one either than to be scrupulously on time or even early. I saved my seventeenth secretarial job with a high-powered advertising executive—finally a *good* job—by being at my desk every morning for his arrival. "*You* here, Miss Gurley?" he would ask, incredulous and pleased . . . he was an *early* one; I had to leave home in West Los Angeles when the moon was still up for the trip to downtown L.A. in order to prearrive him. Punctuality, plus never going to coffee with the other girls so he always had the use of me, are the two things I could successfully do until more knowledge set in; my shorthand and typing were good. After five years as his secretary, he let me write advertising copy. Things kick in. I got happier!

5. DO IT THIS MINUTE, OR AT LEAST THIS DAY

The best way to get noticed and loved before you're brilliant at your job is to do everything instantly. A boss may give you five "instantlies" and you have to decide which to do first, second, etc., but get on with it all. One of my helpers whisks off to the store the same day she hears my need for seven-pound dumbbells, taupe eye liner, plant fertilizer, and Woolite, even though *Cosmo* International would surely not be in peril if she waited, and God knows all that errand running isn't what her mother sent her to college for. You'll be relieved to know the dear child also does research, works with a ton of people both inside and outside the company, and handles just about everything that doesn't absolutely require me, but the point is she not only does the grubby stuff cheerfully, she also does it fast— and I can't live without her.

6. DON'T EXPECT A TERRIFIC SALARY FAST

At Music Corporation of America, the talent agency where I worked
in the band department, my boss asked me one day to take over a
book which tracked bands on the road, recording amounts each
player earned in juxtaposition with the entertainment place he
earned it in so you could tell instantly the Coconut Grove was paying
him better than the Starlight Roof or the Steel Pier. The pay for
me? Five dollars extra a month. Usually you accept whatever is offered to a baby but I turned him down, ridiculous is ridiculous. I
would have been pouring over figures on my lunch hour and, at age
twenty, lunch seemed necessary. He didn't hit me or fire me. I'm
just saying money doesn't pour in *early* even *now* (these thousand
years later) for baby workers.

7. RULE OUT OF YOUR MIND FOREVER THAT COMPETITION IS BAD

Competition may be bad for lazy people but all competing really is
is being "your best self." You aren't doing a smashing job to get back
at Josephine or wait till Peter sees *this*! When you're good, you aren't
taking anything away from anybody else. There are enough rewards
for everybody . . . a company can't *have* too many geniuses.

8. OFFICE MATES ARE A GOES-WITH-THE-TERRITORY BLESSING

Work pals are your daytime family. Bless them and mingle. Just don't
schmooze like a peanut cluster when you should be working or get
to be known as Bad News Brenda, always there first with the ugly
stuff about the company and its people. And what you know about
your *boss* shouldn't be in public domain.

9. JOIN COMPANY GROUP ACTIVITIES

The old team spirit? Yes, it's good to have. I was a total athletic dud,
couldn't hit or catch a beach ball, so nobody ever wanted me on a
team but I showed up and *rooted.* Management kind of notes who's
friendly with her peers. The only group I peered magnificently in
was the one that went to the Hollywood Canteen during World War
II to dance with the G.I.'s and hear Frank Sinatra sing "Old Man
River." MCA founder Jules Stein created the Canteen and encour-

aged employees to go. They didn't have to get out the cat o' nine tails in my case.

10. YOUR ABILITY TO MAKE GOOD DECISIONS ABOUT LITTLE THINGS WILL BECOME AN IMPORTANT ASSET

Small *personal* decisions can begin to contribute right away to your success and happiness—deciding *not* to slither away from extra work they just handed you, *not* to call in sick when you *could* stay on your feet and go to work, not to spend every possible moment in the ladies' room with your pals, *not* to badmouth the people who employ you, even though you think they're idiots. We're really talking about the decision to do what's good for your *job* rather than what might be more personally pleasurable. Anyway, I can assure you that what's *there* in that squirrely little job of yours, plus the "right decisions," will be *enough* to get you to the next plateau and make you an even *happier* employee.

11. AS YOU MOVE ALONG, ALTHOUGH YOU'RE AGGRESSIVE ON THE INSIDE, IT DOESN'T NECESSARILY SHOW

A woman who makes over two hundred thousand dollars a year told me recently, "I used to despair of ever amounting to anything because I thought you had to stride around like Genghis Khan or a member of the light cavalry, be dynamic and aggressive, and I'd never make it." A few women do still pace forcefully, speak dramatically, act important, making the rest of us feel a little marshmallowy. I've seen the pacers, the dramatic speakers clamber right up there for a little while maybe, but usually they clamber right back down because aggression is about *all* they have. You see, there is no substitute for brains plus charm plus *hard work*. You should be "privately aggressive"—just quietly firm up on the job, make the "good decisions," keep your shiny eyes open for places to go. Need, yearn, and *work*—that is the kind of aggression that brings success (i.e., happiness), not acting dramatic.

12. THE WAY TO DRESS FOR AN OFFICE IS PRETTY

There just isn't any reason to hack your way up in tweed or gray flannel if they bore you. Blending in with the furniture is *one* way to "dress for success" but not the *only* way. Whatever you feel you look nice in is what you probably ought to be wearing, provided it isn't slashed to the navel. Maybe it's different in *your* world and you ought to wear all that dull businessy stuff, but I've never seen a woman held back in a job because of what she wore if her brain and drive and devotion were okay.

13. GETTING ALONG WITH OTHER PEOPLE IS 50 (MAYBE EVEN 60, 70!) PERCENT OF YOUR SUCCESS—BUT THAT DOESN'T NECESSARILY MEAN BEING GREGARIOUS OR FUNNY OR EVEN "POPULAR"

Let me tell you about a royal pain who once worked in my office. She never said hello when I met her in the hall. She worked reasonably hard and was smart but never pleasant. One night I was working late, and around eleven I had a *food* fit. I couldn't find anything in the refrigerator where we all store food, and this particular night I started going through people's *desks*. Shameless, but hungry is *hungry*, and I planned to make full confession and restitution the next morning. In Lydia's desk I found the last of a box of raisins and ate the whole thing—twenty-six raisins, stale and dry, and nothing ever tasted so good! The next morning, Lydia was waiting for me as I came through the reception room. "Mrs. Brown," she said, "did you eat my raisins?" "Oh, my God, Lydia," I said, "I did and I meant to bring some in with me on the way to work. I'll get them at lunchtime." She skulked away. Later, when I saw her again, she still looked angry. "Lydia," I said, "did you have special plans for those raisins?" "Yes," she said, "I'm dieting and that was my eleven o'clock snack."

My Susie instantly went out to the market, got a big box of raisins for Lydia (for which she never said thank-you), and the subject of raisins never came up again. On pain of *death* would I ever have robbed that girl's desk again, but what a goose she was! For one thing, a boss, right or wrong, is nobody to humiliate, even though desk-scavengering is pretty tacky. She could without *too* much effort have gone across the street for more raisins, or stolen bond paper to assuage her pique, or whatever! I was not planning to become this girl's biggest life problem, and, more important, this was a chance for the two of us to have a "guilty secret." "Had any more food fits, Mrs. Brown?" she could have asked, or "I left fudge brownies this week and they weren't touched!"—and become a special favorite.

Not that *that's* such a big deal, either, but it doesn't *hurt* your career to have people think you are adorable and charming. To be a pleaser and a charmer is *not* selling out; it is investing in happiness (yours!) through the process of making other people glad to be around you.

Boston psychologist Harry Levinson says, "Abrasive personality is the single most frequent cause for the failure of bright men and women in the executive ranks of business and industry." Some entertainers—actors, singers—behave badly and survive, but they are different from you and me. We simply *can't* be stuffy, snippy, selfish, snapping-turtle little bitches and succeed.

14. DON'T TELL EVERYBODY YOUR PERSONAL PROBLEMS

Share personal grief with one or two office friends you like, but don't burden your employer. He or she should probably know about any serious problems in your life, but don't use him for a daily confessional. I once had a helper who deeply saddened (as well as bored!) me with the continuing saga of her husband's aged father having come to live with them, disrupting the household, being a pain in the neck, etc., etc., sandwiched in with her grief about a face-lift she felt had gone wrong (she looked fine to me).

An office is a home, to some extent; it's where you live every day, so why *shouldn't* people know something about your personal life? Just don't bog *everybody* down with your grief; pick listeners selectively.

15. SEXUAL HARASSMENT ISN'T WHAT IT'S CRACKED UP TO BE

I've got into trouble with my views on this one, but I think offices are places where there not only *is* but *should* be sexual tension. Men and women are there together for hours and hours and knowing he's a man, you're a woman (or vice versa) is part of the fun. If an employer or boss is giving you a bad time with seriously inappropriate sex talk or attention and won't stop though you've reasoned with him and complained to management, then maybe you have to leave. Did no one ever change jobs because of *other* unpleasant working conditions? This is *one* of them. I'm not talking here about somebody with tenure due for a serious promotion being stopped because of gender—possibly grounds for a lawsuit—but about younger employees. May I take you all the way back to the forties when jobs were not easy to get, when you did not do anything to rebuff or offend a boss, even a horny one, lest he fire you. A lot of passes were surely made, but I can't remember anything really heavy or bad coming out of it. One of my bosses at dear, staid Music Corporation of America used to ask me to come in on Sundays to "get rid of this extra work," and he would chase me around his beautiful quiet office with all those fabulous antiques and sometimes *catch* me, but only for a few hugs and kisses. Was that so terrible? No, it shouldn't have been part of the job, but how much trouble was I *in*? Of the millions of naughty suggestions made by millions of male employers to their "defenseless" female employees yearly, I'd say half cheered the girls *up*, half brought the girls *down* but probably nothing bad has come out of most of them.

16. FORGET TRYING NOT TO BE A WOMAN (WHATEVER THAT MEANS) IN BUSINESS

Successful, happy on the job, women remain sexual beings. What you also need to remain—or become if you aren't already—is *charming*. You'll need all the charm you can muster to be persuasive and comfortable to be around, and charm isn't masculine or feminine. If you can make a man (boss, client, employee) feel more masculine and confident because of the way you look at him when he talks, then *do*—you'll listen just as attentively to other women. Rapt attention between the opposite sexes *does* tend to have a sexual quality, however, and so, to some extent, one could accuse you of "using sex" in business when you gaze straight into his eyes. That's okay. The sexual you is part of the *whole* you and doesn't snap off—God, we hope not, anyway!—between nine and six. At any rate, you can *think* sex and still do business—I've done it for *years*! The garbage one reads about keeping sex out of your work! Sex is *there* because he's a man and you're a woman, but that knowledge doesn't make you jump on each other in the conference room or get each other fired. A lot of the time you're going to be concentrating too hard on your work to think about what sex you or anybody else is.

As for sex impeding the workload, I think sexual tension and electricity between men and woman in an office *help* get the job done. Trying to please somebody you're nutty about can be productive. As for not sleeping with the boss, why discriminate against *him*? It's like sleeping with anybody else; there are the good times, the bad times, and the affair probably won't go on forever, but the liaison doesn't necessarily affect the P and L—yours or the company's. Sleeping with somebody influential isn't the way to get to the top, we all know *that*, because, no matter what exalted position somebody crazy about you puts you in, you can only stay there with talent and brains . . . I just think you can sleep with whom you want to—quietly and discreetly (do you really need to tell *anybody?*) without disaster.

17. SUCCESS IS CUMULATIVE

Okay, you don't ever have to do one spectacular splashy thing that has everybody "Oh-my-Godding" and you getting knighted. You get in the habit of working diligently, and one day that puts you in scoring position, in a position to have even *more* fun on the job. You can't just have your eye on the next rung. You have to do what you were hired for efficiently and expand ever so gradually so that you don't upset the rhythm of the people you're working with. And you can't be too brassy. You must have a very careful sense of what you can ask a boss to let you do that is not within your present work frame. A secretary who came to work for me asked instantly if she could attend all our *Cosmo* editorial meetings—those usually attended only by senior editors. I'm sure she felt she was just being enthusiastic, showing a willingness to learn, but it didn't come off quite that way. Secretaries are *not* yet editors—you work *up* to that—and it had a slightly jarring effect (one is put in the position of saying No, which makes a boss feel funny). You may make some mistakes in this business of asking and not receiving— that's almost inevitable. My advice is to volunteer like crazy and also turn in work that nobody asked for—but make it easy and comfortable for your boss to ignore that extra work or say No to your requests. Don't be *irritating*.

Let's say you've moved up a bit, are now having *more* fun in the job because you have more authority and are making more money. *These* rules could apply:

18. GET BACK TO THEM IN A HURRY

People are asking you for ideas rather than an extra set of Xeroxes. Give answers and ideas quickly and it will save you from having to give terrific ones! The longer you wait after somebody has asked for an opinion, the better your answers have to *be*. By coming to some conclusion quickly, they will always feel that from you they get *action*. It may take a *little* time to collect material you need, but don't take too long.

19. IF YOU DON'T KNOW WHAT SOMEBODY IS TALKING ABOUT, ASK!

Obviously you have to be a little careful about being ignorant of something you're already supposed to know. Also, you may not want to ask the person who gave you the assignment or the most important person involved in it, but if you're adrift, get *help*! Bungling along as though you understand when you *don't* is insane and can get you into *big* trouble; you won't be happy. On the other hand, a big-time female executive I know once said, "There's something to be said about not knowing too much. You don't know all the don'ts, so you dare to try where others who know more won't try at all." So *go* for it!

20. IT'S OKAY TO "BORROW" IDEAS FROM A FRIEND WHEN YOU'RE STUCK

Before we were married, I would take my Max Factor television and print ad assignments to David and get "contributions." (Translation: he would bail me out with a lot of concrete suggestions.) I'm *still* borrowing, from David and everyone else, material for television interviews, little speeches I have to make, plus background material for dealing with the editors of international editions of *Cosmo*. Speaking of borrowing talent, David wrote the cover blurbs—every single blurb—for *Cosmopolitan* my entire thirty-two years as editor . . . idiotic not to use all the resources you have. Call it borrowing, call it research, call it talking things over, but do call on people who know more than you do. They can't do your job but can contribute knowledge and ideas that will help generate ideas of your *own* and you'll be *happier*!

21. AS YOU CLIMB, DON'T BE AFRAID THAT SUCCESS WILL DEFEMINIZE YOU

You remain a sexual person no matter how successful you are, that man-woman awareness continues to exist in offices even *with* all parties working hard and making big contributions. Okay, you can accept that idea as long as you're in a minor job, but now, possibly in a new spot that will send you soaring (a *really* happy, good employee!), you are scared to be tampering with the traditional man-woman hierarchy . . . i.e., men must be big, strong, superior (as in *he* boss, *you* underling), women sweet little girls (as in adoring secretary). As even a *minor* executive, you're afraid you'll screw up how men feel about you. That fear is totally unwarranted. Joan Ganz Cooney, president of Children's Television Workshop, who created *Sesame Street* and is one of the most admired women in the country, says, "I tell young women to think about the strong mothers of this world . . . do they not function in a role of complete authority during the most important learning years of a man's life? Does a man think of his *mother* as masculine? In my office, many men have cried with me, and I think they rather enjoy it . . . they couldn't let down the emotional barriers with a male boss. The women don't cry as much. I am an earth mother perhaps, but there's a sort of collegial atmosphere here . . . We talk everything over, we all participate, then I make the final decisions. Does making decisions defeminize anybody? No!" You can be a good employee, have fun *and* be "traditional" in your gut.

22. MAKE YOUR BOSS LOOK GOOD

Wherever you are on the success ladder, you probably still have a boss and always *will* unless you go into business for yourself; even presidents and chairmen of corporations have bosses (boards of directors). Your job, always, is to make that person above you look good at the same time that you get what *you* need from the job. You try to "lighten the load" for him or her—and I'm not just talking about assistants and secretaries lightening the load, but about executives working for other executives. Actually, the better job *you* do, the better it is for the person above you. Don't worry about the boss getting credit for what *you* do. He or she usually *will*, but that isn't as bad as it sounds. People who are good are *good*, and though the boss may not give you public credit, the word gets around. There are many enlightened bosses who *do* give credit and will help you move ahead (and get happier). Professor Eugene Jennings, graduate professor of management at Michigan State University, after conducting extensive research on people who get ahead, says, "Corporate success comes fastest to the person who becomes a crucial

subordinate to an already mobile superior, complementing or sup-
plementing the superior's skills."

What about bosses who will not *let* you make them look good or,
it seems, let you do much of anything else . . . you and they are just
not clicking. We've all had one or two of those and you go crazy.
How can you get anywhere when they are your direct conduit to
success? Well, either they will leave the company—finally—or *you*
do. Doing every possible thing you can for their good and yours is
the only way you can play it for the moment. Maybe they'll get un-
crazy.

23. TRY TO DO THE DIFFICULT THINGS FIRST EACH DAY (THIS IS SO IMPORTANT I'M TELLING YOU AGAIN), BUT IF YOU CAN'T, DON'T!

Usually you don't do small stuff early or you'll empty your energy
pool, but occasionally you have to do the Possible to develop mo-
mentum for the Impossible . . . call the overbooked but has to be
that restaurant to pound for a reservation, do past-due thank-you
notes for party or present, nail the doctor's appointment, etc. I trust
you to prime the pump with little stuff if absolutely *necessary* before
you take off for major, but don't blow the morning.

24. HAPPY EMPLOYEES NEVER SQUANDER (LIKE WAIT IN A RESTAURANT WITH NOTHING TO DO) TIME

Sometimes I take my little Dictaphone along and dictate critiques
of foreign editions of *Cosmo* in the car, sign mail there, call friends
I don't have time to gossip with at the office. Restaurant-waiting is
not for using the cell phone—be reasonable!—but for reading a
folded-up op-ed piece tucked into your purse, writing notes for a
talk, reorganizing the wallet, and making lists. Is it crazy and life-
destroying to be so busy? I don't think so. I decided long ago time
was too precious *not* to fit a lot in. It's okay to "squander" time on
vacation, in bed, or just "thinking," but not waiting for a lunch date.
You also know how to cut short a dragging-on lunch, friend-visit to
the office, or any phone call taking too long. "Organized" sounds
revolting but isn't! The more you fit in, the more you *can* fit in, plus
organized people are usually the ones other people want to be
around because we don't screw up and cause everybody pain.

25. TELEPHONE TRICKS

A lot of your business life is conducted by phone. These are things I have learned about *that*.

- Even though somebody has accepted your call, always ask if he is *busy*. *Always*. "Is this a good time to talk to you?" You may be babbling on and he may be loathing your (necessary) long explanation of the project, whereas letting him call back at his convenience would get you a receptive audience.
- Thank people who are "bigger than you" for calling back. Nothing says they *had* to return your phone call, and the first thing you should do is thank them for calling.
- When *you* call, leave your *number* with your name—even if you think people already have it.
- Don't try to handle two subjects on the same phone call if one of those subjects is gratitude. Don't call up to thank somebody for whatever wonderful thing he did and then, on the same call, ask for another favor. Sometimes you have to make two separate calls, one of them *only* to express gratitude.
- Use your own judgment about whether to tell a secretary what you want or try to get through to the boss. If you're calling somebody you don't know, you'll almost surely need to tell the assistant what you want. P.S. If *you* are a secretary or assistant, charm and compassion are the big two telephone watchwords. You should always act as though you'd *love* to put the person through but can't right now, and should ask if you can do anything to help.
- Be ruthless with the time-wasters—the ladies at home who have nothing to do but gossip, the friends at their offices who are having a slow day. Wind down from the conversation: "Gerry, I have somebody waiting," "Tom, you were so good to call. I'll ring up *soon*." Learn to use cutoff maneuvers. Also learn *not* to answer the telephone. You can have cutoffs on your phone at home. If you're working late at the office, don't answer the phone *there* after five o'clock. It takes courage to ignore a ringing phone, but if you weren't *there* you wouldn't be answering. Just pretend you aren't there.

26. WRITE!

Write instead of telephoning people *outside* your company. A letter
can take a minute or less to dictate; phone calls require chitchat
and tend to expand. Keep your letters *short*, especially to important
people. Write *few* office memos, however. They tend to bore everybody, and the long ones are usually written by time-wasting, defen-
sive people. Write to corroborate instructions, to say that you're
working on a project that's due (the small interim report), or to sub-
mit original ideas so you have a record. Keep whatever you write
short, with lots of paragraphs and white space.

Cardinal rule of business and social life: never say bad, cruel,
crummy, unhappy, unpleasant, critical things in a letter. If they must
be said, try to say them in person or at least by *telephone*. Put the
good things in writing.

27. SUCCESS DOESN'T MAKE YOU INVULNERABLE

The most successful people in the world are still totally, crushingly
vulnerable. So what *else* is new? Superstar entertainers are viciously
attacked by reviewers and the criticism wounds them. Presidents
read vilifications in the *New York Times* and the *Washington Post*
and recoil. If you can feel passion for *anything*—children, family, a
beloved man, your work—you can also experience *hurt* from these
people and things. Don't worry about vulnerability. You can and will
hurt many times, but the hurt can't really *hurt* you. Getting beyond
the hurt, using it to "power" you to your next project can even make
you more successful . . . and happy!

28. AS YOU SUCCEED, KEEP A LOW PROFILE

Some people can hardly get their dear little sweaters and T-shirts
buttoned after their first little success—their *chests* are all puffed
up, you see. Well, we *all* love attention and the limelight, but I think
how successful you can become is probably in direct proportion to
how much you shut *up* about it. Most of us are spurred on by the
need for recognition. In fact, I'm not sure that isn't how most of us
"get there," needing to be loved for *something*—if not for our beautiful selves, then for our beautiful *work*. But, you see, you have to
be rather sneaky about it—you just *can't* go about saying, "Stroke

me, flatter me, tell me I'm *wonderful*," even when you are getting pretty good.

I think you keep two sets of books. In one set, you record the *truth*—how well you are really doing. This is the secret set—just for you and loved ones. In the other set are more modest entries and statements, and these are for *public* consumption! That's just the opposite of how you might think the game would be played. Many people *do* play it the other way; they say all the braggy things publicly, knowing privately that they're not in such hot shape—but if you're good you don't *need* to brag. People usually *know* how well you are doing because they hear it from other people, or they just kind of glean it by how *busy* you are. If they don't know how well you are doing, you can *quietly* tell them, but no hollering and *demanding* praise.

29. SPEAK UP ABOUT MONEY—WHEN IT'S TIME

If you feel you're due, ask. Waiting for them to "recognize your worth" and reward you may take too long (they recognize your worth all right, but may not do a thing about it until you ask). Ask only when you're doing a fabulous job and they wouldn't want to do without you (this can be in some of your earlier jobs, of course; I really don't mean you to *starve*). When you ask, don't stress how much you *need* the money—family responsibilities, car payments, etc. Mention these in passing, but stress how much you love your job, love the company, and want to contribute even more. Outline what you've already done and what else you'll be doing to justify the raise.

Don't try for the crazy top dollar, because even if you *get* it, people will be looking at you funny every time you make a mistake and saying, "My God, we're paying *her* this salary?" They should feel *they* made a good deal. You should feel *you* have a good deal. A salary is only okay if it works for *both* of you. Getting another job offer is frequently the *best* way to get a significant raise but—a crucial *but*— use this device only if you're prepared to accept the other offer. You can't say you're going to go without actually being ready to leave. Also, upping a salary by threat of leaving can work only once or twice—after that the company gets tired of the blackmail and may say Go. It's okay to tell your boss about job offers even if you *don't* plan to leave, or aren't pushing at the moment for a raise. It doesn't hurt him or her to know you're sought after!

30. YOU WILL POSSIBLY ALWAYS WORK HARDER THAN OTHER PEOPLE—AND SPEND MORE HOURS WORKING THAN THEY DO

How can you not accomplish more and be more successful (and happy) if you put the hours in? Yes, you can get stale and dreary if you *never* leave your work; but I have always found that working intensely at something you love simply breeds more success; I believe people who must get away often and lengthily from their work life simply haven't been lucky enough to find the thing they ought to be doing! I can't *imagine* job burnout if you love your work. At any rate, I have never known a really successful person who didn't work harder than other people, or who got very far away from his or her work for very long.

When I was a copywriter at Foote, Cone & Belding—*that* again, but it was my breakthrough job—my six male coworkers used to growl when they saw me curved over my typewriter at 5:30 P.M. when they went home to Pasadena, Altadena, and Alhambra to spend the evening with their families. One of them even complained to our boss that I was taking advantage of the rest of them because I wasn't married and didn't have to go home. Too *bad* about him! I saw him recently and he's *still* going home at five-thirty to Altadena to be a daddy and family man, though his kids are now thirty-five years old.

31. DON'T BE DESTROYED WHEN THEY DON'T "LOVE" YOU ANYMORE

All love isn't romantic; you can love *many* people. I love the captains at Le Cirque, the maintenance men in the Hearst Building where I work, the switchboard girls at the Bel-Air Hotel, several dogs and cats (some of them *passionately*), a few teachers, housekeepers, hairdressers, not to mention loving one's *heroes*—writers, painters, singers, actors—along with "standard" loves—family, husband, friends. Love is good wherever you find it and you can find yourself loving an *office* . . . I surely have.

The thing *not* to do is think the office loves you back unequivocally, the way a mother loves you. They love you as a teammate and worker as long as you're there. Once you leave, nobody may even want to *talk* to you when you show up again for a friendly visit, and if you were *fired*, the chill is palpable.

Office love is for people who are still *in* the office, and who make each other's days more exciting. I can think of no relationship in the world quite like that of copywriter and art director, or editor and writer, when they're getting the best out of each other. Love your office and your office mates. Just don't try to have office love make *up* for the other kinds, or expect it to survive separation.

So are you a happy employee? Do all this stuff and they must surely be happy with *you!*

How to Be a Good Executive

I wrote, unasked, an article for *Fortune* on how to be a good executive. For a long time I'd been perceived as a successful magazine editor, but I was almost prouder of being a good executive and wanted people to know of this talent. Employees—the good ones I didn't want to lose—stayed with me, despite attractive offers from outside, for fifteen, twenty, even thirty years. Though I'd never had any experience as a boss before arriving at *Cosmo* at age forty-three, the boss principles took shape pretty soon in my new job and worked for me all those years. May I tell them to you?

1. Work harder than anybody else.
2. Do the disagreeable stuff first every day.
3. When they need an answer, get back to them in a hurry.
4. Get as much input from others as the project warrants, then you decide . . . no committee decisions. Stay firm . . . no waffling later.
5. Let each department head or person reporting directly to you know exactly what you want from him . . . clean, clear instructions.
6. Praise lavishly even if it was your idea, give all the credit away.
7. Making money for your company is what you are there for. Never get very far away from the product which enables you to do that.
8. Spending company money when required—maybe a lot of it— goes with the territory. Wasting company money is show-offy, indulgent, and dumb.
9. Forget financial bargains with good employees, but you don't

have to be the biggest spender in town. Appreciation of talent, letting the person blossom under your aegis, are big deals.

10. You don't have to know what everybody does well enough to do it yourself. Just try to employ the best people and turn them loose.

11. Before you criticize, find something nice to say about the worker.

12. Leave your door open so anybody can come in, though you may want to visit their offices so you can get out quicker.

13. People's families are as important as their work, surprise! Make it possible for them to be comfortable doing necessary personal stuff during office hours. If needed, pitch in and help.

14. If someone isn't working out, act sooner than later, give him a few months, or a year, not *years*. Softheartedness in letting a puny person stay is bringing down all of you.

15. When you have to fire, know that right is on your side and don't suffer too much.

16. Hiring is almost as painful as—and *more* time-consuming and tedious than—firing. See a lot of candidates before you decide. Mull carefully so you don't have to go through the whole boring process again soon.

17. Thou may not lose one's temper in an office, especially if thou art boss.

Learning on the Job

They (your employees) may or may not learn on the job. Who can be absolutely assured of learning is *you*—if you're a boss—about *them* because you aren't allowed to ask anything personal now in an interview. You may vaguely glean this person is married or living with someone—she *volunteered*, "I can get a ride in with Nathaniel. He has to come up the West Side Highway anyway"—but you will need to discover *after* this person is hired that she is pregnant and will be taking a leave of absence five months from now or that he or she will be asking for a morning off to march in the Save the Spotted Owls parade. Also revealed to you *later* will be who is taking Yom Kippur and who Good Friday—religious to the core—and who is caring for an aged father and will need mornings off to get him to the veteran's hospital. Oh well, it's stimulating to learn on the job.

I don't know exactly what employers are supposed to talk about in the job interview itself these days—the nature of the job perhaps or opinions as to whether Ireland's main Protestant leaders will ever stop putting the Good Friday Peace Accord in jeopardy—but God forbid you should inquire about the applicant's personal life or whether this job is a stepping stone and she will be leaving within the year or plans to stay put awhile—at least until her twenty-ninth birthday, which you also may or may not have gleaned when it's happening. Trying to solicit information as to why she left her last job—as in fired—punishable by death! Perhaps a psychic should sit in during the interview, camouflaged as a television sitcom writer soaking up "atmosphere" for an upcoming segment. With a few innocent questions, he might ferret whether your interviewee is out on probation, a yo-yo dieter, or possibly a spy in the employ of the interviewee's ex-husband to find out whether she is selling the Persian rug she got in the divorce settlement to buy a mink shrug or keeping it on the floor where his three-year-old son can get the good out of it as they agreed. There are ways to find out things in a job interview but current protocol says you mustn't *ask*.

Looks/
Age/
Health

How Old Are You?

We've gotten worse about age. In the 1920s and 1930s a woman confessing her age was thought to be deranged; even in the forties and fifties, confession wasn't recommended. "A woman who will tell her age will tell *anything*," said Elsie Mendel scathingly. In the sixties, seventies, and eighties I thought maybe we'd get a little better. I've always blabbed my age and found it "freeing"—nobody can viciously sneak around behind you, announce your birthday, and embarrass you because you've already told. In the nineties, however, I still run into hampers full of don't-ask, don't-tell age-shy people who include drop-dead attractive twenty-eight-year-old women all the way to mummies.

In order to give a television star a Miss Liberty silver dollar from a pretty complete collection my sister left me—message would be: "that was a wonderful year for all of us when you were born"—I called her office to find her birth year; we're friends and she has been wonderful to me. Wendy said, "We don't talk birth dates around here." Of course the public is mean about women actors' and entertainers' birthdays, but this was *us*. I also couldn't find the birth date of an editor in my office even from the personnel department. No legitimate reason to know, just curious because she'd recently married a much younger man and I wondered how old she was when she got him—I knew how long she'd pursued. Secretary for ten years couldn't help. I'll bet her *husband* doesn't know. Are we ridiculous or *what*? Unlike crooked teeth or a hook nose you can fix, you can't help when you got plunked here. You might as well be ashamed of brown eyes. Even there we have colored contacts.

Short Men

The shorter the man, the harder he tries, don't you agree? He will Make Up for Things with his brain, wit, charm, verve, and the body of a steel cable because he works out mercilessly. The taller the girl, the greater the chance she will be *picked* by one of the short men, possibly a rich short man, to be his Vargas or Petty Girl—but you're too young to know those creatures, let's say his show girl, his sexpot-goddess. Tall girls frequently hate their tallness even when worshipped by short men, poor statuesque things. Fair or not, we short girls and tall men don't have much trouble with our height. We are viewed as how high or low men and women are supposed to be. This height acceptance frees us fortunate ones to get on with weeping our brains out about no bosom or grappling with male-pattern baldness. It evens out.

Composers

How can these angel-sweet sounds and touch-you-to-your-soul words come out of people who look or looked like aardvarks? Lorenz Hart, desperately short, the Gershwins, little porcupine men, Cole Porter, somewhat flashier but hardly hunky, especially after the horse fell on him. Irving Berlin was a compact little cougar. Maybe what came out of them had something to do with longing to look better. They composed for themselves *and* for us, the needy, and, of course, in their genius and in their soul they were and are very beautiful.

Irving was a *big* pussycat in personality. We went to dinner once at Peter Luger's in Brooklyn and he put up with my singing "Change Partners," "Cheek to Cheek," "How Deep Is the Ocean" and a lot of other Berlin lyrics in the back of our limousine with David writhing with embarrassment in front. Later in the evening at the restaurant he sent my running-with-blood steak back and told the waiter, "You take this meat back to the kitchen and cook it the way Ms. Brown told you [cremated] or I will come out there personally and break your . . ." His voice trailed off. He didn't have to make good. They cremated. Darling man. We've got his paintings all over the house . . . he painted lots in his later years. We ate a thousand trout from his well-stocked lake. He gave me the original scores of

"It Only Happens When I Dance with You" and "Better Luck Next Time," my two favorites. He and his peers were beautiful men.

Thin Hair

Having it fall out on your pillow from an illness or chemotherapy isn't what I am talking about. Those conditions presuppose you have enough hair to fall *out*. Thin hair is when you finish your shampoo and there aren't any tangles . . . comb slides right through without one single hang-up. You can pin the whole mop on top of your head with one bobby pin. Mousse increases the volume *infinitesimally*. Others complain about other miseries, of course. Maxine says her knees are too close to the ground . . . you can't have good legs, Max says, if your ankles and knees aren't far enough apart. Althea regrets waistlessness; her waist is only three inches smaller than her hips . . . she'll show you. Pat says life would be brighter if her fingers weren't fat like a six-year-old child's but were long and tapered. Shall we cry, maybe even *sob*, for these gargoyles? Give me, as they say, a break. When you sit down or even don't sit down, nobody is looking at your knees, waist, fingers. Hair they are *always* looking at. As my friend Nancy Collins says, "Hair is *sex*!" What's a miracle is that I have got by in life all these years, at least recent years, without enough hair. Thanks for pretending not to notice.

To maintain current crop, I have a Minoxidil habit that must be just this side of cocaine addiction in terms of maintenance. One skimpy little sixty-milliliter bottle (two ounces) is sixty dollars, and I use two droppersful twice a day every day so a bottle lasts less than a month. Does Minoxidil actually prevent hair loss, encourage hair growth? I'm not sure but am afraid to stop—sort of the same way I feel about vitamins . . . could they hurt? My skimpy hair doesn't seem to be any *worse* than it was two or three years ago before the Minoxidil. It's occurred to me to ask Norman Orentreich for a wholesale price like I do with some of my clothes from the manufacturers. Is a different price for different folks fair? I'm not sure. I just know I've stuck with Minoxidil since it was twenty dollars a bottle . . . shouldn't loyalty get you *somewhere*?

What You Can't Read Can Hurt You

Hair shampooed, curled, and dry, is now lying on top of me like a greasy blanket or melted chewing gum. Seems pretty certain I got one of those little bottles of bath gel instead of volumizer/conditioner in the bathroom of the George V Hotel in Paris and dumped it on freshly shampooed hair. That's *this* week. Last week I couldn't read the recipe on the tapioca box and left out the eggs. Instead of dessert we had a bowl of seriously unthickened milk with little pellets floating around languishing at the bottom of the fridge. Is it possible one has finally to stop stashing magnifying glasses all over the house and stash a few *reading* glasses here and there, possibly an extra pair for hotel bathrobes? How long can you go on pretending things (eyesight) aren't going bye-bye on you?

Divine Dead Skin

Getting off dead skin is one of life's serious pleasures. Exfoliating freshens and frees the skin underneath; scrubbing, scraping, pushing the old skin away is satisfying. When I dropped a metal box on my leg near the shin (don't *ask* . . . carrying too much stuff at the time,) skin, deeply bruised, formed a scab that gradually got smaller, receded, dropped off, leaving skin flaky *around* it. At last, with scab gone, scar healed, the *fun* I had with rubbing away the fluffies! Another pleasure: every Saturday morning I squeeze Andrea bleach from a tube across thighs and calves to bleach brunette hair blonde. Plop on bleach. Leave fifteen minutes, start rubbing. Dead skin rolls off in little pellets. Amazing! I don't sunburn anymore, so I miss the pleasure of peeling away ex-epidermis but we all have bottoms of feet. After a lovely soaking—scrape, scrape, scrape, then bye-bye yesterday's once-live coating . . . hello fresh pink. What's the matter with you? Too prissy to acknowledge where real fun comes from?

Scruffy Posture

I could really complain my brains out about never having been nagged as a kid to stand up straight or sit up straight. Posture was never *mentioned*. Everything *else* was mentioned—"Yellow makes you sallow . . . pink is your color," "Comb your hair before we go shopping," "You're not going to wear *that* to church!"—but never one word about this important thing that could have improved my grown-up looks more than just about *anything*, particularly as I face seventy-eight. Kids whose mothers badgered them or who went to West Point have elegant posture, and it's the one thing you can really do to look better that I have ever figured out: pull in your gut, throw back your shoulders, and you don't *look* like a little old lady. Slump, slouch, pooch . . . you could be ninety. The good-posture people don't even *think* about it . . . from having been nagged, sitting or standing straight is ingrained. I'm too old to think about it as much as you need to *do* anything about it but, of course I *am* thinking and *am* doing.

I signed up with some people who teach "postural re-education," just what I need. They use something called The Alexander Technique created by a young Shakespearean actor in Australia in the last decades of the nineteenth century. Well, whoever created it or wherever he did it, *maybe* it will do a little good. All day long I chant to myself, "Let my neck be free, to let my head go forward and up, to let my torso lengthen and widen, to let my legs release away from my torso and let my shoulders widen out to the sides." During the chanting, posture does behave better but one tends to forget to chant when engaged in daily life, which is most of the time—talking, working, cooking, writing—i.e., you forget posture if there's anything better to do but, as always, I feel better trying than howling. Right this minute my neck is free, really it is, and I'm *sure* my torso is lengthening and widening like a good torso *should*.

Vulnerable—Broken-Toe Department

I don't know what falls apart on *you* but my falling-apart part is toes. Once you break *one*, they all want to get in on the act, maybe because of the attention they get . . . owner can't stop talking about, looking at, pointing to, and touching poor broken toe. Not much you can *do* for them—hot and cold compresses, wear sandals, elevate toesies inside shoes. I mostly break mine in people's swimming pools . . . not big Olympic-size ones like the Bel-Air Hotel or the Oriental in Bangkok, but designer pools, shaped like pretzels.

Last year I broke *two* in Barbaralee and Carl Spielvogel's pool (I never told them . . . nothing they could do *then*, why make a fuss. Possibly they thought I was drunk or being funny with all that hobbling). The Spielvogels' pool has wide concrete-slab steps, not just at the ends of the pool so you can get in and out but all the way along both sides—the entire length. The slabs would probably come in handy if you were trying to escape from a shark . . . who knows what can get you in a Southampton swimming pool . . . but they don't help much with regular swimming. Actual swimming area of Spielvogel pool is a little channel down the middle, the width of your body with arms spread and a bit more. In daylight, with sunlight streaming, you can glance ahead and see whether or not you are swimming correctly *in* the channel—I tend to drift—but late at night in inky black (pool not lit), you can crash. Thinking I was *in* the channel, I gave a good hard kick (not the recommended delicate butterfly kick I haven't been able to get the hang of) with my left leg, toes hit concrete, two crumpled. Maybe my toes are vulnerable because *something* has to be, right? I'm so otherwise perfect. Compensation: the bruising is beautiful. First stage: black and purple followed by chartreuse and yellow then, finally, baby-blush pink again—you could think of your color progression as the four seasons. The Spielvogel pool isn't the only place my toes go. At home one day carrying luggage downstairs, I crashed into a wrought-iron stair rail and took out two. Swimming pools are my bête noire, however, not just for toes. Not a great swimmer as in creamy, splashless, calm, I'm inclined more to flailing, kicking, thrashing, and sometimes I hit the side of the pool, anybody's pool, with the sides of my hands and get all scraped and skinned. Small price. As I mentioned, if you swim *enough*, fettucini Alfredo smothered in Parmesan followed by apple strudel with soft ice cream doesn't show up on you, or not as *much*. I can live with vulnerable.

Older—Good News (*Honest!*)

Maybe the *only* good thing about getting older (old) is that you know how long stuff takes. For a major, or at least longer-than-a-weekend, trip you know there is no way you can pack in one night . . . put the hang-up things on a rack, organize shoes and bags . . . good girls don't take black, brown, *and* navy . . . which will it be, can you sleep in the T-shirt and panties you're taking for exercise, how do you get seven possible cocktail dresses (yes, you've gone nutty through the years) down to two, and can the daytime shoes *possibly* do . . . blah, blah, blah. Grown-up girls fifty or older *know* this cannot all be done in one packing session and you sneak up on it—a weekend plus another night.

Other things you now know: to get across town by car in rush hour takes thirty minutes, *not* rush hour, twenty. On foot, a little less time than car, but on foot from my house to the Sony complex at Sixty-eighth and Broadway (favorite destination) you'll be winded! What else do you know how long it takes? There can be a fifteen-minute wait in the ladies' room of an old New York theater (I have been known to commandeer the men's room with a guard outside if business there is slow), a charity dinner in the Waldorf Astoria ball-room will never get out before 10:00 P.M.—10:45 is more likely. Having more than one person over for dinner even if it's best friend is a two-night proposition in *my* case—one night to get the apart-ment spiffed—big apartment—wine picked, dishes selected, table set, food planned, even if it's coming from the deli. If I tried to do all that in one night, it would be N.B.T. (nervous breakdown time). You know how long to plan for a certain friend's phone call (she's fast, she's slow), to get hair color and blow-dry, to pick a wedding present at Tiffany. I wish there were something *else* age had going for it . . . I'll keep thinking. How about you *know* there is nothing like a cookie/candy/cake fix—*screw* carrot juice and cantaloupe? Now if we could just get *them* to know how long it takes so *they'd* never be late.

How to Grow Fingernails

Most of what people tell you to do to yourself to be better-looking is either (a) too much trouble or (b) only works for people already gorgeous, but this little recipe for strong nails can absolutely happen to *anyone.* I had crêpe-paper fingernails forever, kept them filed nearly to the quick because anything *there* always tore off, and for years covered them with acrylic. Every ten days a manicurist came to the office. Then before surgery one year I had to remove the acrylic shields and decided while convalescing to try once more for natural nails. Off came the shields and there they were, the little creeps . . . my own pitiful skimpies. Take a deep breath, plunge! In a year—yes, it took that long—I had strong, healthy nails. Recipe:

1. Try two biotin (massive vitamin H) tablets every day. Veterinarians first used Biotin to treat the split hooves (equivalent of our nails) of horses. When horses were given large does of vitamin H, the split hooves healed. Tested on human beings, large does of vitamin H benefited nails *and* hair. My dermatologist, Dr. Norman Orentreich, thinks the F.D.A. recommended daily dose of vitamin H is insufficient for the desired effect. He suggests three 2500 miligram tablets a day. (I take two.) Biotin is obtainable at health food stores in 2000 miligram wattage; from doctor's office, 2500.
2. Coat nails *daily* with Nailtique, a crystal enamel, available in drug stores. Once a week you can peel off old enamel and start again—this is fun.
3. Put your fingers in Crisco a dozen times a day; rub it in. Not too messy . . . just a little bit. I keep a can or small container of Crisco in kitchen, bathroom, office john, by my bed, and in my luggage (David says he feels like he's married to an apple pie), have found it more efficacious for nail-growing than hand lotion, Vaseline, or any other product. It really *is* thrilling to grow strong, natural, break-proof fingernails so late in life. Want to try?

A Beauty Present

My beauty present to you is Crisco—plain old-fashioned Proctor and Gamble Crisco—the sixteen-ounce can you make pies with. I discovered this wonderful product as an emollient after cosmetic surgery. I can't remember which surgery, but when scabs formed on your face, you were supposed to dab generously with Crisco. I dabbed so generously I grew fingernails—for the first time in fifteen years. Before that I just had those little crêpe-paper wisps. From using big C. lavishly on my fingers, I branched out to other places: bottoms of feet then stroked around toes and ankles before pulling on panty hose, globbed around mouth at night if no sexual assignation planned, rubbed into elbows, sometimes for hand cream during the day. Nothing is wrong with official moisturizers and hand creams, they're wonderful, but you can be so extravagant with this substitute. A can costs less than $4.00, lasts forever. Once you get Crisco into your life, you may decide, like me, it's your best beauty friend. The product is pure . . . goes down your throat, then to your stomach in pies, pastries, and biscuits, right? Thrifty, innocent, safe, and *smart*!

Breast Augmentation

An extremely aggressive (and popular) Canadian journalist interviewed me at the Four Seasons Hotel in Toronto, not the least interested in talking about anything except whether or not I had breast implants. Looking at my sweatered bosom like a vulture in possession of a dead wildebeest, she fitted in a tiny question or two about my profession and why I was in Toronto (to speak to the Magazine Association of Canada) but quickly returned to her passion: had I or hadn't I? I told her no at least six times, the little bitch. At the time my implants were eighteen months old. I was and still am happy with them but, though I have often talked about cosmetic surgery, breast surgery I have preferred not to discuss. I think that is often the case with people who have had both . . . we'll talk throat, chin, mouth, eyes, nose but implant disclosure would be like confessing a small murder. I'm talking now because I tell you everything.

I wasn't your typical breast-augmentation candidate, if there is such a thing. Years ago I learned to live with a 34A, mostly ribcage. I had help. First I helped myself . . . went through all the do-it-yourself (bobby socks, cotton, little balloons filled with water—one broke one day and talk about slushy!) augmenting. Most of the time the augmenting *did* help . . . one looked bosomier, lusher. Officially padded bras of today are only more professional versions of what I was doing, with reasonable success, back in the forties. Of course, there is *no* embarrassment—I haven't run into it—like that of having a man get hold of a bobby sock instead of *you*. With a steady beau you wouldn't pad, of course, if you knew there was going to be heavy necking that night, but you didn't always judge correctly the way an evening with a new companion might go. Though underwear manufacturers would later construct beautifully padded bras of satin and lace, I never went back to padded after my late twenties because of three wonderful men. The charmer of the century actually convinced me bigger was *worse* (gross!), small was beautiful. He adored my small breasts, could bring me to orgasm just by . . . oh, let's stop! This kind of self-revelation *is* tacky. Another attractive man also declared worship of small; Audrey Hepburn was his idol. He could get turned on by looking at my . . . let's stop again!

Then there was darling David, an unreconstructed small-breast appreciater. Flattering always to hear when questioned, "You don't need *anything*, dearest, you're perfect!" In the early seventies I did check out breast augmentation with a cosmetic surgeon who performed it; even *he* wasn't enthusiastic. Implants could harden sometime after surgery, he said, and you actually had to squash them in your hands—like walnuts?—to soften them up or they could be removed if you preferred. Ugh! I discarded the augmentation option and, mostly because of the "appreciaters," quit wearing *any* kind of bra—free felt nifty. If a gauzy blouse or dress was too see-through and a full-length slip flattened what bosom there *was*, I simply put a Band-Aid across the nipple. Adequate.

So why, June 12, 1995, did I have breast-augmentation surgery? Because fashions that year were so bosom-revealing (now they're *worse!*) I wanted to throw up; it was terminally depressing to watch the goddesses at runway shows reveal everything from the ribcage up bralessly, magnificently. More important reason: in the summer of 1995, my beloved internist, Dr. Harvey Klein of New York Hospital, just happened to mention that good work was being done with augmentation. Harvey is conservative. I zoomed right out and booked an appointment with Dr. Sherrill Aston, soon was being augmented at the same time I had a tiny face lift. If you're going to be away from the office and not feeling and looking red hot for two weeks, why not do everything at once?

I was and still am enthusiastic about the augmentation. Implants were small and appropriate for my body size—I have never had one second of regret, only pride and pleasure. I feel the breasts are *mine*, indigenous to me, the size they should always have been (34B). No friends or office mates ever commented; if they noticed, they tactfully didn't speak. I think likely the new creation is so natural the truth didn't really bang at them. P.S. you mostly do this operation for yourself, not others.

Procedure: Implant, appropriate for your body's present bosom size (nobody is encouraged to go down-pillow gigantic), is tucked in behind your real bosom so what's on top sticking out in front is *you*, including nipples; nipples remain sensitive and appreciative of lovemaking if they were before. I didn't tell David about the augmentation ahead of time, only about the lift; unveiled my beautiful new bosom after I got home from Manhattan Eye, Ear and Throat. Husband: "Helen, how could you do this! You know I loved your small bosom. Could we get them back the way they were?" Wife: "Yes, David, we could but no, David, we won't." He hasn't yet really forgiven me the enlargement and that is the truth.

While I was recovering at home from both procedures, he graciously offered to go on a Zabar's run to bring me rocky road ice cream, couldn't *find* R.R., and substituted toffee crunch. Rocky road is all marshmallow, cherries, and a few chocolate bits . . . face-friendly; toffee crunch contains hunks of real toffee . . . dangerous. I bit down hard, broke a cap, and *that* was the worst aftermath of the breast/face-lift experience. I feel a woman shouldn't have to visit the dentist to get fitted for new caps (dentist had to do *two* since front teeth connected) when your chest and throat hurt, but the new caps actually look better than the old ones and I have forgiven David (whom I blamed totally for the dental experience). Soon I bought a thousand beautiful new bras in all colors . . . I can have cleavage if I want but have rarely worn any of the bras. Having been as free as Lassie all those years—unfettered and frisky—getting all harnessed up in fabric, elastic, and straps doesn't feel good; camisoles and slips are still all I need. To go for augmentation takes the wish, the guts, and money. I'm not pushing, just reporting. God knows how many of your friends and mine and/or how many famous people have had the procedure. I doubt we'll ever know. Few are as blabby as I. For me it was a happy experience. Francesco Scavulla, who photographed 95 percent of all *Cosmo* covers, and his stylist Sean Byrnes were incredibly clever at creating cleavage from virtually nothing by pushing breasts up and together with tape, told me recently, "Helen, we've retired the Scotch tape!"

The New York Hospital Caper

A big surgery eats you up . . . gobble, gobble, gobble . . . like some Jurassic Park monster . . . chomp, chomp, chomp. You aren't interested in anything out *there* because you are a consumed thing floating about in the monster's tummy. Still, although you have no strength, you continue to be you just enough to try to figure out "If I swim upstream, can I maybe get *out* of here?" Did the whale give up Jonah or did Jonah do aggressive stuff to make it happen? I can't remember, if I ever knew. How many days does it take to escape from a whale? I'm into my ninth day since surgery. Such an invasion of privacy, to put it mildly. Unspeakable things keep being done to you despite your being inside a big rubbery stomach, and I'm not just talking about everybody looks at your backside, frontside, bottomside, upside down side all the time; *functions* are incessantly checked . . . more in a minute.

Though I can be pretty blabby about my diet, exercise routine, David's disgusting overtipping, etc., I really did once think of myself as private; now I belong to New York Hospital. I don't have to ask how did this happen . . . I *know* how it happened. At a big wingding at the Metropolitan Museum at which *New York Times* publisher Arthur Sulzberger introduced his bride, Allison Cowles, to several thousand friends (there are those who say Arthur married rather quickly after Carol died—six months—simply to discourage the mob of females who kept calling to say, "Arthur, have we got a girl for you!" Arthur did well; Allison is a peach). Stomach cramps start during dessert, escalate at home until I'm doubled over. I sleep—if you could call that sleeping—on the carpet by my bed . . . a little more endurable I thought than bedding. David, wildly worried, comes down often to visit, is sent away. After a modest stretch of sleep, up to my eyeballs in Tylenol II left over from gum surgery, I'm not feeling *too* awful, begin to exercise as usual but cramps are coming back. David orders me into some clothes, plunks me into the car, we're off to see the wizard, my internist. Dr. Harvey Klein, at New York Hospital.

The pains are now back full strength and I'm almost relieved—pains frequently go bye-bye when you've made an emergency appointment and then the doctor thinks you're an hysteric. Over a period of several hours, Harvey does a swarm of tests and X rays, disappointed that I'm having neither a bowel movement nor throwing up—whatever is in you, you want to come out if you're cramping. No dice. After I have cleared everybody out of Dr. Klein's waiting room with the screamies and a second round of more sophisticated X rays are ordered, we get a diagnosis: a piece of scar tissue from a two-years-ago hysterectomy has wrapped itself around an intestine, blocking passage of anything that would like to come out. Decision: emergency surgery. Head of surgery at New York Hospital, John Daley, is called at home. Elfin, engaging, so low-key you could even say *sweet*, Dr. Daley clomps right over. Surgery begins at 8:00 P.M. Except for a few Tylenol II moments, I have been thrashing around and shrieking for nineteen hours. Four hours under the knife, then into recovery. David has done his death watch . . . awful thing to go through for a loved one. With me from the modest first shriek, David has held up pretty well, bless his baby heart. Like all men he is terrified of surgery, can never glean why any sane person would sign up voluntarily as in cosmetic surgery, but that's another story. Okay, it's been nine days. I've extricated myself from Moby Dick for the moment—maybe he got bored with me and coughed me out. I'm really not worried about recovery—am not expected to die—but have made the (serious) mistake of looking at myself in the mirror.

Dilapidated! *Dilapidated* was my sister Mary's word for how you get when older; everything is different colors instead of creamy, etc.—I wrote about this in *The Late Show*. In the time I've been in the hospital, lines have popped out on forehead and around mouth which look silicone-proof no matter what mega wattage is turned on by another of my genius doctors, dermatologist Norman Orentreich (Silicone now legal again). Tummy pooches obnoxiously, showing its eighteen tiny vertical incisions, which, you are told unconsolingly, may quiet down *some* but, like the face craters, will never disappear the rest of your life. Intolerable!

I have fought aging and flab and a poochy stomach *almost* uncomplainingly with exercise all these years—I've told you about that—one hour and a half daily in two sessions. A lot of my life is fitted *around* exercise . . . when I can squiggle it in . . . will anybody kill if I'm fifteen minutes late getting down to the reception from hotel room? Can I borrow an office while waiting for my TV segment? I commandeered Larry King's office one day . . . his little blue and white striped shirts, freshly laundered, fluttered *all* around. At the airport, can I sneak in fifteen minutes in Delta's ladies' room waiting for flight 106 to Frankfurt, then another fifteen minutes in the ladies' room on the 757 (the standing up, sitting-on-the-john, lifting-knees-to-forehead part, lying down stuff will have to come later)? Possibly. At home, if David is famished, maybe I'll knock off the fifteen minutes standing, do his breakfast, finish thirty-minutes lying down afterwards. Exercise is *me* for whatever compulsive reasons. Almost, almost as weird as the surgery is not being *allowed* to exercise. No *way* they have declared . . . the exertion will impede the healing but, at this moment, the very *thought* of exercising isn't happening. I'm not sure I'll *ever* exercise again . . . you ever heard me say *that* before?

I know I will recover, yes, and some day be reunited with my weights and Body Bar but right now I hurt. They make you push a hard little pillow up against your tummy over and over . . . supposed to hold everything *in*. You blow into a little box to try to push a little ball up to the top. If your breath is strong enough—push, push, push—ball will hit the ceiling . . . mine never does, have my lungs collapsed? Morphine. What a dreamy thing *that* is. I can see how Edgar Allen Poe got entranced. Morphine makes you sleep when somebody is talking straight *at* you . . . not even "funny sleep" but just straight, deep-down delicious apple-pie sleep. Rosalie, my lovely, annoying, petal-skinned Irish nurse couldn't push the morphine pound sign often enough to suit *her*. "You're only getting five milligram doses, Ms. Brown," she would scold. "Everybody else is at least on ten." Then Rosalie would swamp my little system when we were only going for a halfway-up-to-the-clock walk or having a sponge bath, for God's sake. Your tree dripping glucose into you goes with you everywhere . . . walking in the hospital hallway, of course, but also to the bathroom.

With your catheter in you're sure you need to go to the bathroom most of the time. After the catheter came out, I thought I could make it on my own in the john but, having to take the tree in with me, I came close to breaking my neck because I was always getting the tree wrapped around me. I finally learned to take Reno, the lovely *not* homosexual Philippino night nurse, in with me. Two or three times I tried the bedpan instead of hoofing it with my tree to the john but I was afraid I'd stream all over the bed—you feel *totally* out of control lying flat out on your tush on a cold pan trying to urinate. Such a cute little bed pan . . . I didn't try it often but uncomfortable. A catheter is in one part of you, you're hooked up to a tree, and a *tube* is down your throat. Naturally the tube makes you want to swallow all the time and try to . . . testing, testing, is my throat as sore this time as last time I swallowed . . . yes! The *only* treat is a teeny-tiny ice cube, not even a normal size one—just little tidbits of ice maybe half an inch square which melt on your tongue and you are *goofy* with gratitude. Food. At one point I decide if you are what you eat, I'm nothing. . . . I haven't eaten anything for four days! Well, maybe I'm not *nothing* . . . I'm sugar and water! What do people in hospitals do who are used to *eating* . . . as in *food*? I'm never all that used to it, at least I can skip meals, but when some-body has been deprived of food entirely for a few days (just liquids slipped into you intravenously) and you're out walking with your tree in the hospital hall, pass the little trays of food ready to be delivered to the lucky eaters, and look longingly at applesauce, a big glutinous white roll, mashed potatoes in a giant lifeless mound, and you start coveting *this* forbidden "treat," you know you have to be sick, not to mention starving.

The hospital halls are as foreign to me as Danang, fellow patients pretty depressing . . . they probably feel the same way about *me*. I hardly saw *one* who didn't look as though this was about *it*. One man sitting in his room in a wheelchair said over and over whenever you happened to go by, "Help me, help me, help me," thousands of times. I always wanted to go in and help but I knew they wouldn't want me to.

So, you're not scheduled to eat until Friday . . . nine days after surgery and it's only Tuesday . . . I've backed up a little in my tale. Sometimes in my room I gave an entire hour to food-thinking . . . Macaroni and melted cheddar cheese, sauted-in-garlic-butter scampi with rice, but dreaming gets tiresome if there's no fulfillment. When I did finally get put on a diet . . . actual food, as in the famous soft diet, instead of osmosed into you through the tube, you can't get as excited as you thought you'd be. Jell-O should have qualified as a thrill . . . I *love* Jell-O but they make it runny. I ought to tell the hospital how to do *gummy* . . . leave out three-quarters of the water package suggests and it's like gumdrops. I *kind* of enjoyed the ho-mogenized milk . . . a whole glass if I wanted. When did you ever pour out a glass of whole milk and drink it down—135 calories—as a grown-up? I have better things to do with calories. Okay we don't have to talk about hospital food. The ice cream was melted but I promised not to start.

My private nurses were the world's best friends. I ran up a bill of $3,400.00—not a bad little business. They make $425.00 for a twelve-hour shift. I refused to have Rosalie back the fourth day be-cause all I needed was a sponge bath—a $425.00 sponge bath? She was a little irritated. Most of the regular hospital nurses were not real friendly. Not angry—not at me anyway, maybe at life—but just not charmable. This isn't Bergdorf Goodman and you a customer buying a blouse, I kept reminding myself. This is a staff working megahours trying to care for too many people. "Can I have tea in-

stead of coffee?" "Why didn't you ask for tea in the first place?"
"Nobody gave me a menu . . . maybe the soft-food trays arrive all
preordained?" It's a wonder I don't get bitten on the wrist or accused
of sexual harassment. I am so grateful to the nurse who overheard
my pitiful plea and brought me tea, and I keep patting her lovingly
on the arm.

Masses of hospital staff descend on you every day, some *very* early
in the morning. At this same hospital after my hysterectomy, a young
doctor used to visit around seven o'clock every morning, wake me
from sleep, and actually say this: "Good morning, Ms. Brown. I just
wanted to check and see if you're resting okay!" During this new visit
to the hospital, a small crew arrived in the morning, another in the
afternoon. Professional, focused. No laughs. I grow quite fond of
Dr. Chan and his associate Dr. Tracy Kelvo, a twelve-year-old trying
to pass for twenty-two. I didn't know they made doctors that young
and pretty. Doctors Daley and Klein visited every evening.

Everybody is passionately interested in your elimination; every
smidge that comes out is collected. Urine goes into a special compartment of the john, ounces recorded. Probably never again in your
life will you be able to feel your urine is so valuable even though
you'd as soon be valued for something else—teeth, fingernails, personality? What really gets their attention is defecation or lack of.
The anxiety is palpable and why not . . . they've all gone to a lot of
trouble to get you to this stage—four hours of abdominal surgery
can't have been fun for *anyone*. "Did you pass gas?" "No." An hour
later, "Did you pass gas?" "I don't *think* so . . . maybe a *little*." "Be
sure to tell us when you do," they implore. As for an actual stool,
maybe fifteen inquiries over two days. When the tiniest stool—just
a tiny pellet or two—emerges, it's strike up the band! You'd think
this kind of carrying on might be reserved for the birth of a baby
condor! The pellets' arrival simply means, of course, that everything
"took." They got the scar tissue to let go of the intestine, everything
neatly sewed back together . . . the scars *are* neat if showy . . . your
alimentary tract is working again . . . I'm kind of enthusiastic myself!
Nobody talks about what they'd do if nothing ever came out . . . I'm
sure there are cases . . . let's don't think about it.

My darling Dr. Klein who, we could say, along with Dr. Daley,
saved my life, would sit with me in the evenings out on the verandah
of the Baker Pavilion—pleasant, peaceful. Harvey said he had trouble with the forms these days . . . misrepresent a procedure in the

tiniest way and you go to prison. He tells me stories. Until recently, Harvey said, bodily parts were thought of as something to cause pain and trauma—the enemy!—good idea to get rid of as many as you could . . . tonsils, appendix, even uteri. Harvey recalled that when hysterectomies were performed so perfunctorily, four women scheduled their hysterectomies for the same day at the hospital so they could recuperate together and play bridge . . . like booking at the Golden Door.

Harvey said not so long ago in hospitals, everything continuously went wrong. . . . not just on isolated occasions. Before the advent of plastic bottles, fluids for the I.V. machines were suspended from glass bottles . . . occasionally a bottle would crack or get broken and glass could shatter all over the patient. On other occasions patients would be ejected from gurneys or beds when they were testing new automatic equipment. Somebody said at that time that any given moment of the day, night, week, month, or year, some patient was in the air at New York Hospital! Harvey once sent an actress to surgery who wanted her knee fixed so she could continue to dance in the musical *42nd Street*. The night before the surgery her friends had a party in her room, got the magic marker, and marked up both of her legs—one leg said this isn't the one, the other leg had the notation, "Operate on this leg." Sure enough, the surgeon got them mixed up the next day and did the wrong leg. A couple of years ago a young Indian woman patient at Sloan-Kettering was to have brain surgery but the doctor got mixed up with the Indian names and performed surgery on the wrong side of her head. Woof!

Time at last to go home; Susie and Ramona fetched me. We took a few plants and flowers, nothing to steal—I didn't even want the Johnson and Johnson hand lotion in little pink bottles—nothing to remind where you got it, though I *did* relent and lift a mustard-color plastic glass . . . icky color but easier to lift than glass tumbler in my bath at home. The experience at New York Hospital was both gruesome and comforting. You feel glad somebody can do what these people do—can you imagine slicing somebody open for a living? After three weeks at home I was exercising again, told, naturally, it was way too soon. Never mind. Flab comes around faster than a freight train . . . you have to try to get out of the way.

Cancer

I had cancer, doesn't everyone? Don't mean to be disrespectful but a special issue of *People* recently revealed how many celebrities (Nancy Reagan, Betty Ford, Linda Ellerbee, Gloria Steinem, Carly Simon, Linda McCartney [she died], etc.) have had breast cancer (my kind). Diane Von Furstenberg's was throat. In the general public breast cancer now hits one out of eight women, though those figures will go down if more women get the mammograms they are urged to have. Uncharacteristically, I didn't tell anyone about the cancer except my husband, my wonderful assistant, Susie, and three girlfriends. At the office I wanted to continue to be perceived a healthy rat despite my age; management who pays me (well) must always be encouraged to feel they are getting a bargain, don't want them concerned with my vital signs. It's different with you and me. We don't have secrets, though I'm not sure you're as crystal pure as I . . . have you *yet* told me about your first baby face-lift? (If you write, I'll open the mail.)

JUNE 17 (WEDNESDAY)

An ordinary, run-of-the-mill mammogram five months after I got the notice to come in. Though I would never be one of those sillies who doesn't have mammograms, for years I mostly had them to keep a doctor from nagging. I was casual about mammograms because I couldn't possibly *get* breast cancer . . . breasts were too small, cancer likes lush bosoms, I reasoned. After viewing the Enemy—a 36B or C in yummy décolletage—this thought cheered me: she can, I *can't* (get breast cancer). Also I was too healthy . . . one hour and a half of exercise seven days a week, eight hours of sleep, no booze or cigarettes, good-girl diet except for occasional cookie craziness, nobody in family ever had cancer . . . how could it come *near* my dainty bosom? I showed up in June instead of January when notice came in, not to be careless but because I was busy—to Croatia and Beijing to open *Cosmo*, to Mexico City to celebrate Latin America's twenty-fifth anniversary, cruising on the *Seabourne* with David to Bora Bora, Tonga, and Tahiti, then back to the South Pacific six weeks later for *Cosmo*'s international conference in Sydney with editors from all over the world and, oh yes, quick trip to Los Angeles for my godson Harrison Zanuck's wedding.

Showing up six months previous wouldn't have changed the outcome of the visit in any way except they could have had even more trouble finding the cancer because it was so tiny, or maybe it wouldn't have shown at all that early. At the mammogram appointment the technician kept taking extra slides, sending them off to another room to be looked at, coming back to do more. The extras didn't worry me. All mammograms are yucky . . . squeeze, scrunch, press, rearrange breasts on a metal tray . . . hurts! Booked in advance for a sonogram, we did that next. In this procedure, while moving a breast—just my left one—all around and around, radiologist looks into an imaging machine . . . and looks and looks and looks. Nipples are sensitive, so who needs all this wash-cycle motion but nothing was *really* misery-making.

Dr. Miriam Levy, whose clinic this is, now comes in. Hadn't expected to see Mimi. Since an eight-week wait for appointment with her, mine is with a lesser doctor. Mimi reports funny shadows on X rays and in sonogram, wants to do a needle biopsy that afternoon. I wouldn't deny Mimi anything. Eight years ago in a sonogram she discovered the thickened lining of the uterus that led to hysterectomy; my gynecologist, Dr. Thomas Steadman, trusts her utterly. I come back after lunch for the needle biopsy; bosom is numbed, long needle inserted, tissue removed. This doesn't really hurt, procedure just a little unnerving. It's Wednesday, reading of biopsy isn't promised until Monday . . . I could live without the wait. Mimi, a good person, actually calls Thursday afternoon. "Cancer," she tells me. "We found cancer." With civilians I guess you don't say "The results were positive" because positive sounds good and what we are dealing with here *isn't* and you don't say carcinoma because term not understood . . . cancer crystal-clear.

From that moment on, life got different, almost didn't seem like my life. I already had enough to worry about I thought . . . we fit worry in, don't we . . . now I have to make room for this New Thing. Dr. Levy tells me to contact a surgeon. I've kept David informed about the medical development though, of course, low-key is how you play it . . . some people are not the world's leading calm and tranquil in matters of health. After my chat with Mimi in the afternoon, that night at a big-deal dinner at the Museum of Natural History honoring Dr. Rees Pritchett, David's doctor at New York Hospital, I scooched around looking for *my* New York Hospital doctor, Harvey Klein. Harvey isn't there. Phone-tag next morning with

Harvey's office is phone torture. His answering machine offers several options, none of which is to talk with a live human person. Only live human person I ever got was somebody at the answering service whom I'd called several times and left messages. A human person finally said they'd have somebody from doctor's office call, but a Harvey person never called. Not characteristic. He is usually the most conscientious keeping-in-touch there is. He seriously apologized later . . . something way off with the phones that day. Since Dr. Levy said I have cancer and need a surgeon I think I'd better find one. Dr. Steadman can't help, he's in Europe.

I call my friend Ann Siegel, survivor of a lumptectomy eleven years earlier at Memorial Sloan-Kettering, and two months ago a mastectomy, same place. Ann has been doing a lot of work with the American Cancer Society and I figured, in addition to her own experience, would Know Things. Also couldn't hurt that she had given three mammogram machines and three examining rooms to the hospital; a large plaque on the wall at Sloan says, "Mammography/ultrasound suite donated through the generosity of Ann L. Siegel." Annie tells me her surgeon is Dr. Patrick Borgen, whom she highly respects and finds extremely sensitive, gives me his number. You don't pass surgeons' phone numbers around the way you do caterers', dressmakers', and hairdressers', of course, but we're doing the right thing. Explained to Dr. Borgen's office why it was *me* calling instead of a doctor—this particular day I can't *find* one. Office is cordial, tells me Dr. Borgen will be on vacation for the next two weeks. Mimi had mentioned another surgeon at Sloan-Kettering, Jeanne Patrek. I call Dr. Patrek's office and ask for an appointment. She, too, it seems will not be in the office for two weeks. What do they do in emergencies I wonder? Is it like grade school where they send in Ms. Phillips, the substitute teacher? Will I eventually get Ms. Phillips, the substitute doc? While I'm on the phone with Dr. Patrek's office, they tell me Dr. Borgen's office is calling *them* and would like to talk to me. Annie has gone to work. After telling her Dr. Borgen will be away and I'm contacting Dr. Patrek, she called Dr. Borgen himself, found he wasn't quite away *yet*, they will give me an appointment that day . . . that *day*, 2:00 P.M., I suggest 2:15. I want to keep my lunch date. The way things are going, who knows when I'll get to make lunch dates again? Two-fifteen is okay. Now comes the task of getting X rays released from Dr. Levy's office to be studied by Dr. Borgen before my appointment. Phoning, faxing, explaining we need them now, this morning, not some spring day in the millenium keeps Susie and me busy. Dr. Levy wouldn't *not* want the X rays released to Dr. Borgen but Mimi is seeing patients. Phone answerer in her office is in no hurry to track the boss, get me the film released. Susie and I continue to phone, fax, push for over an hour, finally get the release okayed. Michael, my driver, is dispatched to Mimi's office with $75 check required for release, delivers the famous photographs into my icy little hands just before the doctor's appointment. I describe the tepid pace of film-releasing as a big deal because it *is*. Other deals in one's life are surely bigger right now, but I learn the requesting and securing records, data, film will be part of the surgical procedure and tedious enough to make you twitchy.

Dressing in the morning I have decided the pink Ralph Lauren twin sweater set with Ralph scarf will be fine for both lunch at La Grenouille and meeting with my surgeon-to-be, whom I surely want to impress and get to like me so he'll operate on me if necessary. Lunch is the best I ever ate . . . halibut with poached veggies nestled all around, side order of rice (*always*), decaf cappuccino, petit fours numerous enough to plunk several in my purse . . . my purses are always crumby.

Lunch over, we're outside and my lunchdate longtime friend and namesake owner of Georgette Klinger salons, is futzing around. Pushkin, her adored poodle, has been with us at lunch in a carrying case at her feet but is now out of his case on the street looking around with the rest of us for Georgette's car—not there. Georgette wants to walk to her salon, a block and a half away, with Pushkin padding beside her, she carrying his case. Both La Grenouille maître'd, on the street with us and trying to get us dispatched, and I want her, Pushkin, and case to get in my car . . . her salon at 501 Madison is right on the way to doctor's. Negotiations continue until I finally do a tiny scream—"Georgette, I have to *leave*! If you aren't coming with me, you must go *without* me!" Last I saw as I got in the car was Georgette padding east on Fifty-second Street with Pushkin out of his carrier, padding beside her, Georgette carrying his case. Pushkin is about as old as Georgette (85) in doggy years. I wasn't the least sure they were going to reach the corner, called later to learn mommy and child had arrived safely at the salon.

I arrived at the doctor's. Experience not too bad, actually made me feel a little frisky because (a) I got in without waiting (a very big deal with me . . . I'd been warned to bring mountains of reading);

(b) Dr. Borgen was what Annie Siegel said . . . extremely professional, brilliant, and very kind, with a unique way of putting you at ease. Thirty-nine years old, good-looking (doesn't *hurt*), reassuring. The needle biopsy with Dr. Levy has revealed only the tiniest amount of cancer but glory, glory malignancy has been spotted early; (c) he said my massive doses of estrogen (two 1.25-milligram tablets a day, dosage up or down a little, for the past thirty years), probably hadn't brought on this blight so I didn't have to feel like a fool who had given herself cancer (later, other doctors disagreed with this appraisal). Breast implants hadn't done it either; (d) surgery, if performed, would be a lumpectomy, not a mastectomy . . . whew! I get to keep most of my breast; and (e) there's a frail chance he wouldn't do surgery at all.

Although X rays from needle biopsy reveal cancer, doctor would like quickly to do a core biopsy, more comprehensive procedure—bigger needle—either to corroborate or deny Mimi's findings. Dr. Levy's X rays also reveal some calcium deposits in breast, but she thinks those have been there a long time, not worthy of excision, so reports to Dr. Borgen; new biopsy will tell us more.

At this appointment I see radiologist Dr. Andrea Abramson—cute, looks like Rhea Perlman in *Cheers* and *Canadian Bacon*, Danny Devito's wife, not quite as charming as the surgeon, but somebody around there has to play it more grim perhaps. Original mammogram and needle biopsy have been performed on Wednesday, now it's only two days later . . . we're moving right along . . . but Dr. Abramsom says her core biopsy must wait for a week because I have been taking vitamin E which can cause bleeding . . . have you ever heard that? I must come in clean. She requests all slides from previous mammograms (many through the years with Dr. Levy) as well as pathology from last week's biopsy, this work done at New York University Hospital. Getting the previous years' slides from Dr. Levy's office is again only slightly less difficult than getting the last print of *Mata Hari* out of the MGM film library for your personal use. More faxing, phoning, pleading, eventual success. Dr. Jerry Weisman at New York Hospital is happy to release pathology report but hospital (on East River between Thirtieth and Thirty-fourth Streets, connected with Bellevue Hospital) (a) is definitely not in our neighborhood, and (b) could get a little confusing for a messenger trying to retrieve reports from a particular room. Michael is dispatched to get the goods from both Dr. Levy's office and Dr. Weisman's office, takes these baubles to Dr. Abramson.

JUNE 23 (TUESDAY)

Dr. Abramson performs a core biopsy, a little less "fun," though neither procedure is fun, than needle biopsy because needle is larger (like an innertube) . . . probe, probe, probe, click, click, click like a giant Cracker Jack clicker going off in your chest. I didn't ask what was all that clicking, didn't need to know. Dr. Abramson is working like the sorcerer's apprentice, cursing ladylike little curses because every time she gets the needle in the right position to take a picture, she's in danger of puncturing my breast implant (the only person beside David who *ever* complained about them). I doubt Dr. A. is thinking about my appearance as a result of possible puncture and subsequent loss of saline solution (flat-chested again) but doesn't need solution squirting around inside me to complicate her photography right this minute. Lunchtime and we're through!

Though doctor said absolutely not to, I would usually have gone to the office—if you aren't running 103° and are ambulatory what's to stay home about—but somehow indolence has crept in to me; I went home. Couldn't find anything to do but make tapioca, eat it, reorganize a closet, then get seriously dolled up to pick David up at his office at the unholy hour of 6:00 P.M . . . I never leave the office before 7:30 P.M. We dine at the Gotham Bar and Grill . . . halibut again, their tall Everest crispy green salad, biscotti (some in my purse for later), decaf cappuccino then to see *As Thousands Cheer*, a sweet, semiscruffy little off-Broadway production of an ancient Irving Berlin bonbon. I fill David in on day's activities, cheerful as Bugs Bunny.

JUNE 26 (FRIDAY)

Dr. Abramson calls at 9:30 A.M. to say core biopsy has confirmed what earlier needle biopsy revealed; cancer cells in left breast; she has arranged an appointment for me with Dr. Borgen the following Tuesday to talk about surgery.

JUNE 30 (TUESDAY)

Dr. Borgen is again reassuring, tells, me he will be excising only the smallest amount of tissue, a simple procedure; I won't stay in the hospital overnight. Doctor doesn't think chemotherapy will be in my future but, yes, radiation will. If you've got to have *one*, I know enough to know he made the more palatable choice. A date for surgery is set two days later; we have moved like a subway train and I'm grateful. Next day I have my hair colored, who knows when again. Stopped on Sixty-first and Madison to buy Teuscher chocolates for Marvin Hamlish who has done something wonderful for me. Schlepping to the office in the rain I lose a wide gold bracelet. Traffic so snarled I got out of the car and plunged along the street, clasp not secure and bracelet slipped wrist. I lose jewelry a lot and the pain is *beyond* inappropriate. I know jewelry loss isn't a top-drawer tragedy, especially this day, but why should I get all my priorities straight and get sensible *now*?

JULY 1 (WEDNESDAY)

Finally, a few tear splashes. I haven't been superanxious about this new Life Development because (a) I have been grateful to have such superb doctors on the case who have moved swiftly; (b) the procedure won't be that comprehensive—they'll save the breast—and (c) more likely I've been a little into denial. People as healthy as I am— I've told you about all that healthiness—plus "small bosoms don't attract cancer, they got the wrong person" have sustained me, but now I'm coming around to acknowledge it's me who got cancer and worrying like any Normal Person with Cancer would. It's tough fitting *in* this arriviste problem, busy as I am with the old ones.

I'm the luckiest woman alive to have the career I have at age seventy-six, busy busy busy opening new editions of *Cosmo* around the world, critiquing two dozen international editions every month (saying where they are going right, going wrong), getting paid a gangster salary, phones somewhat quiet but haven't stopped ringing as they would for somebody putting out a product each month, but occasionally I get my feelings hurt and think how it was—made-a-big-fuss-over editor of successful magazine—and how it is *now*. Cathie Black, the president of Hearst Magazines, has taken Hearst women editors and publishers off for a girls' outing in Phoenix, invited Erica Jong, Faye Wattleton, Naomi Wolf, and Linda Obst to be guest speakers. It wouldn't occur to Cathie that *I* might know a little wisdom to pass along? Okay, maybe I'm old-hat, but Erica isn't exactly *new* hat. David has been my stalwart companion in this medical development, hasn't acted like a little boy who might be losing his mommy, has listened grown-up fashion to my various medical reports, never mind he is worried like any normal little-boy man despite my reassurances.

Where he is really superb is with one's professional life, and right now
he has to put up with my whining about Cathie's conference. "You're
a company girl," he reminds me. "Nobody thinks you can add anything
to this conference . . . forget it!" I already know that's true, but having
him say it makes life okay . . . he is no bullshit, doesn't dissemble, very
very good at job stuff.

In the past week Ann Siegel has been a great help. Having got
me to a top surgeon at the country's top cancer facility, she talks
with me daily, hourly, minutely if I wish about what's coming next,
has even sent over a special squashy-natural falsie if I should happen to lose my breast, along with coconut lemon cream pie from
Cipriani. Arnaz Marker, my exotic Pakistani princess-friend, has
visited and submerged me in Reiki, a hands-on spiritual healing I
didn't ask for, but felt if it made Arnaz feel better, go ahead,
couldn't hurt. Charlotte Veal, my longtime dear friend, has called
daily. Nizza and John Heyman have taken David off to dinner to
keep him cheered up.

JULY 1 (WEDNESDAY)

It's the night before surgery. I read the *New York Times* Sunday
book-review section we get in advance. "To be conscious is to suffer,"
writes Patrick McGrath of South African novelist J. M. Coetzee's
latest, *The Master of Petersburg.* Mr. McGrath says that in each of
his novels, Coetzee, "has created figures who stand starkly silhou-
etted against a vast, harsh landscape and an equally harsh political
system . . . belittled and dehumanized by both. His prime concern
has been with survival, spiritual and physical, the scraping of meaning and sustenance from the most hostile of environments. In his
newest book, Mr. Coetzee's grimmest yet, he suggests a new degree
of darkness in an outlook that has yet to find much to celebrate in
the human condition." Well. Though not South African like the novelist or Russian like Dostoyevsky, the novelist's new chosen subject,
I must have had some good times *sometime* in life, haven't I? This
night, facing surgery tomorrow I'm definitely in the Coetzee "to be
conscious is to suffer" mode. Of course, I can feel that way *not* on
the eve of surgery but just enduring ordinary life-silliness. Am I really
going to get whomped some day by something *big* so should save my
Coetzee outlook for more special occasions? Possibly. Maybe the
surgery will turn out to *be* one but let's don't hope for *that.*

JULY 2 (THURSDAY)

Rolled out of bed at 5:30—yes, A.M.—two and a half hours before my usual pop-up. I know millions of people rise uncomplainingly at this hour, but early-rising for me is root canal. Exercised harder than usual. Dr. Borgen has said exercise couldn't hurt . . . he'd have a nice worked-out body to work on later in the day . . . I told you he was cute . . . plus this will be my last time for a while. Making up, picking shoes, panty hose, earrings, big time-eaters usually, not necessary . . . saved time *there*. Michael, my sweet, bearded, twenty-six-year-old new-daddy driver, had to get up at 4:30 A.M. to subway in from Queens, pick up car from garage, fetch David and me at home to arrive at Sloan-Kettering at 6:40 A.M.

At the hospital a sludge of people are in reception area waiting for M.O.'s (marching orders). A nice Irish girl does my blood pressure; I do my own urine, bring it to her. Told nice Irish girl she must read *Angela's Ashes*, incredible book about the joys and woes of a poor Irish family, my husband making the movie, etc., wrote down book title and author on one of my cards. She didn't scowl, though I'm sure she has plenty of other ways to spend her money, sending her the book would have been classy, telling her to get it herself wasn't . . . am I going to suddenly get class this very day? David was a good waiting companion, we talked about movies. At 9:15 A.M. I made the right decision: send him to the dentist, not have him wait through each procedure and schlepp me to the next one; he left. We saw each other again at 4:30 P.M. when surgery was over and I could pretty soon go home. Around 9:30 A.M. first procedure—localization (putting a needle in your breast, moving it around to mark exact place they'll be excising) about to begin. Supposed to have been 8:00 A.M. but delays began early and escalated. Right now, as I wait for localization (you sit in chairs with lots of other people) I'm so icy cold they wrap me in a cotton blanket (no yumminess *there*) and send me to a "warmer" room where will be done ultrasound imaging instead of, or rather *before*, scheduled localization.

Waiting is tiresome. I couldn't read because hadn't brought glasses, assuming anything I brought to hospital I would lose or would disappear. I finally plop my blanketed self out in the hallway to try to get things moving; I *am* pushy. Some worker out in the hallway . . . an orderly? janitor? asks me why I'm out there, I'm not supposed to be. Weirdly enough, after hearing my protests about delay, new best friend actually fetches me a doctor—can you imagine?—at least a doctor in training. Tim—I don't remember his last name because he said just call him Tim—is major cute. Australian, thirty-six years old with a great hairline . . . hope he gets to keep it . . . most don't . . . Fiancée, he said, doesn't know whether she wants to live in New York. I'm thinking Kate, Kate, come to your senses! Let your to-be husband establish himself *here*, then back to your hometown *later* with New York medical experience in his resume. I tell him to tell Kate that. Tim takes me to a proper room and begins the imaging. Lie on your right side on a slab while doctor manipulates nipple on your left breast and looks at it in an imagining machine—I think it's called sonography. I'm getting used to all the attention to this breast, never my favorite, right one a little bigger. Next you lie on your back, not shriek-making painful, just uncomfortable—like lying out on the pavement in the rain in your underwear I would think.

Next comes the localization . . . putting the needle (a fine wire) in your breast that lets them know the exact location of the abnormal mass and this hurts. I wept and shrieked when the needle went in, soon calmed down like a good girl. What do you know? An hour later they have to do it over. My understanding at the time was that the dye used was a crummy bunch and that's why they had to do it over. You don't want to fuss at them about this . . . wouldn't want bad dye in there. After writing this account, to be sure it's accurate, I sent to Dr. Borgen who says, "There was not actually a bad 'dye lot,' they always use two types of dye—a blue dye called isosulfan dye and a radiolabeled tracer called ninety-nine technetium sulfur colloid. The two dyes are complementary and when one does not work the other virtually always does. It is a belt and suspenders approach that we have popularized here at MSKCC. One dye worked better than the other, further, the dye doesn't go into you—into the breast tissue—until after you are sedated in the operating room." I figure he might know what he is talking about. I just know it's getting to seem like the Longest Day. By the time I get to the operating room we are pitifully behind schedule. Surgery had been scheduled for 11:15 A.M., it is now 2:30 P.M. and delay was explained to me at the time as having something to do with arrival of the "wrong dye" and they had to wait for the right one, albeit dye not going into me until later.

Whatever, at 2:30 P.M. I'm wheeled on a gurney into a operating room and it's not exclusively *me* in there. Lots of tables, bustling staff . . . multiple surgeries are performed simultaneously all day long; I'm glad to be getting on with mine. They give me something called twilight sleep. Needle hurts and I cry, but quiet down as I get into the twilight. Lumpectomy takes about fifteen minutes to perform and the sentinel node (nodes under arm as in lymph) biopsy takes another forty minutes. Pathology requires about fifteen minutes to tell the doctor the status of the sentinel nodes; you're in operating room about two hours. Before and after I woke up, blood pressure machine is checking away. Right there attached to your bed it squeezes you regularly—cute. I got a painkiller, really didn't hurt much after that. At 6:15 P.M. David took me home. I'm pissed at Margarita, our usually divine housekeeper, who isn't at apartment on my arrival from hospital, wanted the day off, okay, but now also wants Monday. Is this any way to treat a fragile, banged-up employer? Well, I'm not fragile or banged up enough, or dumb enough to say no to her request. Margarita is good and doesn't do rotten things very often. Breast surgery doesn't affect your motor skills; I can get the refrigerator door open, fry an egg. That night half an extra-strength Tylenol was all it took to put me to sleep. It's over! The cancer surgery is *over, over, over!* Relief, relief, relief!

Steri-strips (Band-Aids) are on the skin over my incision, on top of that a gauze dressing to seal the area, over that a surgical bra with Velcro in the center . . . I am sheer glamour! Two days later it's show time . . . I gingerly remove the surgical dressing and look at my left bosom . . . it's there! Discolored, tender and *there!* (Maybe some of the "there" is swelling but I think enough of the real thing is intact). I'm ecstatic! They didn't take all of me or most of me or even a big *hunk* of me . . . this wonderful surgeon has been ultraconservative. Cut is just on top of the nipple . . . you can barely see it.

Monday I stay home, Tuesday to the office. This whole cancer experience has been so pippypoo and undramatic. Diagnosis and quick action meant everything, even if procedure itself and some of the preliminaries were not an afternoon at Malibu. Wednesday, I see Dr. Borgen. I'd so looked forward to this appointment—had brought my little list: When/where is radiation (I won't be having chemotherapy, thanks God). Can I be fitted in before others and not wait my brains out? (I'm spoiled and guiltless about getting in without long waits.) Can I exercise? Will he give me a Premarin replacement? Can I stop wearing this binding, boring bra that replaced bandage? All questions answered satisfactorily but Pandora's box flies open and a baby gruesome pops out: in the tissue removed and biopsied during surgery, doctor says other microscopic cancer cells were found . . . two small malignancies; possibly others are in there in the neighborhood. Dr. Borgen says he, Beryl McCormick, radiation oncologist, Larry Norton, head oncologist at Sloan-Kettering will look over all the pathology and pictures together and decide whether more surgery is indicated. He doesn't think so because so tiny but this is an option they must discuss; they may decide on chemotherapy but no surgery, chemotherapy previously not on the agenda. I ask: if they found new cancer cells in the biopsy during surgery, why didn't they just take them out at the first surgery? The extra-tiny cancer cells were only discovered under great magnification by the pathologists several days after surgery, he says. They didn't know they were there at the time of surgery but took tissue out as a precaution. Only by taking this extra tissue can they confirm the safety of having conserved the breast in the first place. Well, there they are, the extra little cancer creatures. If they do new surgery, will they take my whole breast? No, just go in a little further than they did before. But if new tiny cells were found near the old ones, too tiny to detect until surgery, couldn't still *more* baby microscopic cells be someplace else in the bosom, tiny but with growth potential? Chemotherapy would take care of that. Doctor and his team must decide whether surgery, chemotherapy, or possibly— *still*—only a round of radiation.

I'm passing out. How will I live until these megadoctors have their conference—obviously they have bigger stuff on week's agenda than me—and tell me what's next? My breast is still so sore I can't bear to think of their opening me up, going in again—dig, dig, dig. Never mind whether I can bear it, I will if I have to, but I can't get out of my head if we take out a little more from same area, what about the rest of the breast . . . couldn't it also harbour teeny-tiny cells . . . will I need more surgery later a little deeper in same area *and* chemotherapy to zap the possible growing-in-there minuscule cells, not detectable now with regular core and needle biopsies but gaining strength? It's all so confusing. I thought I was through, through, *through* except for radiation . . . ecstatic when I came home from hospital just one week ago and now it's bye-bye euphoria, hello gummy. Why couldn't I have a clean bill of health? Why doesn't cottage cheese taste as good as brownies? This is Wednesday. Thursday I'm pestering the daylights out of Roberta Baron, Dr. Borgen's nurse, to get me an answer from the Big Three. I don't want to go through the weekend without knowing what's ahead. I ask her would I rather have the cutting than the chemo—not fair to put a nurse in position of answering this question, that's for her boss. Roberta, an angel girl, goes so far as to say she doesn't think chemotherapy will be decided on but *possibly* a little more cutting . . . could you screech? I make myself think of people who have struggled with more serious cancer . . . now alive and happy. Who am I to be such a wimp? Doesn't help. It's Friday afternoon and I've sweated through Wednesday, Thursday, Friday morning waiting up a storm for the call that will say more surgery.

I'm sure you're sick of this little drama but I can't remember a Friday morning as bad as this one ever. Love trouble is icky, job trouble is sickening. I've never had children trouble which has to be the worst, but this particular waiting is awful. Glancing at a mirror I could pose for Max Beckman—tired, sad, haunted. I critique the Indonesian and Czech Republic issues of *Cosmo,* send a friend's article to *Travel and Leisure* I've promised to, answer mail, try to be normal—I'm dying. At 4:30 P.M. I finally call Roberta Baron. They might all go home at 5:00 P.M. or have gone already, and I tell her if I don't get word before the weekend, I'm in shards . . . she has to help. Roberta gives me the news: the three doctors have decided not to do surgery or chemotherapy, only radiation. I gulp joy gulps. Dr. Borgen calls at 5:00 P.M., to confirm what Roberta told me. I thank him fervently. Radiation is scheduled to begin in three weeks, will continue for six weeks. I call up Annie, Arnaz, Nizza, Carlotta, David first, of course. Poor baby has suffered though he's tried not to ra-diate—whoops!—communicate gloom. Now we are going to forget all this foolishness and have a great weekend.

You'll be relieved to know you don't have to go through radiation with me—there isn't that much to report. Everyday, five days a week for six weeks, you show up on the fourth floor at the radiation de-partment at Sloan at 425 East Sixty-seventh Street and wait your turn, but you don't wait that long. Every patient has a schedule carefully worked out for him saying what time to show up and, mi-raculously, staff pretty much sticks to schedule. Only one little time did I wait longer than twenty minutes, sometimes only five. Once called, you go to a locker room, exchange your clothes for a hospital gown, have another tiny wait to be called into the radiation room.

A plastic mould has been made of your shoulder and upper arm that you will lie on to get radiated. Getting moulded two weeks previously has been big-league discomfort but only takes a couple of hours. Once moulded there's no more bad stuff. Called inside, you plop on the table and two giantburger machines, one after the other, swoop down to within two inches of your face and chest. Not the sweetest scene for a claustrophobic, but they never hurt you. Technicians, different on different days, are young, friendly, beyond efficient . . . I guess you don't make mistakes with those machines. We talk about Monica's rottweiler, Freda, about Al's soon-to-happen wedding.

After six weeks of radiation, they give you a few days off, then back for six more days of booster zaps. During my days off I went to Los Angeles to do *Politically Incorrect*, swim my brains out at the Bel-Air Hotel, have a major lobster salad drowning in mayonnaise and fudge brownie groaning under chocolate-chip ice cream room service debauch. The reception room at Sloan was always tranquil. I brought this manuscript to work on, made a few new friends. Can the radiation experience have been almost pleasant except for why you were there and the time it takes from one's life to drive round-trip to Sloan and do the routine, perhaps an extra hour and a half a day? Almost. To this moment I still don't seem to identify with other cancer patients. Never got out of denial? No, I think I did. I was just one of the lucky ones diagnosed quickly, disease quickly zapped. I've almost had more trauma with gum surgery . . . gums don't grow *back*. I also don't dwell on the possibility of my having given *myself* cancer with the heavy dosage of Premarin for thirty-three years. Occasionally a doctor suggested taking less but nobody slugged me. Okay, I'm absolutely through with this story . . . you've been wonderful! The cancer breast is still a little swollen, presumably from surgery, though that was five months ago. I hope it stays that way forever. Oh yes, my gold bracelet hadn't fallen off in the street after all but was lodged next to a plant in my office where it had fallen off, clasp broken, as I was getting out of my coat . . . we found it last week. Don't expect any more good news from me . . . this is *it* for the moment!

Food / Diet

Deadly Potion?

If aspartame should ever turn out to be carcinogenic or something rotten like that, I will be the first person dead. I use four to six packets a day of Equal and tablespoons more in granulated form that you can sprinkle on cereal or rice pudding. Equal . . . what a lovely creation. If it weren't for Equal, I would weigh three hundred pounds, for I could never give up sweets. I know you're supposed to wean yourself from loving sugar but who would want to . . . it's much too pleasurable and I've got those magic chemicals to make life sweet sans calories.

Stop Picking on Me!

If I were the food designated as "fat," I'd be plenty pissed these days. I never get anything but bad press while much worse stuff than me hardly gets a bad notice. Did you hear about the wine causing liver damage? Maybe in far-off France, but in our country grapa is Gracious Living. Does sugar get any hate mail? A recipe in *Reader's Digest* this month calls for a cup of granulated sugar in cheese cake, enough sugar to rot teeth, blow up the stomach, send eater into navy blue funks . . . talk about empty calories. Fat is actually necessary to lubricate our bodies . . . we'd rust without it. We toss around insults about butter, margarine, and mayonnaise, not so much about grease. French fries have to be fried in grease (hot oil) yes, but (a) you can pat them pretty dry with paper towels, and (b) giving up fries isn't a big deal, like never dribbling a smidge of diet margarine onto your English muffin again. A hamburger patty can also be patted/squeezed dry. Still, "Lowfat!" "Lowered fat!" and "Fat content reduced!" scream from grocery shelves and magazine pages. If I were fat, I'd be thinking of heading for another country until the fat-fright blows over and the ninny nutritionists find somebody else to victimize. We'd *miss* the little bugger.

Basic Nutrition

Candy calories are worse than chicken-salad calories, I think, even if they tote up the same. Candy cals are even worse than liquor ones because you eat more candy once you start (as in sugar addiction); with Scotch and soda you can have just *one* if that's what you've decided on. With candy, it doesn't matter *what* you've decided. Once a champagne truffle is there in front of you, you take more. Candy calories are also worse because candy doesn't do a thing for you once inside but make fat—no food value whatever. Chicken salad cals, better still plain chicken cals, fish cals, veggie cals nourish and fill you up so you don't want so much. Can you imagine pigging out on broiled scrod and brussel sprouts? The way to manage non–candy shoveling is not even to *look* at candy. Look the other way when it's passed. I can be this pure because candy isn't my problem, *cookies* are.

Not everybody wants to eschew candy, of course. My favorite crazed-diet person is Alex Mayes Birnbaum, whose diet consists of cigarettes . . . numerous . . . she still smokes, a scoop of M & Ms for breakfast, enough regular food to get *by* for two more meals. Alex's trainer comes three times a week for two-hour sessions. Between trainer-times she exercises. The woman is petunia-thin and never sick. She recently walked 26.2 miles in Anchorage, Alaska, for a Leukemia Society of America marathon. When is all that badness going to catch *up* with our heroine? We don't know. Call it arrogant, call it lucky. I hope she lasts forever or at least as long as *I'm* here because I love her, she is interesting and different from the pack.

Life's Little Good Things, Food Division

The way a *little* oil spreads over so much lettuce, raw spinach, parsley is one of life's happy mysteries. Put in just a capful of flax oil—my favorite—plus a glob of rice vinegar and you've got enough salad dressing with baby cals to handle salad for two people. That's because the oil *spreads* like a real friend. Lots of low-calorie salad dressings are out there but this one's purer. Second blessing: diet Jell-O. Instructions say one package serves four people, ten calories each— are they nuts? Make one dish of gummy Jell-O with less water than called for from one package (forty calories) all for *you* with a dollop of Dannon's light yogurt on top, fifty cals total. I have this treat every weeknight just before midnight and two on Saturdays and Sundays.

My Food Plan—Don't Retch!

Yes, skinny is sacred to me. It's what I can do to stay cute and young and, a *bit* more important, *healthy*. I don't get sick or get colds, as we know. Considerable research indicates that calorie-deprivation isn't a bad idea for older. Skinny may or may not make you live longer but, coupled with exercise, it seems to discourage illness. I hate exercise. I'm not good at it, not athletic, but do an hour and a half total at two sessions seven days a week—one bout the minute I roll out of bed, another after lunch at home or office. I've just advanced from seven-pound dumbbells to ten—is that thrilling?

Food plan: Breakfast: one egg fried in Pam, one slice of seven-grain toast with half a tablespoon of diet margarine.

Lunch: Tuna salad, sometimes chicken. Margarita makes up a tub of both for me every week. One or the other goes to the office in a B.P. bag for lunch at my desk, chopped apple on top, a few raisins. Second course is half a cup of low-fat cottage cheese, apple and mozzarella cheese chopped in.

Around 6:00 P.M. I have a mozzarella-and-apple snack. If we're home for dinner—perhaps around 8:00 P.M.—I cook for David, bring his simple little repast on a tray, don't eat *with* him but have something satisfying before going to bed around midnight. Are we weird or something . . . separate dining times *and* separate menus? Lean Cuisine meatballs and spaghetti, chocolate milkshake made with Optifast for hubby; a different selection for *me* later—when we could have a live-in cook? Definitely weird but we're out too many nights a week for me to happily pay a live-in who's home alone chomping away on filet mignon and Sara Lee cheesecake. Order-in doesn't appeal either . . . arrival time at apartment of food and people has to be coordinated, cold cash shelled out or charged . . . too lavish.

After bringing David his dinner in the den—waiting for me he watches CNN, reads papers and mail—I may plop down for a little visit but have lots of things to do before bedtime. Yes, I bring work home but it's a tradeoff—I do personal things all day, now must read, return phone calls, shampoo, lay out clothes for next day *and* night if dinner will be fancy . . . I dress at the office . . . write household instructions for Magarita.

If my weight's okay, dinner for me might be muesli with chopped prunes, dried apricot, six unsalted almonds, dusting of Equal, and a cup of whole milk. Delicious! If weight-fighting, it's back to tuna salad with one slice seven-grain toast and half a tablespoon of diet margarine. Dessert *every* night is that whole package of sugar-free diet Jell-O in one dish just for me—one envelope couldn't possibly serve four as directions suggest—with a dollop of peach, lemon, strawberry, or whatever Dannon light yogurt on top. Fifty cals—heaven! My Saturday routine is sleep eight hours Friday night, get up, exercise for an hour, skip breakfast (fix David's), work on this book—which consumes me and I love doing—until earliest 2:00 P.M. for lunch, maybe three or four, then on to the joy of eating; later a snack at midnight.

If you're very busy doing something you really like, no responsibilities or stress, you work right through a meal and, at the late lunch, have something pretty big and satisfying. I'm not of the school which believes you can be all filled up and clam-happy every instant, that you never need to have a hungry moment to be the size you want to be. A little human sacrifice comes in there somewhere. I've been doing Saturday and Sunday breakfast-skipping for two years. Repeat: skipped or postponed meals don't kill you longing-wise or health-wise if you do them selectively.

During the week I never skip breakfast before going to the office because it hurts too much. Going foodless from, say, 8:00 A.M. until lunch at 12:45 or 1:00 P.M. you get all edgy and funny, start having "I'm not quite there" conversations. My 150-cal breakfast holds Monday through Friday but Saturdays and Sundays, because I'm home doing something soul-pleasing; i.e., writing, I find I *can* skip breakfast to keep weight down (a delicious lunch comes later).

If I've put on two or three pounds during the week, I want them off *now* before they are joined by evil companions in the next few

days, so on a weekend I skip breakfast (as usual) but instead of
something yummy for lunch later at two or three, it's protein *only*,
also protein for dinner. Menu: one-quarter pound ground sirloin
sauteed in Pam, Kikkoman soy sauce splashed on, scoop cottage
cheese, apple (only nonprotein item) chopped on top or made into
applesauce, sugar-free Jell-O. Same routine Sunday, by Monday a
couple of pounds will have gone bye-bye; you don't really suffer eating this little; protein gives you a nice full feeling.

Am I recommending this ridiculous eating plan for *you*? Absolutely not . . . are you crazy?! More gradual dieting may work better
for you, but I couldn't *do* what you do to get off the weight. I'd never
get through more than three days of fish, skinless chicken, and all
those prissy things you're allowed to eat all you want of—greens,
green veggies, yucky between-meal snacks like raw carrots, celery,
cauliflowerettes with lemon juice—ugh once again. We do what
works for *us*, right? I know I've got to stop after a day's, no longer
than a week's binge.

Sometimes I stop in the middle of a lovely foreign country, traveling for business or pleasure, because damage has been done and,
rather than face heavy-duty giving up for days or weeks back home,
I'll stop cold, skip the hotel breakfast, go for broiled fish at lunch,
also dinner, start lunch or dinner late in the day. Follow this plan
for at least one day.Does this food plan sound pretty prissy and grim?
Skimpy maybe, but it isn't grim. I *like* all the stuff I eat at home or
on the road, plus David and I are in restaurants a lot for lunch and
dinner, that's where the yumminess is. As I mentioned, we've never
wanted a cook at home. I'm too cheap—they gobble expensive
stuff—and I don't want someone around all the time. With a cook
you'd be constrained to eat home, not in some of the best-on-the-
planet New York restaurants. Food plan in restaurants: Perrier with
ice and lime wedge while *they* drink. Many people *don't* these days;
a waiter can leave with an order for six Diet Cokes and one martini.
First course: green salad with dressing on the side, spoon on a tea-
spoon or two. Restaurants usually drown their salads with dressing.
I *have* a first course, not so other people won't be uncomfortable
with the empty space in front of me, but I *like* to eat. Even for me
consommé is too seriously sacrificial; salad is fine. Main course:
broiled fish with lemon juice and lots of salt (low blood pressure lets
me splash on salt), green veggie (ugh!) or a little pile of rice, occasionally pasta. Pasta is a challenge. You can't ask a restaurant to

bring you half an order if it's your main dish and I can't leave anything on the plate—if it's there it's *mine* and I'm going to eat it. Frequently I plop part of my dinner on somebody else's plate, generous little thing. Plopee often plops it right back, they've met my kind before. Dessert: a ton of decaf coffee while others eat profiteroles smothered in caramel. Lately I've switched to mint or chamomile tea because I've decided decaf is dangerous. Either restaurant doesn't bother with fake or manufacturer didn't bother to get out enough caf—at 3:00 A.M. you're still thrashing. I never pass up the petit fours, my sin, but hope others will capture a few before I dive in, not leave me the whole disaster. Careful eaters are not always careful in restaurants, you know that.

At dinner parties you eat. A plague on hostesses and their self-centered little souls. They never understand we don't eat their exquisite food not because we have no taste or taste buds or are trying to make them miserable (they've cooked, they've slaved) but because we are trying—desperately!—not to gain weight or maybe even knock back a pound or two. The hostess could be trying to do the same thing but not at *her* dinner . . . knocking back has to be at somebody else's expense. Nearly all hostesses, me included, equate loving and appreciating them with whether or not we've had a second helping of their beef Wellington and banana pineapple surprise pie. They understand your need not to blimp up but would you please take your abstinence elsewhere. It wouldn't be a bad idea if hostesses gave you a *choice* of honeydew or batter-fried scampi for your first course like a fine restaurant. Oh, why don't I shut up? It isn't going to happen and I'm getting hungry. Even my beloved "21" which never used to give you a free anything—not even a drink for their oldest customer's ninetieth birthday—is now sending dessert, compliments of the chef, and they have the chutzpah to say "no calories" as they serve mango sorbet swimming in raspberry crème. Bruce, how about cookies at the table with coffee? These I can slip into my bag for *later* . . . you don't try that with mango sorbet.

Being skinny doesn't make you popular. In a survey reported in *USA Today*, the people at the top of the list others didn't want to look like were: Janet Reno, Roseanne, Tipper Gore, and me. I guess Janet because she isn't a standard American beauty; Roseanne is chubby pudgy; Tipper, who knows, but she'd slubbed up a bit for a while and perhaps talked too much about losing it; and me I'm sure because I'm skinny . . . out there doing what the polled ones could but won't, and nobody wants to be reminded. What the denigrating/ insulting don't know or want to know is that skinny, with exercise, to tamp down the food, you can eat pretty good. You can't have it *all*. No hors d'oeuvres for me even though I love them. I've chosen desserts over booze but always have a few sips of wine when it's served; sometimes I drink swallows of David's Scotch and water. Another man would drive a fork right into your wrist but David is so happy to see me "drinking" he shares gallantly . . . justifies his having another drink? I do binge . . . badly . . . but never beyond two or three pounds and then, as I said, atone. The exercise is always there to help a person keep her body taut and young and, I'll bet you've *heard*, exercise burns *some* calories. Like religion, I think whatever works for the dieter is his business. I guess my diet to me almost *is* a religion. Tita Cahn, attractive widow of composer Sammy Cahn, said that since she had begun dating producer Mace Newfeld, going to dailies every day, then on to dinner—sometimes with the cast and crew—she couldn't possibly not put on weight. Lili Zanuck, to whom she said this, told her, "Tita, it isn't the dailies or the cast and crew parties that put on the weight . . . it's the food you put down your throat." Right.

P.S. Exercise Doesn't Provide a Free Binge

There is no free lunch in lots of life's places, but none less free than eating everything you want and assuming you can cancel out the subsequent weight gain with exercise. After sinning, I've climbed a thousand hotel stairs, eschewed the escalator at airports schlepping luggage up the stairs, danced my brains out, walked from here to Kansas City (or so it seemed) to atone for sin—*your* atonement might be tennis or football—but the scale doesn't read the way it did before the debauch. I don't think you *can* cancel bingeing already in your tummy with exercise later, you're going to need to cut calories to unblimp . . . ugh! But I feel differently about swimming; in addition to what you usually do, I find swimming a great little cal burner, not pippypoo splashes but a good half hour of hard, heavy swimming, lap, lap, lap.

I don't have a pool but check instantly at a new hotel, convention center, friend's house, wherever, to see if *they* have one. The Bel-Air Hotel pool in Los Angeles has saved me from serious chubbing all these years, God bless its toasty blue depths, its exclusiveness . . . nobody but me splashing there after sundown. I'm not a great swimmer—smooth, calm, controlled. I'm a *terrible* swimmer—splash, kick, gasp, gurgle. When I flop around late at night, a hotel employee usually strolls by to instruct, "Swim close to the edge, please Ms. Brown." They've noticed the flapping, but I think I'm the world's luckiest. Moon shining down through the palms, night-blooming jasmine wafting its nighttime fragrance—splash, splash, kick, kick, gasp, gasp, gurgle, gurgle.

Tomorrow I'll still be me, not a big pink lollipop despite the hot fudge sundae on American Airlines coming to L.A., chocolate chip cookies, cooked on board, carried from plane to hotel—my beloved flight attendants always give me extras—Mai Tais, Chicken Gui Que (*not* slivers, big whole *almonds*), fried rice, monkey bread with peanut butter, snowball (different name for hot fudge sundae) at Trader Vic's, macadamia-nut shortcake under bananas and kirsch, eggs benedict, and tortilla soup in the Bel-Air dining room. If swimming isn't convenient, I don't think there's anything this side of finger-down-the-throat-and-throw-up-right-away that works as efficiently but bulimia causes major medical problems, you wouldn't want to go near it and it is also ghastly unpleasant. You can't *not* sin, we know that, so it's sin-and-swim. You have to swim a *lot*, but it's the dieter's best friend.

Airline Food

Some people are so fussy they take their own food on airplanes. Isn't that *too* fussy—and wasteful? You have to pay for brought-on food, which defeats the joy of having everything except the tickets paid for when you fly as opposed to trains, which charge for food, booze, and your tip. First thing you know, people who bring food onboard planes will start trying to tip flight attendants. Attendants won't be allowed to *accept*, but a few might just cave some day, which will make the nontipping rest of us look cheap.

I never met an airplane meal I didn't eat. You might plan on being real hungry when you check in for a coach flight, but I love all airplane food because I don't have to cook it, everything is their responsibility. In first class it may be better than what I'm eating at home. Recently in its zeal to be new and frisky, cuisine-wise, American Airlines whipped mustard into the mashed potatoes. You might as well whip *mayonnaise* into the mashed potatoes (we're talking *fat*) and the penne with olive-and-tomato sauce seemed to have been cooked all the way from New York to San Diego, we're talking *mushy*, but never mind their occasional lapse from Cordon Bleu—they mostly do just fine. Then there's the hot fudge sundae you wouldn't have anyplace else on earth except aboard this plane, would you (are you crazy?), but it's right at your elbow on a cart saying, "Take me, I'm yours!" How could you *not* obey, besides you've got God knows what waiting when you get off the plane (speech, sales pitch, family crisis, face-lift) and your seatmate is having one with everything—caramel sauce, chocolate *and* strawberry syrup—rude to make him eat alone. An hour or two later come the baked-onboard chocolate chip cookies served with a glass of cold milk just before landing, the loveliest, rottenest thing an airline could do to a calorie count. And because flight attendants and I are friends, they frequently give me extras in a little package to take home. I've thought of asking to be buried in an L-1011 like the Texas woman who was buried in her Cadillac Le Baron. I've spent many a happy hour and happy *years* in airplanes.

David

Making Movies

He's back at the Bel-Air Hotel—1:30 A.M. New York time, 10:30 P.M. California—and calls, having just returned from a screening of *Canadian Bacon*, his new movie about the U.S. government declaring war on Canada to put recession-pinched America back to work. Canada is handy and *can* sometimes be annoying . . . their celebrities are getting too celebrated (Peter Jennings, Dan Akroyd, Alanis Morissette), Canadian food is terrible . . . did you ever hear anybody say, "Honey, let's send out for some Canadian food?" Their skins are too white, jokes too tepid, etc. My husband has been working on this movie for two years and I can tell from his first little five-letter word—"Helen"—you get to know a loved one's mood instantly by voice inflection—that it hasn't gone well.

Canadian Bacon came to David as an original screenplay from Michael Moore, longtime citizen of Flynt, Michigan, writer and director of a brilliant documentary send-up of General Motors called *Roger and Me*. David thought the new Moore project Had Something, spent two years with Michael trying to find a backer. Despite David's track record, each new project brings new migraines. He and Moore would go out like hopeful Willie Lomans, shoeshine and a smile their umbrella, sample case in hand, to see, and subsequently be turned down by studios. Finally Madonna's company, Maverick Productions, decided to take it to Propaganda Films who agreed to finance it. From the first hours of filming, problems sprang. Steve Golin, Propaganda's chief, and Michael Moore developed a hate for each other that threatened violence on the set. Other serious challenges: Rodgers and Hammerstein music from *Oklahoma* couldn't

be used and songs of numerous other important lyricists and com-
posers slotted throughout the film were also too pricey for their
peanut butter budget, and yes, their star, John Candy, died shortly
after the film was completed so none of his lines could be looped,
standard procedure with major actors after principal photography is
finished. Finally, after six months of postproduction, *Canadian
Bacon* is shown with temporary music to a preview audience. Disaster. This is the night David called and said, "It isn't working."
Immediately afterwards, however, he said, "A bad preview doesn't
mean anything . . . the score will make all the difference." Music was
added and it *didn't* make all the difference; at next screening audience still hates movie, many leave midway through. Still another
screening is held, zero enthusiasm but my ever-courageous, not always realistic husband still says not to worry, poor screening results
also happened to *The Crying Game*, a low-budget movie that later
became a hit and they fixed it by getting a gimmick. Gimmick: audience is exhorted not to tell people who haven't yet seen the movie
about the ending: (major-sexy love-object girl turns out to be a boy.)
What *Canadian Bacon* obviously needs is a gimmick, something the
audience will talk—or be told *not* to talk—about. "But David," I
remind him, "Gimmick or no gimmick to talk about, *The Crying
Game* was a good movie, nominated for an Academy Award. *You*
liked it, your friend Lewis Allen saw it five times. That was all because of a gimmick?" Special angle couldn't hurt, David insists. His
idea is to open the movie in a theater that runs low-budget brilliant
imports, nonhullabalooed product. "You know how critics get orgas-
mic over an obscure film while denigrating a sure-to-be-blockbuster,"
says my husband. Sure, sure. Ironic, David invoking critics. He hates
critics like celery strings between your teeth unreachable by dental
floss combined with stomach cramps and sinus headache, but now
thinks critics could possibly be useful. Why not? Critics who hate
so much that is good might actually like this love child if seen in an
art house and then write great reviews, word would get out, and
we're sailing home!

Brave, vulnerable, (sometimes *invulnerable* because he closes off
the hurt and disappointment) David. Forget art houses, the movie
doesn't capture audiences in art houses, Sony Theatre complexes or
any other viewing site. It is a *good* movie, David insists to this moment, he's glad he made it, he *likes* it. Maybe such loyalty is like
loving, not to be disrespectful, a brain-damaged child, flesh and bone
of oneself, child of your soul.

I won't take you through other disappointments David has also loved—*Myra Breckinridge* with book and screenplay by Gore Vidal starring Mae West *and* Raquel Welch, *The Cemetery Club* with darling Ellen Burstyn and Danny Aiello (wives visit dead husbands at the cemetery every Thursday until one of the wives defects). I loved floppy *Watch It* and brought my staff to see it. Betsy Perry said it was "dark." That should have warned us, dark you don't want to hear. The picture never opened, i.e., didn't have a great first week or any week. *The Girl from Petrovka* starred darling Goldie Hawn, but darling Goldie couldn't float it. So my producer husband is the bravest, dearest, most touching creature I have ever known. He breaks my heart. His failed movies break my heart. But then there are the hits and joy happens.

My favorite movie of David's and Richard Zanuck's is *The Sting*, Paul Newman and Robert Redford at their delicious best. Also their *Jaws, The Verdict, Deep Impact*, and David's *The Player* and *A Few Good Men* brought money, kudos, P and P (pride and pleasure). David also made the deal for the writer and the rights for *Driving Miss Daisy* but left it for Richard and Lili Zanuck to produce (and win an Academy Award) when he and Richard broke up their partnership. David executive-produced *Daisy*. The producer team received the Thalberg Award, industry's highest honor for a producer, and lots of other awards; several of David's other movies have been nominated for best picture. Although he tells me it is a wretched business and I observe first-hand that it is, about half of the world seems to want to be in it. David sees maybe two dozen kids of illustrious parents a year who want to get into film, not as actors but to *make* movies. Wherever you are in the world, when you don't know the language or the people, if conversation gets around to movies you've all seen, you're home free. But for people *in* it—and I observe one of these from my bed, breakfast table, shower, a million shared cab rides, and other togetherness places—the business isn't always fun.

What does a producer do? The real producer, like my husband, finds the material—book, play, or original screenplay—options it, hires and starts working with a writer, maybe goes through two or three more writers (don't mean to make them sound like popcorn), before a script is right. Then with your good script, you start trying to interest a director, may contact many before one commits, after which come the casting and *making* of the movie with subsequent griefs. When the Hollywood Film Festival recently honored David and Richard Zanuck, David mentioned that "Real producers have become overshadowed by the proliferation of unearned producer credits going to managers, agents, financiers, and other nonparticipants in the actual process. Credits [you see these on the screen] are cheaply given or are demanded, but real producers bring home the bacon: they bring home the subjects that attract the big players." Of course, the real producer does have to find somebody to put up the money for all this carrying-on and to commit to distribution (no good just having a movie in the can).

Once a studio or its satellite expresses serious interest (commits to the project), they can say no anyplace along the line to script, director, actors proposed by the producer. Only a few top-echelon executives can say, "Yes, go ahead with your selections," but before big cheeses get a chance to evaluate what you're turning in, pygmies get first look at ideas and material. Easier and safer for them to negate than give their boss a yes and get stuck with a possible subsequent failure, be the one who encouraged the clinker getting made, apparently not penalized if they have failed to move along a ton of product. In David's case, the early naysayers along the way are often under thirty . . . quel ignominy!

My husband's big strength is recognizing material. Before *Angela's Ashes* was a *New York Times* bestseller (120 weeks as I write), would anybody suppose that a little book about a deprived Irish childhood would make a movie? David thought so and teamed with Scott Rudin, who felt the same way, and together they put up their own money to secure the rights. David and Dick Zanuck worked on *Deep Impact* in various stages over a period of twenty years. Before becoming a producer, David found and nurtured material for Twentieth Century Fox—*The Sound of Music, Butch Cassidy and the Sundance Kid, The French Connection, Patton, Cleopatra,* lots more. For the past few years he has had a deal with Paramount Pictures giving them first look at whatever projects he proposes, and his last four movies, after an initial investment by my husband, have been financed and distributed by them—*The Saint, Kiss the Girls, Deep Impact,* and *Angela's Ashes,* all hits. He and Sherry Lansing, head of Paramount, have a good relationship and have had good luck together these past few years.

As a little girl in Little Rock I saw three to five movies a week— they made lots then and admission was ten cents weekdays, twenty-five cents weekends except the Saturday matinee when the ten cent tab held and you got a free Snickers or Milky Way. Right *now,* plopping into the Sony Lincoln Square complex at Sixty-eighth and Broadway—sixteen screens and you can see two movies if you like . . . three? . . . followed by a sweet little supper at Café Des Artistes or Santa Fe is my idea of Something To Do. David doesn't much enjoy *going to* movies . . . I can understand that viewpoint since he's all mixed up inside them, but I'd rather give up my driver's license or exquisitely-matched-to-my-own-hair favorite hairpiece than surrender my Sony pass.

David and Me and *Cosmo*

One Friday night in March 1965, David, author Irving Wallace, and I are walking up Park Avenue, having just had dinner at Christ Cella's on Forty-sixth Street and in front of the Waldorf Astoria, having started with mere tears, I am now into sobs. "I don't want to be a magazine editor," I explain. "I just want to be a bestselling author like Irving (all Irving's books—*The Chapman Report, The Prize, Seven Minutes*—always made the bestseller list, then became movies). "Honey," said my husband, perhaps for the twelfth time that night, "you've had your bestseller [*Sex and the Single Girl*] and maybe you can do that again, but, meantime, why don't you just take this job and see how you like it." "I already hate it," I said. "I want to be a bestselling author!"

Well, one could not *not* take the job. I have a contract with the Hearst Corporation for one year to edit *Cosmopolitan* and if—or *when*, I believe they said, let's not quibble—the magazine failed I could use up my contract writing articles for their other magazines— *Good Housekeeping, Harper's Bazaar*, etc. This agreement had all come about because of the stacks of mail I had got from my bestseller (S.&S.G.), and I was trying to answer all the letters myself. The book obviously worked because it said you don't have to be married to have a great life, that single girls probably have a better *sex* life than their married friends. Everybody single I knew was involved sexually, fairly satisfactorily, with *somebody*, and I just wrote what I knew. All other publications and advice-givers at the time said if a single girl *had* a sex life, she might as well get on the bus, go to Grand Canyon, and throw herself in and, if she were having an affair with a married *man*, forget Grand Canyon, just go to the kitchen, stick her head in the oven, and turn on the gas.

Watching me type my brains out one night (to my new friends

from the mail who wanted even *more* advice), David had said, "You ought to have your own magazine, then you could answer everybody at one time." Not being of sound mind, we thought you could *start* a magazine, and we sat down at the kitchen table—David did the advertising plan, me the article ideas—and did up a format—twelve typed pages which he took all over town to try to get somebody interested. Nobody was, but he heard the venerable *Cosmopolitan* was about to fold and got in touch with my publisher, Bernard Geis, who had worked at *Esquire* magazine with Richard E. Deems, now president of Hearst Magazines, and Berney got our magazine proposal over to Hearst. They didn't want to start a magazine either but thought we might superimpose our format on their beloved *Cosmo*— once a great literary journal (Ernest Hemingway, John Dos Passos, John Steinbeck, etc.) now hemorrhaging money. We signed an agreement. Back to the soggy Friday night. When we got home, David said, "Honey, a year isn't very long, you know. You just go in there Monday morning and try like you always do, okay?" Contractually committed, that's what I did, telling myself all weekend it would be like going to prison; 365 days later I could be free and out in the sunshine again. That was a few moments ago. I stayed at *Cosmo* thirty-two years as editor-in-chief, would have paid *them* I loved the work so much. Having started my career at eighteen, at age forty-three, I found what I should be doing in life.

Mentholatum Kisses, Monte Cristo Cigars

David has been putting up with Mentholatum kisses since the day we were married because I can't live without M. I've learned you shouldn't put it in your nostrils—bad for delicate membranes—but don't give me Chapstick, Vaseline or lipstick for lip comfort, has to be this menthol magic. David's "can't live without"? He smoked at least one Havana cigar a day when we were married and I said I didn't mind—he has even said that's why he married me. I really *didn't* mind—maybe my membranes weren't that sensitive—I've always felt pass-along smoke is overrated as a troublemaker.

The first year of our marriage, I smiled sweetly through nightly coils of smoke, sometimes smuggled the contraband Cuban treat in from Europe in my lingerie case. One winter night we are returning to New York in a limousine from a party in Westchester, David is happily puffing away like a four-year-old with endless soap bubbles to make. It's getting a little *dense* back there. I roll the window down one smidge—too cold to go further. David looks at me as though he had been stabbed . . . "Et tu, Brute?" he asks. Yes, I guess me, too, brute. I could see his point. He smokes less now than a few years ago, whereas I'm still mainlining on Mentholatum. Some people are better keepers of bargains than others.

The Old A.C. Standoff

David says he can't sleep without air-conditioning . . . I barely can sleep *with*. The A.C. makes a racket, no heavier than airplane noise, my husband points out, but you aren't supposed to *have* airplane noise in your bedroom. Plus A.C. makes me *cold*; body temperature comes *with* the brown eyes and deep half-moons. Though you can adjust a jawline, cap teeth, or plop in purple contacts if you like, you can't alter much of your basic equipment after they give it to you. At our house we have worked out an arrangement: air-conditioning stays on from April through September, me snoozing under half a down comforter and inside a sweater if icicles are imminent. I talked myself into this generosity because I figure David can't get *cooler* by sheer will but I can get warmer with *stuff*. Other part of arrangement—I'm not *all* altruism—no air-conditioning in the car unless temperature is over ninety.

Michael, my driver, is cold-natured like me—how did I fall *into* this paragon . . . he drives superbly, too! Michael and I scooch around New York in a roasting Mercedes, graciously turn on the A.C. a block or two before we pick up somebody except David. Sometimes we roast David for a few blocks to make up for the iced bedroom unless he seems to be passing out in front of us, then the A.C. clicks on. The car was a twenty-fifth anniversary present to me from the Hearst Corporation, so it's mine. When David and I buy a new one, I'm contemplating blankets and Thermos bottles of hot cocoa . . . present air-conditioning agreement sure to be abrogated. Michael is on his own.

David's Saturday Morning

Husbands. They *do* aggravate. There he goes . . . second newest suit from his nifty Mr. Ned collection. Mr. Ned custom tailors fine Italian fabrics into spiffy New York City threads for a lot of business-men, and David has made the best-dressed list six times to my *none*, is even in the hall of fame . . . bravo for Mr. Ned and David. Accompanying or accessorizing the suit is a white collar, blue-striped Turn-bull and Asser shirt (now $350.00 per . . . what you save at Mr. Ned you spend on the shirt), scarlet Sulka tie with *no* pasta stains . . . a little unusual at our house, Tiffany lapis-and-eighteen-Karat gold cuff links I gave him for his birthday . . . he looks like a page in *GQ* and where he is off to? The Seventy-ninth Street crosstown bus that picks him up across the street from our apartment on his way to his beloved practitioner of shiatsu, Yukiko Irwin, on East Seventy-fourth Street who will smash and soothe away all his tensions until next Saturday morning. David, you've heard of dress-down Fridays in offices? Perhaps. Wouldn't that kind of dress code apply to you on Saturday mornings? Is Mickey Mouse a reptile? This is a man who reserves his navy cashmere blazer with the antique brass buttons to wear on a cross-country or round-the-world plane trip, a tie knotted right to the Adam's apple the entire time. Coming home from Bali he mistakenly packed all his ties, heaven save us, and bought a tie in Sydney Airport with little kangaroos all over it for the remaining nineteen-hour trip to JFK, much of it at night. And this is a person who calls *me* rigid because exercise comes before all else in life?

Early Birds

Every husband and wife negotiate, don't they? The day when we did what *they* said, no questions asked, take no prisoners, left town with World War II as women "manned" defense plants to make vessels and ammunition to help our boys win the war, proved how strong we were, and also brought home paychecks. One of the things my husband and I negotiate is when to show up. If the reminder card for a dinner party says 7:00 P.M., we're pushing the buzzer at 7:10 P.M. I've lost *that* negotiation. Yes, hostesses are sometimes damp from the shower, still mulling over what to wear as they pop out, horrified and terry wrapped, to greet punctual us.

I *used* to come out a little better with charity dinners at the Waldorf. If card said cocktails 6:30 P.M. to 7:30 P.M., dinner at 7:30 P.M., I had David negotiated to arrive at 8:00 P.M. when people actually went in to dinner, but recently he has renegotiated me to get to the reception earlier so he can have a drink—you can't do

that easily later at the table—so lately we've been arriving at 7:15
P.M., me going almost immediately to the ladies room to hide out
until dinner. Waldorf ladies' room is roomy, you can call up girlfriends from seated pay phone if nobody else using, not too big a
sacrifice for a mate.

Where I have failed utterly in negotiating is that we now get to
the airport not just reasonably early but two hours ahead of flight
time even for domestic. Typical! We leave my office in New York
City at 4:00 P.M. to make a 7:20 P.M. plane from Newark, New
Jersey, to Paris, arriving Newark at 4:50 to wait in airport two hours
and thirty minutes. Why do I tolerate such waste? A truck once
turned over on the Van Wyck Expressway when we were catching a
plane for Tokyo, tied the traffic up for over an hour. Having left
home our usual three hours before flight time, we didn't even have
to breathe heavy . . . that incident was all the corroboration David
ever needed for flagrantly early departure from home to catch planes.
In my tote bag for these occasions I carry manicure essentials, mend-
ing, lists of friend-calls to make . . . you have time for *deep* chats . . .
enough reading to stock a small library. I have usually completed my
fill-up-the-time assignments long before flight is called.

Though David and I are a joke among friends and traveling companions, I sort of don't mind early arrival at airport, so I haven't
negotiated hard. If traveling alone, I slice the before-time a little
thinner, arrive only an hour before the flight, but airports aren't the
place I long to have breathtaking "just made its." Missing an entire
cocktail reception before a charity event is my idea of a brilliant if
I can negotiate it. Missing an international flight would be dopey.
David and I are now negotiating how many movies one can see in
one day. My ideal is three, David's is none. He's in the business but
complains a lot about having to go to the movies at *all*. Does this
make *sense*?

You Gave Already

"I don't have the strength to get in the pool right now," says my
mate, calling me in New York from the Bel-Air Hotel which contains
one of the three most glorious swimming places in the world, you've
heard me on that subject. "Don't forget I've swum three times already this week."

Ah yes, the old "I've already done it three times this week, what do you want from me?" routine from somebody who is supposed to be crashing off a couple of pounds but finds it disagreeable. "I quit for six weeks . . . I proved I can do it," says Claudia, looking me straight in the eye as she lights up a Virginia Slims. Keeping on keeping on . . . the thing that separates the skinny and the non-smoking from the rest of the world. Where does the self-discipline come from? Eight parts vanity, two parts concern about health, I think. Whatever gets you to do it or not do it doesn't matter. In my husband's case, it's eight parts concern for his health on my part, two parts vanity on his. He knows he looks better when he can see over his stomach. I will keep nagging and, no doubt, keep being "rationalized."

Nicknames

My nickname for David is Basker, as in Baskerville, as in *Hound of the Baskervilles*. As a bride, I learned quickly that men *eat*. My usual dinners for *me*—cottage cheese with sliced pears, Campbell's chunky chicken gumbo soup, Stouffer's chicken pot pie—were not going to do it, the man wanted lamb chops, steak, hash browns, apple pie, preferably à la mode. In the famous Conan Doyle novel, the hounds howled more than they ate but ate when they *could* . . . i.e., when a visitor could be snatched unawares. Not so different in my house. My Baskerville howls until something substantial is put down (*not* tuna salad with lots of celery chopped in), then he eats it. I have no nickname. The only one David ever gave me was Bird-brain . . . can you imagine a man calling his wife Birdbrain even in front of company? I spoke to him about this and he quit. Now I just get H.B. "Ready when you are, H.B." In high school I had a cute nickname—Guppy—Guppy Gurley . . . because Florence Stanley and I once wore tiny fishbowls on our lapels that contained live guppies. How we could do such a cruel thing, I don't know. The nickname stuck but that was a long time ago. I wish somebody would think of a nice new one for me . . . I call everybody pussycat, whether they are one or not.

Is this a cute baby?

Cleo Sisco Gurley (mother).

Ira Marvin Gurley (father).

With sister Mary, ages
five and nine.

With Mary at our house
on West Fifty-ninth
Street in Los Angeles
(where gophers plowed
up the bedroom floor),
1945.

With grandmother Jenny
Sisco, uncle Jack Sisco,
Mary, mother Cleo
(seated), in Osage,
Arkansas, where
everybody but me
was born, 1944.

Mary and me at her
home in Shawnee,
Oklahoma, 1980.

World War II sweater girl (padded), 1944. Picture went to
multiple boyfriends in the Army, Navy, and Marine Corps.

Jon Engstead photo (with Spam) that helped me win *Glamour* magazine's Ten Girls with Taste contest, 1953.

Shorthand—130 words per minute, if you please! Photo for *Glamour* magazine, 1952.

Beloved boss Don Belding, president of Foote, Cone & Belding advertising agency. My seventeenth and last secretarial job (for five years), 1952.

I finally got him! Wedding day,
Beverly Hills City Hall,
September 1959.

Bernard Geis, publisher of *Sex and
the Single Girl,* and Letty Cottin
Pogrebin, who helped talk him
into it, 1962.

Book jacket, *Sex and the
Single Girl,* 1962.

(Photo copyright © 1962
Peter Samerjan)

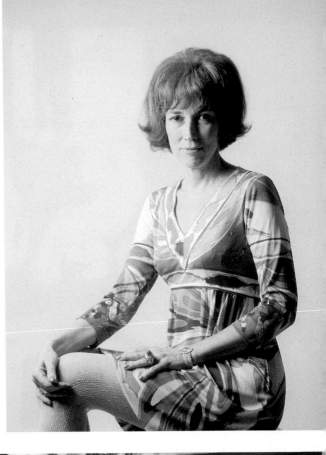

1966: The Emilio Pucci
dress I will be buried in.
I have nineteen others.

Below:
Gregory and Samantha helping me write (or not helping
me write) *Sex and the Office,*
Pacific Palisades, California,
1963.

(Photo copyright © 1963
Time-Life Inc.)

Early panel show with Peter Lawford, Sybil Burton Christopher, an actress whose name I can't remember, Woody Allen, and me, 1965.

Autographing party at Lamston's Madison Avenue for *Outrageous Opinions of Helen Gurley Brown*, 1967.

Joan Crawford was shy, and my good friend. I literally held her hand when she spoke for the Sales Executives Club of New York, 1968.

Sexy Rex Harrison at a party in London for the royal premiere of *The Prime of Miss Jean Brodie*.

(Photo copyright © 1967 PIC Photos Ltd., London)

With D.B., Richard D. Zanuck, Daryl F. Zanuck, and Queen Elizabeth for premiere of *Doctor Dolittle*, 1967. She was friendly.

(Photo copyright © 1967 PIC Photos Ltd., London)

Chez nous for a television shoot, 1973. I'm usually not this dressed up at home.

I raised Regis Philbin from a puppy. At first encounter—San Diego, 1962—I told him he was an *enfant terrible*; he still is. We've visited often since then. This photo was taken in Los Angeles, 1981.

Best boss in the world,
Frank A. Bennack, Jr.,
president and CEO of the
Hearst Corporation, 1980.

Rally for Equal Rights Amendment
ratification by all states, steps of
New York Public Library, 1981.

Up all night with
Larry King for his five-
hour radio show,
1982. I have visited
him often on his tele-
vision show.

Francesco Scavullo shot 95 percent of the cover photographs for *Cosmopolitan*, 1975.

Jane Pauley, Diane Von Furstenberg, Faye Dunaway, H.G.B. Women's conference, Tokyo, 1980.

Original crew for *Good Morning America,* 1975: (standing) John Lindsay, Geraldo Rivera, Erma Bombeck, H.G.B., Jack Albertson, (seated) David Hartman, Rona Barrett, Nancy Dussault. I did the show weekly for two and a half years.

Left: Liz Smith and Barbara Walters at my "Twentieth Anniversary at *Cosmo*" party, 1985

Below: Erica Jong, Francine du Plessix Gray, H.G.B., and Gloria Steinem at *Cosmo International* conference, New York, 1982.

(Photo copyright © 1982 Camera One Photographers)

Elizabeth Taylor let me interview her for a profile in *Cosmo*. She looked ravishing! Plaza Athene, New York, 1986.

The team that put it together: *Cosmo* executive editor Roberta Ashley, managing editor Guy Flatley, art director Linda Cox, and photography editor Larry Mitchell, 1996.

Malcom Forbes gave me a ride to a party in SoHo on his motorbike the week he died, 1990.

Above: With guest host Sammy Davis, Jr., on *The Tonight Show,* 1979.

Right: Abu and me at Camp Abu—the camp is named for him—in Botswana. One friendly pachyderm!

Below: John F. Kennedy, Jr., at Trophee des Arts gala, New York, 1988.

(Photo copyright © 1988 Patrick McMullan)

Love of my life—sometimes major irritation—David Brown...
Is that how it is with husbands? Sunday morning at home, 1999.

David's Tipping

There is no financial craziness crazier than my husband checking out of a good European hotel. You watch your retirement plans leave town. Having been told tips are included in the hotel bill, he pays no attention—maybe the money never gets to the people—tips American style. Recently somebody told him European housekeeping *isn't* on the bill . . . quel thrill! He now hands out his usual pack of twenties to anybody who gets in line . . . the night maid, day maid, an apprentice or two. Complicating his giving a bit is that he is never quite sure how much a franc or lira is worth in dollars but a handful or fistful of either makes up for lack of money-exchange expertise.

I wish tips lined up like they *used* to: one dollar per bag for porter who carries luggage to your hotel room, five dollars max; two dollars per night for the maid. A dollar to the doorman who puts luggage in car. My husband and I no longer discuss tipping. I glean from smiles on faces of the recently tipped he is tipping the way things *might* be, say ten years from now; I don't expect to be *back* at this place where he just gave the man who delivered the cleaning a down payment on a Subaru. I figure some day I may be typing manuscripts for some author with a deadline (I'll have to learn the word processor) or maybe waiting tables; we are going to need every dollar I can rake in. In restaurants I've occasionally thought about trying to get in on the waiters' take. Why would I do that? Well, I do help out . . . sweep dirty dishes off the table and stack them on nearby tables if service is slow, hand any restaurant personnel that happens to be flying by dreggy drink glasses or empty Perrier bottles. Bruce Snyder at "21" and Julian or Alex who own the Four Seasons are used to me and are always cordial about my helpfulness but so far none of this is persuading David to put a little something on the tab for *me*.

David's Further Tipping

He did it again today. Ninety-four-dollar lunch check, with tips, $150.00. We quarrel. "It's for *everybody*," he says. "The waiter, captain, maître d'." "There *is* no captain," I point out, "and maître d'–wise, are you talking about that person at the desk who is obviously making a little Christmas money between classes at NYU? She's not going to *be* here when you come in again . . . this isn't Le Cirque or the Four

Seasons." We are at the Union Square Café on East Sixteenth Street, formerly Brownies' Health Food Store, where we once bought all our vitamins. For lunch today we have had everything that wasn't running around on a leash in order to run *up* a $94.00 tab—drinks, wine, three courses apiece, cappuccino. My mate turns icy. "It's nonnegotiable. Tipping is what I *do* and will keep *on* doing and I don't want to hear one more word about it!"

Still seated at the table, the only thing keeping me sane is the challenge of trying to figure out what percentage of $150.00 *is* $56.00, the tip. Let's see $150.00 into $56.00 or is it $56.00 into $150.00 or is it $56.00 into $94.00? Forget it. I am simply not *up* to this arithmetic challenge, I just know the tip is way out of line . . . out of *sight*, and I would be out of *control* except the computation is keeping me busy and reasonably calmed down for a minute.

Okay, I think I've got it. He's managed a 60 percent tip at this nice little neighborhood restaurant; uptown is even crazier. His ultimate out-of-controlness was at Le Cirque this year when I took South African *Cosmo* people to dinner there. "*I'll* pay," he said. "I don't like your counting out money at the table [I like to pay cash]. You can pay me back when you get reimbursed." I'm supposed to turn in a check for six people for dinner; $763.98 including $150.00 for waiter, $150.00 for captain, $150.00 for maître d'. I'm telling the truth. Has Sirio Maccioni stopped paying the help possibly, and David has decided to take over? I deducted David's tips from the bill, added a modest 20 percent, and turned tab in. David says he tips massively to make people happy. I say he does it to make people happy and himself a big shot. *Possibly* he is more right than me. Restaurant personnel do tend to smile a lot when he comes in.

Losing It at Marks

Anger can cleanse and also get you in a whole lot of trouble. People despise, fear, denigrate you when you let loose, then they fling at you the lowest form of recognition of another person . . . pity. For these reasons I don't fly off very often, at least not in public but for David, I will occasionally make an exception.

We are having dinner at Marks, a private club in London . . . lovely old 1922 mansion, sink-into cushioned couches in reception area, where you have quail's eggs and cocktails before dinner, cushy banquettes in dining room, where you have the most wonderful roast beef hash there is and make that split pea soup as well. We have feasted tonight on pheasant but David is frustrated because there is nobody to tip; service is included. Sometimes in a European restaurant he pretends service *isn't* or situation ambiguous and he goes right on tipping, but tonight service arrangement clearly printed on check and he *knows* tipping isn't expected . . . what to *do?* He will tip the girl who brought the rolls and butter. He calls her over, deposits a ten-pound note in her chubby paw. "David," I say, "that is twenty-two dollars in American money, are you crazy?" "It brings me pleasure," my husband says. "I like to make people happy." "You are making me *miserable*," I reply.

Check paid, we leave the dining room, but in Mark's lobby I am still railing. "You are trying to buy love," I fling at him. "You are so insecure you think people will love you if you give them lots of money, and actually they *do* for ten minutes, but other people get loved without bribery." My voice has risen two octaves and I am just warming up! "Stop it!" my beloved commands and, under his breath, "You are embarrassing me with these people (Mark's maître d' and head waiter). I'll never be able to get *in* here again." "You are embarrassing me in life altogether!" I assure him and take off.

The night is mild and I head for Regent Street, stroll around Selfridges for awhile, finally work my way back to Claridges, find David in the bar. I'm now cooled down. David isn't mad but seriously sad. "Helen, you've made it impossible for me to ever get into Marks again," he mourns. "They don't like people making scenes." "You can go back without me," I suggest. "I'd be embarrassed to ask for a reservation," he says. Yes, it was ugly, that little temper tantrum and I wish I hadn't. Three months later David has got back into Marks, several times, yes, without me. Whether or what he is tipping the bread girl I don't want to know. Is out of control maybe like sneezing, do you suppose? Involuntary and sometimes you *have* to.

Thrift at Our House

We use ratty bath towels because they still have good in them. Unraveled at the edges but still thirsty. David uses them to humor me—thrift is in my DNA—seeming to ignore the ravels but then one morning, while trying to pat himself dry (not enough whole thirsty fabric to *rub* himself dry), he will say, "I'm going to the office wringing wet again! How can you send a man to work who isn't dried *off*!" Parting shot at breakfast, "Couldn't you bestir yourself to visit Bloomingdale's today maybe and pick up some towels or are you waiting for me to steal some for you at Claridges?"—haughtily drops name of London Hotel where he will be spending a few days. "Bloomingdale's isn't the *point*," I explained for possibly the three thousandth time. "We have brand new towels in the linen closet, I just don't want to use them until the old ones are *finished*. I promise to take them out of circulation *soon* and we'll use them for rags . . . nobody ever has enough rags." I haven't got over the cleaning woman telling me horrifiedly her first morning, "Ms. Brown, you people ain't got no *rags*!" and explaining her needing them for dusting, polishing, scrubbing, all the things you do with rags. I've been trying, quite successfully, to develop rags ever since—never mind damp David.

Listen, the man had maybe fifteen cents when he married me and even acknowledges that my thrift has made him more comfortable financially, whether stringy bath towels have actually contributed to the new comfort or not, we don't know. I don't want him to start showering at some other woman's apartment, of course. Maybe some of my oldest T-shirts—not old, but *oldest*, so faded you can't read the words—"So many men, so little time," "I'm the head pussycat around here," "The Best Gets Better Together—Revco," etc., etc.—anymore would make rags. I'm thinking, I'm thinking!

Lying

I just do social lies mostly . . . "It was a wonderful bar mitzvah." "I love your hat, your brother, your new rumpus room and can well understand you and Larry spending thirty thousand dollars and a year of your life on it." There's also the lie-to-yourself deception necessary some days. "I feel strong and confident like a bear, not a pitiful gored little rabbit and will go right out there and *show* them!" "This party is fun . . . I'm having a great time [don't get too near the bathroom or you might start in looking for the Motrin]."

But there is also the low-down, you-don't-have-a-decent-reason-to-do-it kind of lying and deception, and this is that kind; me filling the empty Mountain Valley water bottle with tap water, putting it back in the fridge and passing it off as the Real Thing. I did that for years with David. He loves Mountain Valley, prefers it to Evian, and often used to rave about its great mountain taste, whatever that is . . . "from your home state, honey, up there in the Ozark Mountains." He was seriously happy when I poured him a tumbler of it, but how could I resist cheating? (a) New York water is rated to be some of the best in the country; (b) I always knew David couldn't tell the difference between the local and imported; then we get to (c) Mountain Valley water costs $2.98 and I tend not to be a squanderer. My wont was to buy one bottle of M.V., when it was finished refill with New York City tap, keep doing that until label got a little scruffy from water spilling over it, buy a new authentic Mountain Valley, start cycle again. I always made sure to have the real thing *or* the fake very cold since it tastes better (more authentic!) that way.

What tipped me over into craziness? I don't know. One night at dinner with some friends at La Grenouille—very festive, very expensive, hosts paid—we were telling stories about the high price of Persian melons, condominiums, Concorde tickets, Hermes scarves, and how you could cut corners if you were smart and I just up and told our little group about the Mountain Valley water switch. David laughed along with everyone else—the joke was on him—all those years he'd thought he was drinking good Mountain Valley water from the Ozark Mountains in Helen's home state and actually swilling down New York tap! When we got home, he got real—not abusive, accusing, or angry but from his deep pain he told me of his disappointment. He said I could have told him I had a lover and he wouldn't have been much more upset. This was a sacred ritual—his appreciating that bottled water and me supplying—now I had cynically betrayed that trust and hurt him. I had a choice: keep on with the deception . . . Mountain Valley costs $2.98 a bottle and he really can't tell the difference between Brand A and Brand B or go straight. I chose straight. The waste kills me, but if I was dumb and show-offy enough to confess my secret to make people laugh and cluck a little in the first place, spilling the beans to innocent David at the same time, I didn't deserve to get away with my thrift any longer. Also it's one thing to deceive by action, another to lie when or if confronted as I might be. Got any secrets? Don't tell me. I can't keep my own.

Travel

Round the World in Seventy or So (Let's Don't Count) Years

(A FEW TRAVEL MOMENTS)

Opening up new editions of *Cosmo* all over the world (thirty-nine now) has provided lovely travel, but I started early. At age six Mother took me from Little Rock to Denver on the train one summer so she could attend Teacher's College in Greeley. It wasn't St. Moritz but it was travel. At ages eleven and twelve, I trained it again with Cleo to the World's Fair (A Century of Progress) in Chicago. Yummy. We'll skip a few years. In my twenties there were many treks from Los Angeles to Caliente with girlfriends to see the bullfights (oooooooooof!), with a boyfriend to Mexico City, same goal (another oooooooooof!). Twice *Glamour* magazine brought me from Los Angeles to New York as a winner or runner-up in their Ten Girls with Taste Contest. Was seeing this magical place the first time, staying at the glitzy Waldorf Astoria, the most exciting trip ever before or since? Maybe.

At age thirty-four, borrowing $500.00 from my boss's wife, Alice, adding a few saved pennies of my own, I toured Europe all alone for four weeks, brave little person. Like many things I've tried in life, I didn't know what I was doing at the time but nice memories and one or two gruesomes have been reaped. Cambodia is the next planned trip for David and me. Sometimes I go someplace just because it's famous, no huge longing, but how would you not sign up for the temples of Angkor Wat now that Pol Pot has retired, so to speak, and tourists are no longer in danger of bumping into the Khmer Rouge. I can't be a major source of travel help for anybody.

Early in life I was inept as a land crab and now other people help *me* but I hope you'll let me recall a travel adventure or two you won't want to *duplicate* and add a sensible thought or two. To be avoided: falling over a dead man behind the Taj Mahal in the dawn's early light (the time they said to get there). He wouldn't have looked much better in the sunshine. Also to forget: the memorable day David's foamy shaving cream blew up in the luggage while flying with us and we spent much of our day in Bombay scrubbing, scrubbing, scrubbing with hot wet towels, everything the foam had encountered—blue serge suits, raincoat, suede address book, etc.

Among the *good* encounters, *two* cars, one for the bodies, one for the luggage, given us by the king of Morocco when we visited his country, both produced by using the old H.G.B. chutzpah (you have your own). The psalm says "Ask, and it shall be given you; seek and ye shall find"; I've often found that adage to be true. This particular chutzpah meant calling up somebody met at a party a few weeks earlier (friend of king's) one thought might be helpful in working out details of a planned trip. For the same trip, chutzpah also convinced late magazine tycoon Malcolm Forbes to loan us his Castle Mendoub in Tangiers where six of Malcolm's motorbikes shared the palace with us. Looking across the garden at breakfast you could see Gibraltar. The king's (economy-sized) Mercedes picked us up at the castle for a drive to Casablanca to have lunch with a dentist and his family at their seaside mansion (Moroccan dentists apparently do well), another fix-up by the party person, then to Marrakesh to dine in the Casbah (one more fix-up) in a young designer's pad that used to be a harem . . . domed ceiling, wall-to-wall couches, evening prayers floating in . . . sexiest place I'd ever seen.

I have evergreen memories (the kind you *don't* want) of David in Rome in the Coliseum, roaring like a lion because our guide didn't speak English while costing us 230,000 lira. David wasn't roaring at the guide or the price—he doesn't roar about things like that—but at me for having attached myself to a tour troup (am I going to waste the whole afternoon?) without paying.

The first visit to Beijing in 1980 was a thriller when streets were filled with people in padded Mao jackets swooshing about on bicycles, our tour bus virtually the only thing moving on more than two wheels. Fabulous fat babies and two-year-olds with ribbons in their hair dressed in fluffy ruffled pinafores and petticoats charmed us later indoors. *Outdoors* I feel I trekked more of the Great Wall than anybody since the conscriptural laborers of the Ming Dynasty—I just couldn't get enough; the Wall was sweet and foreign but somehow not foreign at all. You have this feeling of familiarity huffing and puffing on the Wall, gasping at the Eiffel Tower, kneeling in St. Peter's, touring mad King Ludwig's Bavarian aerie, watching the guard change at Buckingham Palace because so many paintings, photographs, movie film have shown us these places. The tombs of the pharaohs in Luxor were awesome but so was the hissy-tantrum had by our Egyptian guide because, having had it with trying to absorb the history of every pharaoh from Ramses to Tutankhamen, we had asked for just a little quiet please to lean up against a monument and gurgle air. Guide said we were trying to cost her her job and she would report us to the tour booker . . . eeeek! Frank Sinatra sang under the stars in front of the Great Pyramid in Cairo the next night. Old Blue Eyes warbling "Chicago" and "The Lady Is a Tramp" made up for guide grouchiness.

We've had many *colorful* guides. A Jay Leno–in-training in Israel did riddles while pointing out the Jaffa Police Station and Casarea Ampi-Theatre. What is the smallest room? Mushroom. What is the biggest room? Room for improvement. What is a receding hairline? Twenty rabbits walking backward. We were eventually dropped at the Knesset where Shimon Peres, the Israeli opposition leader at the time, visited with us. Tour guides are mostly pros who can't be lived without, surely not by grassy-greens like us.

I'm winding down now with my travelogue, but may I recall the night I met the Queen Mother, Queen Elizabeth II, her hubby, Prince Phillip, Margaret Rose, and Tony Armstrong-Jones at a royal premiere of *Doctor Dolittle*. Mother liked me. "Your Majesty," I said, "Her Majesty the Queen looks just like you . . . a very beautiful young woman." (She wasn't so young). Did I know how to chat up a Queen Mother or *what*? London was as magical that night for me as it must have been when a nightingale sang in Berkeley Square or Will Shakespeare did his thing for the *first* Elizabeth.

Of course, there are eagerly-looked-*forward*-to disappointing travel moments. If I lecture in Sao Paulo, will sponsors send David and me on to Manaus on the Amazon to see crocodiles and other animals? Deal. Ensconced at the Tropical Hotel in Manaus, we leave predawn with pilot and guide in a small boat for the jungle to see beasts, half an hour later reach what looks like a promising jungle, scamper ashore, drop our bags and food provisions at a small frame building, take right off for animal sighting. Machetes distributed, one each for boat pilot, guide, David, and me. David freaks, figuring we will kill each other, get killed trying to spear an animal, or the pilot and guide will have us for dinner. Usually he's more trusting of other human creatures but machete blades do gleam, and our twosome isn't skilled in weaponry.

Trek begins, moves along at an insect's pace, husband muttering the entire way about speeding things up a bit, guide stopping to describe every leaf and flower. The trees *are* magnificent, though many being mortally choked by killer vines wrapped around their middles; black tree stumps testify to marches of termite armies. Wild animal count? One chirpy bird (Francesco chirped back to the bird). The only thing the birdie had to look out for was humans—no other creatures who might gobble him *or* us ever showed, two tiny spiders were spotted crawling up a tree. On inquiry about animal activity, Francesco said he had never *seen* an animal on one of his treks (machetes now seemed *totally* unnecessary . . . nothing to fight off, chop down, or scare away). Is it possible I should have had a little clearer picture about what we could expect to show up down here in the jungle? Yes, of course, but I had simply trusted Sao Paulo hosts to send us to a fascinating rhythm animal compound. Maybe somebody mentioned "nature walk" but I wasn't listening carefully, didn't ask is that all there *is?*

On returning to our small frame building for the night, David has a new freak. No gin and tonic, for God's sake, and we are talking fancy hotel back there on the mainland that had assembled the overnight dinner and breakfast provisions, had they no brains whatever? At first he was so angry—him visualizing G. and T. back there on the trail, me kudo and warthogs—he wouldn't even drink the cold beer provided, but finally forced a little down. Ready for sleep, my roommate insisted on closing and locking our door. Why? Afraid of being killed by something in the night, but what? No beasts. Poor little Francesco who whistled back to birds? Hardly. Close and lock we did. During the next 98-degree six hours the noisiest air conditioner this side of a 1930s New Orleans brothel sustained us. The toilet, once flushed, never stopped telling you it had . . . you know how some toilets like to show off . . . gurgle, gurgle, gurgle for twenty minutes.

Next morning we rose early—who slept—took our little boat out to the Amazon. Having failed me with animals, I now hoped Francesco could produce alligators, where are they I asked, I want *alli-*

gators! Francesco said he hadn't seen an alligator in the ten years he'd been at the hotel. There was one *once* out in the river (one we are now on) but it left years ago. No birds in the area either, he explained, in case I'm about to ask. Insects all left when the river became covered with acid . . . birds would have starved. My husband, still anxious, said to hold on tight to the boat as we chugged Amazon-ward, but what could harm me if I fell in? Snakes were not discussed . . . probably they had left town with the birds. When we got to the mighty Amazon, it featured no behemoths of the sea either, only large vessels of commerce. Back at the Tropical we did see a nice little assortment of chimpanzee, orangutan, gorilla, baboon—everything you could wish for monkey-wise—in cages out back of the hotel. There was one small leopard, imported no doubt, and a wrap-around king cobra (we didn't ask to see his papers of origin). Of course one can always visit the animals in the Central Park Zoo back home but I don't like to see them in captivity however well cared for.

Before and since Menaus we've done three animal safaris in southern Africa. The last was at Camp Abu in Botswana, the camp named for head elephant Abu. At the camp you ride on the backs of elephants in howdahs and observe other animals all day long . . . they *do* show. I was elephant-aloft two days, David one. When my small camera slipped out of the opening at the bottom of the howdah and into a stream, I didn't even know it was gone until the driver (who sits on the elephant's head) got my attention, handed me the camera, said Catherine, Abu's sister, had picked it out of the stream with her trunk and turned it over to him. Cathy got some peanuts. Are elephants smarter than us? Probably. I should have one as a pet to help me find the things I lose all day long.

Now for a few more thoughts about travel, some a little *helpful* I hope, others just reminiscences, opinions.

Travel on Business

I never get over the wonder of people *sending* you to another city, paying for the trip, the classier the accommodations the greater the wonder, though Marriott or Holiday Inn are just fine with me if that's the budget. I always vaguely wonder if the company couldn't have got it done from home or suggested you do it when you were going to be in the other place anyway or even perhaps picked somebody more worthy to go. Lots of conferring by television hookup now, of course, but I have been sent so often to so many places even when younger and in not-important jobs, I can barely comprehend how much money companies spend sending us around. Am I critical? No. Ungrateful? Never! Happy down to my Manolo Blahnik sandals which were partially paid for, no doubt, by the travel *for* the travel. When you don't buy a meal or spring for a taxi days in a row and do this several times a year, sandal money builds up.

I have never been a company spender or sender, however. For thirty years as editor of U.S. *Cosmo* I never let the fashion editor go to the collections in Paris and Milan when all her peers were taking off. "Though your pages are important," I told Sandy, "we aren't a fashion magazine. What the *Cosmo* girl will wear and love will be what you see on the runways and in showrooms in New York, not the runways and showrooms of Europe that feature Chanel, La Croix, and Versace, though these designers will influence U.S. design." Sandy whimpered until my last year as editor when I finally got her a coach ticket to Paris and she stayed with friends. I'm glad people weren't so frugal with *me*.

In traveling on business one surely should fit in a little sightseeing . . . Paul Revere's embarkation point in Boston, the Liberty Bell in Philadelphia. When will you be back there? Working on the Catalina swimsuit account for Foote, Cone & Belding for three years, the agency would send me out to work in department stores across the country actually fitting swimsuits so I'd know what I was writing about. The Alamo looked pretty good after I'd squeezed a sixteen into several size twelves (she insisted) in the afternoon, explained the difference between Lycra and spandex to the unenlightened. It's called getting the good out. As for regular travel, not so many travel agents now with the advent of computers and proliferating online information. Best way to select a T.A. is to have one recommended by a friend. Be sure to contact the specific person they mention, not just agency itself—not all agents are created equal.

Destination

You've decided on the place but is this the season? Don't sweat season. Perhaps you wouldn't plop into India during the heavy monsoon months or Antarctica for Thanksgiving, but if a promising exciting trip is offered, cheap, cheap, cheap, "off season," pack! Europe in winter is no colder than Christmas in New York, and you know how tourists swarm here for theater, store windows, pure excitement at that time. London is just as delicious. Trade winds in Honolulu cool things down mornings and afternoons in July. Research your destination ahead of time, of course. You know you want to see Tivoli Gardens and the Little Mermaid in Copenhagen, hear the nightingale floor squeak in the Shogun's Palace in Kyoto, but you can't see *everything*. Map a little plan at home, refine when you get there.

You need to check every airline going to *your* destination. Each will have different fares for different departure days, variations if you stay over Saturday and Sunday. You can also comparison-shop on-line, log on and say you will pay $200 for a one-way ticket to London or whatever, see who responds. Companies now buy up block tickets from airlines, offer these cheaper than you can buy direct from the airline. Check their ads in newspapers or consult online.

You know, of course, to get a seat assignment at the same time you book the flight. With preassigned seat there's less chance of getting bumped if flight gets overbooked; also, if you're fussy like me, you'll want to pin *down* your aisle seat, not wind up in the center section or wherever you don't like. Obviously picking up tickets in advance is best even if just the night before. No use waiting interminably in lines at the airport to get tickets written.

Packing

Travel writer Alex Mayes Birnbaum sings my song . . . pack heavy! How many times have you heard the opposite . . . bring the bare minimum. The *New York Times* once put it this way: "When preparing to travel, lay out all your clothes and all your money, then take half the clothes and twice the money." Alex and I are probably the only travelers in the world who would advise lack of discipline in packing, but I have found the thing you throw in at the last minute—woolly sweater or shawl, there might be *one* cold night—you will live in five days in a row, the sun never came out. The silk frock (everyone said bring only shorts and T-shirts) will turn out to be perfect for a party the governor of the island decides suddenly to give, you the only one in the group with a scrap of glamour.

Sure, you can buy whatever you didn't bring, but the dress or swimsuit may cost twice as much in the city you're in as the city you left, and who wants emergency shopping when you're supposed to be viewing the ruins? Can you lift your bag with all that stuff? Who cares. Frequently you aren't carrying your own luggage anyway or use little wheels. I'm not recommending *more* bags, just fitting more *in*. Pack-minuscule people get so bored with their clothes, with two cities still to go, they want to throw everything in the incinerator and may actually do so when they get home.

Once arrived at a hotel, unpack *everything*, tuck it in closets and drawers. Living out of bags to avoid later repacking, you're rummaging noon and night to find the navy shoes, the lavender headband and, ready to go home, you'll have to dump everything out of the bags on the floor to repack anyway because, after bag-living, nothing will lie down flat and fit in the bag the way it did before the rummage. I cover hang-up dresses, suits, and pants with plastic drycleaner bags; they take no room and discourage wrinkles. Maybe you don't *have* hang-up clothes but flatten everything out in a suitcase. Fine. I couldn't do that to the Chanel suit I'm planning to make last the rest of my life and be buried in if anything happens to the Pucci shift.

Travel Anxiety

I never go anywhere without it! The anxiety hangs around like an old dog at the back steps—you don't know where it came from and why doesn't it go back there—or a garrulous, embarrassing relative you'd rather not be connected with but everybody knows he's *yours*. With all one's travel experience, the anxiety is wildly inappropriate but, of course, trip departure has to be a lot less anxious for anybody not doing it with David.

My husband needs a staff to bark orders to and, since all we have is *me*, there are just too many orders for one barkee, not to mention his primordial need to get us to the airport two hours before flight time. David's commands at the airport consist of "Put that on the conveyor belt, don't put it on the conveyor belts, the porter will get it, get out your passport, put your passport back in your bag, wait here while I get newspapers, don't eat any cookies (in Ambassador lounge), you'll spoil your appetite, use this phone, you don't have to

go to a booth, why don't you go to the ladies' room *now*, we're boarding in a few minutes" (actually twenty-five), etc. David is usually *not*
dictatorial (a little bossy maybe) but his travel nerves have arrived
at the airport *with* him along with me and *my* nerves.

This is what I vaguely worry about:

1. Will we get to the airport on time? Yes probably, with *him*
   in charge but all day long before a flight I'm a little uneasy.
2. In the lounge they forget to send you down on time or give
   you the wrong time to remember to go down yourself.
3. You go to the wrong gate and they actually let you board the
   wrong flight.
4. You skip the club, go directly to the (right) gate, sit in the
   boarding area but doze, drowse, or read so intently, flight is
   called and you don't get *on* it.
5. You go to the right gate, get on the right flight, but two
   people have been assigned your seat.
6. Carrier won't have anything but Diet Coke onboard, refusing
   to realize some people want to stay skinny but also don't
   want to stay hooty-owl awake the entire flight.
7. Flight attendant won't let you take any small bottles of
   scotch or brandy off the plane though you are only having
   diet soda or Diet Fresca (if they remembered to stock) while
   there.
8. They won't have enough of the entrée you ordered—only
   two chicken cacciatore brought on board and you'll be stuck
   with gummy pasta.
9. Though your luggage is tagged, it will go to the wrong city.
10. Luggage will go to the right city but somebody will take it
    from the conveyor belt when you aren't watching or before
    you arrive.

All but numbers 6 and 8 of these worries are totally worthless, of
course. My actual experience with booking (dear Susie does all this),
departure, and flying is *quite* satisfactory, sometimes wonderful with
just a gleep or two along the way, which I'll insist on telling you
about in a moment, but I never quite kick the vague uneasies.

As for leaving a country with problems, I think my friend Berna's
experience takes the Oscar. Berna tried on a fetching turquoise and
opal ring in the arcade jewelry store in the Schiphol Airport in Am-

sterdam. Tight squeeze but she made it. Close to flight time, she decided not to buy the ring—too expensive and she had one a lot like it at home. Alors, ring won't come off her finger. Soaking hand in crushed ice for fifteen or twenty minutes might have done the trick but no ice and no fifteen minutes. Berna could have bought the ring but, even if price was right, who wants a ring you can never get off your finger? Everybody twisted and twisted . . . ring finally came off before plane took off and knuckle was totally crushed. I get squeaky with relief just knowing it wasn't *me*!

P.S. There is no such thing, in my opinion, as checking too often to see if you have your tickets and passport—every five minutes would be about right. Hope you don't have the bad luck my friend Linda Harrison Zanuck had on her way to the airport. Making sure she had her passport while walking out to the car, she left passport on top of the limo while looking in back to see if luggage was stowed properly in the trunk. It was. Linda got in the car, took off, passport fell off at Wilshire and Sepulveda Boulevards where and angel found it, recognized the Zanuck name, called Richard Zanuck's office at Twentieth Century Fox, Richard's secretary rushed to LAX to reunite Linda with passport. I keep mine in a nifty 5" × 10" beige and brown straw folder that snaps shut, easy to spot in the Vuitton tote and lift out from all the other stuff that's in there with it.

Airport Stress

When you are having a bad time at the airport—often used to be St. Louis or Dallas for me because I was always changing planes there to get to or from Oklahoma City and New York to see my sister Mary and there wasn't enough time between connecting flights . . . plane left takeoff city late, no gates available on arrival in hub city, weather has done its worst, blah, blah, blah and you are running steaming, hissing, anguishing, one tends to become so dependent on person at counter who can possibly fix you up on next (already over-booked) flight or maybe squizzle you onto original flight you're late for just ready to taxi to runway—you get like a POW or kidnap victim with his captor. Wanly smiling, cajoling, writhing, wheedling, bribing (I promise: *Cosmo* will do an article about American Eagle!) hoping to gain a little favor with this power player, you are *pitiful!* Some-times it works. Once seated in your new plane, drink ordered from docile, power-limited person, you're yourself again, a princess among devoted subjects, no longer the pawn of a terrorist . . . I'm *back* . . . it's *me*! One day I'm not going to be a panicked, slathering, weak, and pitiful person at the airport counter of an airline with limited space and options for the likes of me. I'm also never going to feel rejected when Julian gives me a table along the side instead of a booth in the grill at the Four Seasons or wince when they draw out the blood at Met-Path. I will learn bravery.

Arrival for the Flight

You have your own rules about getting to the airport early or possibly (more dramatically) late. You like to play it "cooler" (stodgy) like David and me or "hotter" (last-minute dash); I would have a coronary last-minute dashing, thinking they might go off without me. I used to like to be *reasonably* early but, long-married to my partner, we are frequently on tap for overseas flights two hours ahead of time as I have mentioned. Alone, he arrived at the Moscow airport before the lights were on and at Air France for the Concorde before the airport was open . . . a night watchman let him in. I'm just as happy to have missed those *two* "cools."

Airplane Crime, Petty Theft Division

Toward getting a little sleep, I feel two blankets, two pillows (three are better) are minimum for airplane happiness. Flight attendants don't supply these. Too busy early in the flight plus one pillow, one blanket would be max you could get from them. Your one pillow is probably already in the seat. I start collecting pillows and blankets from overhead racks and behind last row of seats in first class the minute I get on board. (If paying for my own ticket, I fly economy). You don't steal from other seats—tacky. If stopped during the raid or looked askance at by an F.A., I simply tell her, "I'm in 3H. I'm not getting off the plane once we take off, so you know where to find me and the pillows in case you need some back."

How to make your bed for max comfort: place one pillow at small of back even if seat is padded, another behind your neck. If fortunate enough to have a third pillow, choose between placing it under ankles—in my case resting on top of Vuitton tote on floor or—I prefer this—hug pillow to chest or tummy. Place two opened-up blankets on top of you. There! If you're in a stretched-out seat for overseas or fancy domestic flight, maybe you don't need as many pillows but I still like them, especially under bent knees or under ankles. Sometimes I buffer between backside and armrest if that's how one's body is turned. We're talking sybaritic here. We're talking why am I *telling* you this? Now *you'll* be stealing all the pillows.

Feats in Flight

Some people think the neatest achievement on an airplane is to make love in the john (the mile-high club). That isn't the neatest achievement. What *is* is getting your panty hose off and a pair of regular panties *on* (so you can be comfortable during the flight) right at your seat under a blanket without anybody across the aisle knowing what you are doing. Of course, you have to be sitting by yourself to do this. Why not do this exchange in the ladies' room? Because you were just there and forgot to take the panties *with* you, ladies' room now occupied (trying out for the mile-high club?), another person waiting, you don't know *when* you'll get back in, lunch trays now being set up and you don't want to miss anything. So I'm sitting with a tray on my lap, making panty for panty hose switch even more challenging! If you're wearing slacks, you wouldn't even consider trying the exchange, but I'm always in a dress . . . more comfy with nothing hugging your waist.

Why not skip the panty hose and just wear panties to the plane in the first place? Because some of us feel better in the Admirals' Club in stockings, not just in legs, plus we don't want to land in Detroit, London, or Newark in twenty-degree weather bare-legged. Never mind that I am the only person who has ever had trouble with a panty hose switch because I'm the only one who ever wanted to make one, you now try not to attract the attention of people across the aisle as you squirm, wiggle, and pull. Getting the panty hose *off* isn't so bad . . . you're working with gravity. After they're off, feet and all, comes the killer: slipping panties on over your feet, pulling them up over your hips by unobtrusively lifting buttocks off the seat under your tray. Yes, it can be done. Later, before deplaning, having suffered successfully for the cause (comfort in flight), you now go to the ladies' room, panty hose in handbag, put them back on for the landing. Who is in the ladies' room this time is not the mile-high try-outers but a flight attendant putting on full makeup before meeting a beau in San Francisco—a touch more in a moment—or somebody with elimination problems. Finally, attendant or troubled one comes out, I go in for last phase of the Great Panty Hose Panty Switch, accompanied by lighted messages *and* voices sternly suggesting I get back to my seat. One deplanes properly reassembled and never mind nobody cares . . . *you* know, *you* care, you are having it *all* . . . flight comfort and landing-chic, okay?

The Silent Treatment

Never mind people you don't *particularly* want to talk to or not right now, you're reading, nothing is more worrisome than sitting next to a man—it's always a man, women are more polite—you don't want to be involved with but he won't leave you alone, keeps interrupting and you're going to kill him, except *possibly* sitting next to a man who pays no attention to you whatever and he doesn't even have a briefcase or laptop open for work but is *reading*. Happened to me between Dallas and New York last week—the man read *Newsweek* for three hours, including lunch. I didn't think, sensibly, isn't this *heaven* . . . no conversation! Or even what is the matter with this person not wanting to talk to me. I thought what is the matter with *me* . . . not cute enough? Young enough? Giving off boring vibes? Having disciplined myself as a shy person always to talk to the person next to me on landing if we haven't spoken during the flight, I told this sphinx over La Guardia roughly what I've just told you—that I try *not* to talk to seatmates on planes but when somebody doesn't want to talk to *me*, as was the case with him, I'm thinking what's wrong! I go on. For once in my life, I tell him, I haven't brought along enough to read and would actually have welcomed the talk. "Oh," he said, "do you want to borrow my *Newsweek*? Here . . . you can have it now," and the man actually handed me his magazine. Maybe it's just as well we didn't get anything started. Would it be going too far to say it might not have been a thrilling conversation?

I've lived about a thirtieth of my life on airplanes . . . I'm crazy about them, not because of yummy destinations necessarily, but I like to fly. You can read, eat, sleep (if nobody bothers you as in talky husband), not be responsible for anything. Once in a while I let myself do a crossword puzzle. I adore them, but they don't get you anywhere so I ration. I've had good and bad seatmates (David, I love you as a seatmate despite your talkiness). Sidney Poiter at the height of his movie fame sat next to me on a TWA flight from Los Angeles to New York and I "protected" him for hours from greedy, grabby (almost) flight attendants. He didn't seem to mind being protected. Jimmy Stewart, the beloved actor, was across the aisle when he'd just met Gloria McLean, his soon-to-be bride and she was flirting with him like a wild person. Fun to watch.

I exercise on planes. Occasionally I scream at somebody. On a flight from Paris with Kim St. Clair Bodden and another *Cosmo* international editor, we were seated in business class when a baby across the aisle started to be fretful, then went all the way, yowl, yowl! Waked from a serious sleep, I went to the mother, reasonably, graciously, said I knew what a challenge it must be to care for a baby in flight (I hadn't a clue) but I hoped she'd do her best to quiet the child (some babies like to fly), that I had a long day ahead when we got to New York. Mommy, while not totally hostile, was totally disinterested, said not a cooing word to her baby who finally did quiet down; I went back to sleep. At the second wake-up . . . baby now has his second wind, yelling up a storm . . . I grittily stayed in my seat. How often can you remonstrate with a mommy who hasn't got the word *soothe* in her vocabulary and is also apparently deaf, but I am pissed. Other passengers don't seem to mind baby or be particularly sympathetic with me . . . talking to each other, watching movies, etc. Glowers at mother get me nowhere, naturally, but the baby finally stops crying again, all tuckered out I assume. I will myself to sleep again, takes a little doing. At the third wake-up—yowl, yowl!—I blast out of my seat, fly over to mother and baby, scream at baby "Shut up"! I guess it was quite a sight . . . grown woman screaming at tiny infant . . . Kim and Florence are trying not to know me. The baby and I both quiet down about the same time. When I told David this story his first words were, "Oh, my God, what if she was a *Cosmo* reader!" I tell him I think chances are very slim. If she'd been reading *Cosmo* she'd have known how to quiet a baby, especially a male one.

Take Your Pet Along

On a recent visit to Buenos Aires to help them get their *Cosmo* shaped up, Kim St. Clair Bodden and I again traveled together. She's a peach. We don't talk much in flight; I read, Kim watches movies. No baby screamers this time, but the trip was not unalloyed quiet. Kim's seven-year-old son Graham's pet had died recently, and to make him feel less bereft and petless, Kim had given him a cyber-pet—a compact electronic "creature" the owner can actually talk to, feed, send out to play, etc. Cyber hadn't been working properly when Kim left home, so she plopped it in her handbag, told Graham she'd get it fixed soon; Cyber went to B.A. with us. Okay, he may not have been working properly in New York, but in Kim's handbag in flight he was efficient enough to wake me up four times to tell us he was hungry, needed to go to the bathroom, etc. Who needed a real live baby to guarantee ones being alive, alert and . . . sleepless!

Supplies for the Airplane

I will borrow a friend's (or even a stranger's) comb or lipstick in an emergency, not the least bit fussy, though the borrowed-from might like to fuss, but I think packing hand lotion and moisturizer in your tote-on-board bag for a trip and not depending on the airline's is a good idea. (I'm talking first class, of course, which I've only flown in recent years, coach only does soap). People steal anything, from the john that isn't nailed down or at least use it all up before you get there anyway. Airlines do the best they can, I think, but have lots of other things than bathroom supplies to check in flight. The cologne in a john I was recently in smelled like root beer—possibly not a big demand for this flavor so it had got stale; hand lotion was kind of fungusy. Not too much trouble to take small bottles or tubes of your own from home (you could figure this out for yourself?).

Advantage Miles So to Speak

One of the best things about flying for *me* is that you don't have to tip, no matter *how* they hustle and scurry for you, at the counter or on the plane. The second best thing, for a woman at least, would have to be that you don't have to mess with food, bring a drink, or even a snack to anybody (most of us do some of that at home for husband, lover, child, guests). Not only don't you not have to mess with food, you don't have to get anybody a pillow, newspaper, or blanket, Ms. Wonderful or Mr. Wonderful will do that. I'm still always a little incredulous that somebody would want this job, though there is a waiting list in many companies for those wanting to sign on. I guess nobody considers the work demeaning because it has a different name than serving girl, waitress, or maid.

Flight attendant, rather than the old stewardess designation, surely says what he or she does, attends you in flight. One reason asking flight attendants for something is such a pleasure is they mostly don't seem to mind, so you don't have any guilt the way you would asking anybody else. So I guess getting paid well, free pleasure trips for you and your family, lots of time off, and you don't really *mind* heating up all that frozen food, collecting dirty dishes, fetching two drinks per person, pouring all the wine, sometimes getting it poured on *you* or the customer and having to mop up doesn't keep these from being desirable jobs. I have had wonderful visits with flight attendants, many of whom are *Cosmo* readers and I consider friends. I take phone numbers and keep track of several. My attitude seems a little inconsistent with this story but I'll just mention insanity time when I got whopping mad at a flight attendant coming home from London recently.

She got on the *plane* with *attitude*, I swear, but, attitude or not, she didn't deserve *me*. Long, arduous day before departure. Waiting what seemed a day and a half for dinner, tray arrived with fat sausages and runny eggs; maybe an hour before, I had actually ordered baked salmon and polenta. "What is *this*?" I asked, seriously alarmed. "We ran out of what you ordered," she said, as though dealing with a spoiled child. "You *what*?" I asked. Having paid $4,491.00 for a first-class ticket from London to New York—well, my company paid—I thought she could have come back and discussed the substitute dinner, not just sprung it on me. I decided to live right up to her spoiled-brat evaluation. "I can't *eat* this shit," I declared and dumped the tray on the floor, splatter, splatter, splatter. Poor David. Upon leaving plane, flight attendant could go home to River City and never see me again, but David is stuck with his embarrassment and *me*; I thought he would die. He is infinitely kind and considerate of people, *always*—me, frequently, though not in his league. So two attendants mopped up the floor, then they filled out a report about the "incident" and asked a lot of questions. When somebody causes a disturbance in flight . . . I could have been a terrorist! . . . they file a report. David said we would be contacted by a representative and, no doubt, be asked never to fly the airline again (and lose all those Advantage Miles?). I did apologize *hard* for my act . . . "rude, outrageous, unconscionable, not called for" were words I used; flight attendant didn't forgive, who could blame her? As I said, I felt she was snippy before the failed dinner but nobody deserved *me*. Airline never contacted us. David, sometimes weekly, at least monthly flies with them and was probably considered too good a customer to lose. It's a wonderful airline and I have my own thousands of Advantage Miles. Since we can get back on, as far as I know, I'm thinking of Sydney next spring—they have a reciprocal agreement with Quantas.

On one other occasion I did get seriously snippy with a flight attendant and this time I didn't apologize but felt I'd struck a blow for other frequent female flyers. On a flight from New York to Tokyo, then on to Hong Kong, I have been in the air eleven hours, in the plane for fourteen and a half, grounded two and a half before takeoff with a little engine trouble. I am sleeping as peacefully as a raw carrot in a Cuisinart, occasionally managing to doze off. After an hour or two of not really sleeping *or* being awake, I go to the john. Outside the two first class johns—both occupied—are three people waiting. We don't talk. I, for one, am trying not to wake up totally. Five minutes pass, somebody comes out of a john, somebody else goes in. Procedure repeated, same john, and five minutes later another exchange, same john. Everybody's in and out but me. Having had quite enough, thank you, I give the continuously occupied john a solid whack on the door and stand back. Rude, yes, but sure enough, out comes a dewy, fresh-faced, perfectly coifed, put-together flight attendant who could go straight to the Okura to tea and make other sippers look dowdy and tired. "Madam," I say (imagine calling a twenty-three-year-old flight attendant madam . . . pure five o'clock-in-the-morning hauteur). "Your timing is exquisite . . . close to Japanese perfection. You could help negotiate the balance of trade disagreement between Japan and the United States. While four first-class passengers who have paid $6,163.20 to travel from New York to Tokyo, in my case New York to Hong Kong, on this great airline are standing out in the hall getting uremic poisoning in the middle of the night in the middle of the Pacific, getting so totally waked up they will never sleep again, you are in there working on being Miss America for our arrival in Japan." I didn't say it quite that well but close, because I have been practicing saying it for a long time as I have encountered other flight attendants doing a complete makeup job for arrival in Istanbul, Los Angeles, or Rome while I wait out in the hall.

I haven't had a moment's regret about my rudeness, haven't looked back. I plan to pound on more doors as I flush out more flight attendants or other selfish ones. How can I respond to nature and maybe put on a *touch* of blush if you're in there doing the full before and after?

I *didn't* get a man out of the airplane john when we were taking off from San Francisco for New York, though I should have. Plane hadn't lifted off, john occupied during our entire wait on the ground. I pouted and gave him hell when he came *out*. He said he hadn't had time to shave at the hotel, thought this was the perfect spot. Men can be just as selfish and silly as *us*.

Fellow Travelers

I like a man to have something to *do* when he gets on an airplane. It is inconceivable to me that he could just get *on* . . . just *be* there . . . expecting flight attendants and me to entertain him. No book, magazine, a report to finish? *Ce n'est pas possible!* Real men frequently bring laptops. Yes, I know about people hiding out in work, and work really works on airplanes. I'm hidden out in mine nearly at all times and maybe that's bad, but you know I feel you need something else besides just *you* to turn on the world so let this man, please, be buried in his papers, delve into his dear briefcase, do floppy disks. Regardless of his workload and even in summertime, should my seatmate be wearing lime-green socks and white shoes, he also has to be a pass-by respect-wise. There virtually is no way I could communicate with a man in green socks even when we are having lunch.

Airplane Love

Airplanes are sexy, do we all agree on that? Sequestered with someone before unknown, pleasant and male (or female if you're a male) shoulder to shoulder for a few hours, the air is full of possibilities. He has to be *acceptable*, of course. Life-buoy bellies or triple-digit double chins need not apply but physical perfection isn't required. A friend of mine summed it up well, I think. "Falling in love in midair presupposes no penalties, no obligations and no privileges but is definitely organic," he said. I never met a future boyfriend or lover on a plane but have had some great chats.

A man across the aisle coming home from London on the Concorde gave me a computer. Two weeks after I was back in New York at my office arrives the most darling IBM Think Pad. His card said, "I couldn't stand to see somebody as successful and accomplished as you working in such a primitive way [across the aisle from him with manuscripts, pencils, eraser, editing my brains out]. You'll find you can accomplish a great deal more in flight with this small laptop. Sincerely—signed name." I had Susie call Radio Shack immediately to see what the Think Pad cost. About $3,000.00, she said, with attachments. "Am I supposed to sleep with him?" I asked Susie. Although sympathetic to his cause—Susie doesn't understand anybody being computer-illiterate either but, as long as one of us— she—is whizzy with high tech, we get our work done—Susie said she didn't think so. Subject never came up.

Computer friend and I have lunch occasionally. He isn't Fortune 500 but does head an international equipment leasing company with offices throughout the world. After a brief round of lessons with the Pad, it's now on the floor of the closet in my office thinking its little brains out without me. Someday I might give it a shot, take it flying, but I like to work with actual *paper* and wouldn't have paper until a floppy disk was transcribed when I got home. I know people like me drive computer geniuses nuts.

My airplane friend produces art masterpieces using his array of computers and special printers on canvas, has the ability to "texture" his works of art, giving them an air of authenticity. First he tells me he carefully photographs a particular oil painting in the Musee d'Orsay or the Louvre using a high resolution digital camera. Once back at his laboratory/studio in Princeton he can add special effects, adjust the lighting, fine-tune the background and, as he modestly put it, "correct any mistakes da Vinci or van Gogh may have made in their efforts to produce a masterpiece." Once all the adjustments are made, he prints the colors and subtle shades. "Colors," he points out, "that just didn't exist in the time when these paintings were originally done." He therefore "creates a richness that the original artist could only have hoped to achieve had he had the proper tools." Does Bill Gates know about this? My friend also "improves" music on his computer, by adding strings, removing brass, etc. People as clever as he need appreciators, right? That's *me*. Happy to appreciate as long as I don't have to try to understand what the hell they are doing.

Creepy Time Down South

Yes, you meet interesting people in travel . . . and the other kind, too. Between flights in Memphis one day, a man came up to me in the terminal and said, "You look much better than your photographs, Ms. Brown." "Thank you very much," I said. This remark is always meant as a compliment. He then told me he was an optician, owned an optical company, began to pull out a photo of him with Sophia Loren—in *his* glasses presumably—from his wallet. I waited quite patiently for the extraction, didn't have much else to do for forty minutes. Picture extracted—she looked very nice—he then told me what he had said to Sophia, trying not to be too impressed by her celebrity, no doubt. He said he had said, "I suppose you wipe yourself like everybody else does, Miss Loren." I handed the photo back, didn't wait to hear what Sophia had said to *him*. I always talk to strangers—some chats more rewarding than others.

Traveling Alone

An older married couple is not a bad bet for creating a conversation with if you are traveling alone and about to go out of your mind with your own company. The less you talk to anybody on a trip the more clammed-up you get—just like at a party you attend alone and don't talk until finally you have to *plunge* before your vocal chords disappear. Pick a couple on the plane or tour bus. If they're long-married—you can't know just by looking, of course—most of their conversation will have been used up years ago and, if they've got hold of any new stuff, *it* was probably used up last night at dinner ("Do you think this mahimahi was fried in Vaseline?"), they can *use* someone to take the focus off each other. Just get up on your knees, lean over the back of the seat, and ask *anything* . . . does this bus go back to the hotel or does it go where we're all supposed to have dinner (doesn't matter if the tour conductor just announced). What year did he say they started excavating Pompeii (ditto, the tour conductor just said), any banality will do. After a little chat, if the couple wants to grab on to you, they will. Maybe you'll dine together. If they don't, they won't. Getting their attention doesn't take a brilliant opening foray or lion courage, just lonesomeness.

The Hotel Scene

Travel writer Alex Mayes Birnbaum says, if the budget is tight, better to stay in the worst room of the best hotel than the other way around. A once-upon-a-time maid's room, converted (big) hall closet will do just fine, and you'll be *in* that great building with its splendors, seeing interesting people instead of in a scruffy place (they do all change the sheets every night), possibly with riffraff or sixteen-year-olds on a bicycle tour. On arrival at the best hotels in the world—Claridges, Hôtel du Cap, Plaza Athene, Vier Jahreszeiten, Villa d'Este or wherever—I always feel a *bit* intimidated, just a little stitch in the stomach. It isn't the price. I can pay or somebody else will, but the personnel at the check-in desk speaks English better than I speak *anything* and isn't *that* friendly. The thick glass entrance doors pushed open by massive gold handles, carpeting up to your ankles, chandeliers they might have pinched from Versailles . . . awesome and impressive! If there is a tiny touch of a country-girl angst going on in that lobby, I'm not sure that's bad. It's *okay* to be impressed by the worthwhile. I think Alex is right.

Hotel Reservations

Don't arrive without a fax or letter saying your reservation is confirmed. That means no matter when you arrive, a room will have been saved for you. If you don't get in until 11:00 P.M., say, and don't have anything in writing, they may have given your room away. If you don't get in at all that night, of course, you'll have to pay for the confirmed room, but that's better than arriving at 11:00 P.M. without a confirmed reservation and sleeping in the lobby, unless you think lobby-sleeping is a good way to save money. (I wouldn't have put it past some people in olden days.) Disasters happen.

A few years ago David and I arrived at the Oberoi Hotel in Cairo without a piece of paper guaranteeing anything, were part of a Pan Am/Revlon junket. Other junketers had not yet arrived and, since junketer's overseer was seemingly unknown to hotel (how could they locate somebody they didn't know?) David and I were not welcome, rejected. Sulking, exhausted, we sat in the Oberoi lobby with our luggage, discussed going back home that night when a young woman from Boston, not part of our group, recognized me from television and said we could sleep in her room if we liked—there *are* such people. We quickly said yes to her offer and were ready to take our bags upstairs when others from the U.S. group arrived, some with enough clout to get us a room. Hotel finally located our junket-manager out on the tennis court getting the *good* out of, no doubt . . . the little scamp. I'm never without a confirmation now.

What You Can Expect from a Hotel

After you're shown your room and don't like it (the Chinese laundry view from your one window), the hotel may attempt to find another room—same price—but the next one may not be an improvement (a third smaller, the view is a beer billboard). If you're willing to trade *up* a bit (more bucks), hotel will usually accommodate. After you've settled and realize you're across from the elevator, clanking open and shut is driving you mad, hotels are *pretty* good about changing your room without a trade-up if they can find other space. Television, radio, feuding are blasting away in the next room at 2:00 A.M.? Call the desk and ask *them* to quiet the people down. More effective than pounding on the wall or arriving in your bath-robe with a scowl.

European Johns

Flushing European toilets, I sometimes think the London ones are not going to make it. They determinedly get up the ambition to *try* but sometimes you fear the effort is going to be too much of a strain and they will *konk*; usually the john comes through, but one is nervous. Flushing in Istanbul, what's in the bowl comes up to the top and floats around a while and you really *do* think, Oh my God, it's stop-up time or, worse, this john is going to blow *up*! Eventually the facility comes to its senses, takes its plunder down the tube. I am not overly prissy or concerned about plumbing, theirs or mine, can pee behind a tree if necessary, but getting acquainted with each new john on the road is an adventure.

Another bathroom drama might be called "Wake Up Your Roommate." Bathroom light switch in many hotels is *outside* bathroom door so, middle of the night you get up to go to the john, turn on switch, open the door, light streams out, and wakes up whoever you left in bed. Same thing happens when you leave bathroom. Open door to return to bed, light streams out before door can be reclosed and switch turned off, reawakens roommate in *case* he has been able to get back to sleep. Maybe you're not going to the bathroom middle of the night as often as I. I've told David we need *suites*. I would never go for separate bedrooms in a hotel but *bathrooms* I could be talked into and would even pitch in with the bill.

Emergency Hotel Food

I don't ever find airplane food so unappealing I will take sandwiches from home like some people I know. Certain friends never *don't* make a Zabar's run on the way to the airport. I bring tide-over food for the hotel. Arriving middle of the night one needs only a snack; room service is too ambitious. Toted food is a fine hunger-husher, can make a small breakfast if needed. My bring-along food is Polly-O part-skim-milk mozzarella cheese slices (cheese holds up fine until put in hotel refrigerator), apple slices, ditto. Cheese is protein, apple vitamins, very sensible. I would never tote dried apricots, chocolate chip cookies, energy candy bars—anything really *good*—any more than I would stock them at home. We're not supposed to have food-fits in travel, notwithstanding hotel minibars feature miniboxes of

Godiva (the price *alone* is a deterrent). On book promotion one year, I carelessly left all my mozzarella and apple slices home in the fridge. Discovering survival food missing when we got to La Guardia, David crash-dashed into Queens to get a supply. Small eaters may not be big eaters but you don't want to be with a food-deprived one too long—they get mean. David was wise to make the dash.

Bidets

I never get over how *vulgar* they are—I mean the vagina is all opened up and *up* there to get itself hosed out—and, by contrast, how conservative and private the English people are, for example. I met my first bidet at the Green Park Hotel in London ($4.00 a night with crêpe paper curtains) on my first trip to Europe, which is why London comes to mind. The bidet is so indigenous to the French I wouldn't be surprised if they ate out of it, but I simply can't picture a sixty-year-old English lady all flung out like a turbot over her bidet. Never mind. Perhaps she participates out of duty, like going to the gynecologist.

I fell *out* of my first bidet at the Green Park. Regular bathtub down the hall but cost a shilling (fifty cents) and you had to call a maid to take you there. I filled up my bidet with hot water and got all of me into it I *could*. "All of me" consisted of feet and backside, not at the same time, of course. I stood up in the water-filled bidet, leaned over to pick up the soap, and fell out. Nothing damaged. I have a bidet at home now and still have to be careful not to get scalded. Seated, you reach behind you to adjust the hot and cold levers, can easily misjudge (once *again*) which is which and it's *ouch!*

Stealing

You have your own code about what to steal from a hotel. Mine *now* is the stuff on the basin—shampoo, conditioner, bath gel, lotion. Those supplies aren't stealing, of course. You're supposed to use them while there, but I've found if you immediately put them unopened in your makeup bag, housekeeper may replace on the basin and you can use the replacements while in residence, tote the originals home. I pour hotel hand lotion into a jar I keep for that purpose, shampoo into another. You don't get new soap by hiding the unused, paper-wrapped bars, but don't do that anyway because you need soap for hand washing and showers when you get to the hotel and package must be opened. If a pretty big bar of soap—virtually unused—is still left at going-home time, I pat it dry, put it in my makeup bag to fly away.

Some kind of saving madness? Certainly, but no guilt. From never having had enough stuff for a long time, I'm still catching up. Rationalize, rationalize! Sometimes I take one fluffy washrag. Okay, that is stealing but considering the bills David and I run up and pay—whoppers twice or thrice yearly at Claridges, many times a year at the Bel-Air—the washrag-heist doesn't seem *that* bad. David wouldn't agree; he isn't told about it. Yes, stealing is stealing but, considering my previous acquisitions—bath towel or even bath mat occasionally—is the washcloth *too* woofy? Oh the hell with it, I know you're with David!

Stealing a Bathrobe

I did do a major heist two years ago—stole a bathrobe from Claridges. It isn't any riskier to steal a bathrobe from Claridges than the Sheraton or Hilton. Standard procedure is that you can *"steal"* your bathrobe, but housekeeper tells housekeeping, who reports to management, who puts it on your bill. In my case Claridges maid didn't realize what had happened and, because hotel had shorted me in a money exchange earlier in the day, I felt justified to steal.

Scenario: I had gone to hotel desk with ancient pounds and asked if they would change for new. Though London banks *won't*, hotel graciously said they would. I got my new pounds, went back to room. Later cashier telephoned to say he and his boss, maybe the comptroller, would like to come up to my room because they'd given me too many new pounds for old. I hadn't counted, just gratefully accepted what they had given me, left in envelope; I said fine. The hotel money men came up, I gave them their envelope back, they took half the pounds out, left me the rest, said thank you and goodbye. Later I started doing a little adding and subtracting according to what they'd explained to me about the exchange rate and realized, with the rate of new pounds for old, they'd left me fifty too few new pounds, short about $80.00. Truth. I'd worked hard on my counting and figuring. Called downstairs. Cashier said yes, they did seem to be over in their cash count for that night and he would give me all the pounds they were over. He brought up the "overage" with a bunch of flowers; I thanked him. Poor man had probably been through hell with his boss. I counted the money after he left and I'm still short fifteen pounds, roughly $24.00. Hmmm. The Claridges maid, for whatever reason, has left three terry robes in our suite. David had been living at Claridges several weeks on location for *The Saint* and I guess my showing up made the maid want to be sure we were both well robed; there are now two robes on hooks in bathroom, I was wearing a third. Don't know whether housekeeper knew a robe has been snatched; this one didn't report. I just hung robe in my garment bag and and took it home. The robe is worth maybe a little more than $24.00, though it isn't new. I am reasonably content. I always wanted to steal a bathrobe from a hotel but never wanted it on my bill, robes are overpriced. Actually, I never wear the Claridges robe. It's kind of a talisman.

Money Changing Abroad

The best place to change American money into foreign currency is at the ATM (automated teller machine) on the streets or outside the banks of most major foreign cities. Although you can change money before leaving home or in the bank, hotel, or airport where you're going, the exchange rate at an ATM is best. You will *need* local currency for cabs and even for tips. Whereas a U.S. dollar bill or five used to bring smiles, even grins, from somebody carrying your bags, the dollar has been so devalued nearly everywhere in the world except in Eastern Europe you're more likely now to get snarls, even hisses.

Shopping

Pay with a credit card in other countries whenever you can because they get the best exchange rate when converting local (foreign currency) prices into dollars.

The French

Yes, people in civilized parts of the world are still different from each other—looks, religion, philosophy—even if we're more homogenous than before. The French, for example: The "help" in French restaurants are often *still* somewhat hateful, in my opinion, definitely not there to make you like yourself and sometimes act like they'd rather you not be there altogether though you pay their wages. In most three-star restaurants in France or their equivalent in the U.S. there is at least one maître d' and one captain who are as handsome as Tom Cruise and Ben Affleck will be ten years from now, looks in direct ratio to their arrogance—the more of one, the more of the other . . . they're *mean*. Sometimes I try to figure out *why*—I didn't do anything bad to them.

A historian once told me all you have to remember when you get your feelings hurt is that the French are that way even to each *other*. He explained they're mad because they never won a war—had to pull out of Vietnam, Napoleon was slaughtered in St. Petersburg, bested in World Wars I and II—imagine having Nazis occupy your city, let alone if your city was Paris! Well, whatever their motivation to be snippy, whenever you order, I find you never get a smile of approval, not a hint that you have been anything but gauche—the blanquette de veau might have been alright yesterday but only hopeless hicks would order it *today*. The loupe de mer is superb tonight—push, push—though you aren't a fish person (I'm a fish person but some aren't). I was planning on chicken of which there are thirty possibilities and you are sure to pick the wrong one—poulet d'estragon instead of poulet au champagne. They don't quite say you are a joke, they just look it. I'm also not crazy about the leisureliness of French dining. Yes, it's a three-star restaurant and how often will you be there on this visit or possibly ever again, but I had planned to do a little something else during my stay in this city than spend three days—whoops, I mean three hours—dining just one little night. I might prefer to prowl the safe, fascinating streets, even go back to my hotel and read in bed or loll in their tomb-size tub in an ocean of hot water.

At—I'm not going to say which one but a very tony and famous Paris restaurant last year—I had a touch of a dustup with the captain, who felt my salmon should be rare when I had ordered bein cuit. Little Rock girls don't eat rare *meat*, let alone fish. Fish came out about the color of Lancome's Code Red lip color when poked into, fish went back for further cooking. For the next fifteen minutes during which guests were urged to start eating but felt uncomfortable doing so without me, I got all the way through my pelvic exercises and thought through the rest of my life as the others finally caved in and ate. At dessert time, if there is anything a French restaurant is reluctant to do, it's serve *you* coffee at the same time they serve others profiterole and tarte au citron, you not having dessert; for them coffee is *apres*.

I did get one-up with a snippy French headwaiter once—the memory burns bright. At the remarkable and glamorous Tour d'Argent on the left bank of the Seine, a tiny green worm was crawling around my salad greens; I pointed him out to this particularly snooty person. The man went white, he went crazy, he brought champagne for the table and enough new salad to start your own salad bar. Joy! Redemption! Do I detect a little country-girl provincialism around here? Alas, yes. Surely relationships would be helped if I spoke French, and also I'm spoiled.

At La Grenouille in New York, surely one of the best French restaurants in the world, Jean Pierre would bring me all the courses at once if I wanted, get me out in thirty minutes, always supplies "beaucoup de ris" for my quenelle without being asked. David's being a good customer probably helps gain cooperation. David, as I have mentioned, never met a waiter, captain, or maître d' anyplace in the world he didn't overtip, and maybe he's right that there is no such thing as overtipping if you can afford. He is relatively inexpensive as husbands go, doesn't keep a mistress, (do you ever *know*? I *think* I know), a yacht, or potential derby winner in a barn in Connecticut eating up a storm.

Speaking of snootiness, in London's tippy-top restaurants and clubs you sometimes still get the frozen-pudding smiles, glacial hospitality, a sneer in there somewhere trying to get out. I suspect some of the older maitre d's are mildly male chauvinists even now, with a sort of "how did *you* get in here, little girl?" attitude. Still, I respect their taking their jobs seriously, for considering it an honor to serve customers in a splendid restaurant, service a respected profession in the U.K. They're also good at getting the staff to move its tail, no excuses for lollygagging ("something unfortunate is going on with the chef this evening"). In a good British restaurant the customer is king right this *minute*. I can stand a little class system if I get to be part of the class.

Zonked

Arriving in another country after a long trip I don't know anything to recommend except hot bath, hot tea, fresh grapefruit juice, sleep up a storm. Others say don't ever *sleep* on arrival, stay on your feet until it's *their* bedtime—those are stronger folk than I. I think sleep is a summer breeze . . . you gobble it up whenever it's there and a little power nap before lunch or dinner in your new city couldn't hurt even if they have to hit you with a crowbar to wake you up.

Coming back to New York after a trip is so sweet. I start feeling elated coming through customs (especially since I have nothing to declare these days—cheaper here so I don't shop overseas). The joy and pleasantness builds on the Triborough. Seeing the spires and lights of New York City again I think Wow, pow, you made it in that city, kid . . . you must be okay. I can actually feel the city saying welcome home. Once in the flat I unpack immediately rather than wait a single minute, though I know people who hide their luggage for *days*. I find opening the mail, sorting the newspapers and magazines, facing what has to be faced next day at work sweet drudgery even in a zombie state.

Scientists have said you need a week to get back to normal for each hour's difference in time between where you were and where you now are. Depending on who's on daylight savings time, that means five or six weeks to get unzonky after a trip to Europe . . . seems about right. Jet lag is such a clichéd explanation for why you're feeling like a sea turtle in the middle of Bloomingdale's, but I'm not sure readjustment doesn't take even *longer* than one-week-per-hour of time change. At least you have some excuse to yourself for not being whizzy for a while.

Moments on the *QE 2, Sagaford, Rotterdam, Seabourn*

What about other forms of travel than planes? Many passenger ships have this neat arrangement whereby a well-known person or someone with a professional specialty can lecture aboard and get the trip free. I can handle that! What I can't handle is the seasickness, in my case as close to terminal as it gets. There are supposed to be things to do ahead of time to prevent seasickness but I never remember to check them out, have a little faith anyhow. On board the

Sagaford sailing from Hong Kong to Shanghai, I wake up in a pitching boat, soon hit the floor to try to exercise as usual, am quickly forced to crawl into a corner to try *not* to throw up, lose the battle, call a cabin attendant who gives me tablets to put down my throat *now*, a suppository for other places later; I am hair-pulling-out seasick for an hour and a half before medicine takes hold. Husband enters stateroom as I am entering the afraid-you'll-die, afraid-you-won't stage of seasickness and says, "Honey, they say coughing and seasickness are all a matter of discipline. If you don't want to and will yourself *not* to, you won't cough or get sick." I suggest he go up on deck and will himself to throw himself overboard, get help if necessary. No one who hasn't participated can know how terrible seasickness is!

There are lots of old people on most cruise ships, almost like a floating retirement home—crutches, wheelchairs, canes . . . you could be at a geriatric convention. Ultrasuede is the uniform—orange-peach, pea green, lavender. Get behind a nonambulatory passenger on the stairs and you can plan on taking fifteen extra minutes to get to the dining room; invalids have to be pushed *up* the stairs and ladled *down* them. We were just at the bottom of the stairs one night when a group came out of a stateroom with wheelchair and the person they were planning to put *in* it, he on crutches. Parting him from the crutches and lowering him into the chair kept us out of the bar another ten minutes because you can't push past or step over . . . rude. Am I an intolerant bitch? Not in this case. I think what a glorious thing it would have been for my invalid sister Mary to travel on one of these ships and then impatient people could complain about *us*. Alas, by the time I got enough money to pay for sea travel or enough reputation to be asked to lecture, Mary was obese and couldn't go on trips except for a few miles from home. She would have loved it.

Ships have something for everybody. If you're mildly antisocial like me, you can read in a deck chair or cozily in bed in your room and watch the clouds and flying fish go by. My friendly, but shy, husband likes to visit the bar before dinner where other friendly folk are and usually a really good saloon singer, maybe a boy *and* girl, performs; cruise ships make you daffy with great food and multiple choices. Besides choosing and eating and choosing, what else do you do with your time? On our last sea voyage (*Seabourn*) we visited five islands from the ship—Tonga, Roratonga, Bora Bora, Morea, and

Papete (Tahiti), all jungle-ly, waterfallsy, cratery—am I getting too cute? Climbing up on a truck I tore my knee open—shame! I'm usually not klunky but next day I still got all the way up a mountain leaning at 45 degrees with people a third younger than me. One of our group went home and checked my birthdate in *Who's Who*, sent me a snapshot of the group, pointing out my friskiness at such an age. Thanks.

Hope we can do a transatlantic crossing on the *QE 2* again. Very Deborah Kerr and Cary Grant strolling out there on deck in your chiffon evening gown, chiffon stole floating all about you (assuming you don't break your neck in your heels). I'll have to work on my lecture. Last time agent said just talk about your book, *The Late Show*, tell what you do to stay young. I told them: work hard, exercise, lots of sex. My group may have made it on the last count . . . everybody seemed to like each other, and there's limitless time to do whatever you have in mind on a boat. Not sure about the other items. Most of my fellow passengers were retired, many from big corporate jobs, and, from the looks of the looks of the belt and slack extensions, exercise wasn't a big priority in their lives. Maybe I'll switch subjects.

New York Buses

More transportation. I love New York buses. Big, shiny, clean, classy, well lighted . . . the fare is a New York blessing. For seventy-five cents and a transfer, senior people like me can ride virtually all over town. At sixty-five I hesitated just a few weeks before dropping in three quarters instead of paying $1.50, thrift finally triumphing over vanity. No driver ever challenged me, but I have lived comfortably with the insult in exchange for the benefit. Yes, I have a car and driver now but don't like to keep Michael waiting for three hours at night while we're in the theater and having dinner after. He has Jill and baby Michael to get home to, plus I'm not huge on overtime.

Sometimes—often as I can persuade him—I drag David onto the bus, particularly after the theater. On Eighth Avenue at Forty-fifth Street we jump on the number 10, in ten minutes get off at Eighty-first and Central Park West across the street from our house. Savings: $6.50. David thinks I'm crazy but what can he do (please don't give him any ideas!). If Michael's off or David is using the car, sometimes I sit in the back row of the same number 10 and go to work. Bench seat is straight across back there and toasty (over the wheels). I like toasty. Recently I was wedged between a man in the back row reading a paper who stuck out over his seat possibly twenty-five percent, his paper even further, and a lady who took about a seat and a half. The two of them together could have paid an extra fare but it didn't matter—I'm vain about being small. The lady was so bulky she couldn't get her legs together—or maybe she wasn't trying . . . we are talking solid wall of flesh here. I'm fascinated! Further along the row, another lady has hairy legs, I mean really hairy, like a little forest of hair up to midcalf—where her skirt came down to. I've never seen anything quite like this before, absolutely hypnotizing. Also on the bus are neat businessy people like me, of course, but I'm not interested in them.

More adventure: Two weeks ago I was waiting for a crosstown at the shelter at Fifty-seventh and Broadway with a lady having an animated conversation on her cell phone—at least I assume there was somebody on the other end, she did all the talking. In ten minutes the bus came along. Seated on the bus, cell phoner started a new conversation, her voice carried. I told myself not to do it, I'd be sorry, but finally I shot up, crossed over the aisle, said to phoner, "You know radios are noisy and buses don't allow them because they disturb other people. Your conversation is just as disturbing as a radio . . . did you ever think about that?" My fellow passengers are listening raptly and I don't know whose side they are on, possibly I will be hissed or hit. Surprise. The phone lady's eyes light up. "You're Helen Gurley Brown," she says, sweet as a taffy apple. "I've always wanted to meet you!" We chatted, my newspaper went unread. Sometimes pushiness is *not* penalized and I *like* buses.

Another baby bus adventure: Coming home from the office one night around 11:00 P.M., I had an entire bus to myself—no other passengers for eighteen blocks—eerie and fun; no bookmaker would give you odds on this happening. Another night I failed to get off at Eighty-first Street. Usually, when you've made a run often, even if you aren't paying attention, an inner beeper tells you when to press the button but I was raptly reading, came to my senses at Ninety-sixth, disembarked. Longish walk—fifteen blocks—back to Eighty-first, but Central Park West is wildly walkable, especially on a sweet, mild night . . . took off my heels and stocking-footed it. You can be eccentric at my age, nobody even *notices*.

Limousines

I think of limousines as glassy black worms oozing through the city streets, inside the worms are important people with, presumably, important things to do. Sometimes I'm inside a limousine not feeling important. I *am* feeling accomplished. Finished with a television show or party, headed directly for the airport and party clothes not for flying, I know how to get down on the floor in the backseat of a limousine and change clothes, even panty hose. Driver doesn't notice or care; nobody can see in. I was with a limo driver the other day—Michael on vacation—who didn't like traffic. Who does, but he was freaking. "Lemme see if I can lose some of this traffic, Ms. Brown," he says. What he loses, I fear, is our way back to New York. We are headed through St. Albans, Jamaica, Richmond . . . places I've never seen on my way to or from La Guardia and John F. Kennedy—before that Idlewilde—Airports these past thirty-six years. We are sluicing through back alleys, through quiet neighborhoods, people washing cars and dogs, picnicking, far from the creamy, if clogged freeway. I may argue with a taxi driver once in a while but never a limo driver. We are home about forty minutes later than the trip usually takes. If we had a subway or train from the airport, I would probably be on it. Oh, who am I kidding? With my pack-heavy M. O. we'd need two people to get the luggage on the train. Why do I think David wouldn't be one of them?

Other Travels

One more travel happening. I've been to Moscow twice. In 1986 Ted Turner took a few friends over for the Goodwill Games after the U.S. didn't want to participate in the Olympics. Even then people on the street were friendly, though a guard sat on every hotel floor to check you in at night . . . like a den mother. I took David, successfully, to a restaurant on the subway, got us on and off without trauma by counting stops (hotel instructions). I surely couldn't read the Cyrillic curlicues on subway signs but T. G. (true grit) and cheapness work everywhere. Next trip to Moscow was in 1994 to launch *Cosmopolitan* in Russia, maybe the thrillingest of all our launches because who could have expected such success in that country, just a few years away from the Cold War? The magazine was gobbled up like women were *starved*. We got seriously lucky with our two young editors, Elena and Ellen, one Russian, the other the wife of the young Dutch publisher who had already started (successfully) an English-speaking newspaper in Russia. For the 850th anniversary of Moscow, the girls put out an 850-page magazine, 650 ad pages—they knew how to hustle. Fun to schlep their beautiful heavy magazine all over New York burning calories and showing off. Now it's time to go burn some more calories, flop around on the floor, and exercise, not show-offingly but determinedly. Calories are done in more by gall than by doing it perfect. Ciao!

Smatterings and Spatterings

Life Joys

Sex, sleep, and food are joys not enjoyed by rich people any more than by poor people, and if you're going to give me rich-people's-food-is-better-than-poor-people's, those three-star restaurants, that foie gras, the unborn lamb, don't bother. If you aren't used to rich-people food, you don't even like it . . . too prissy and fancy. Sex and sleep have no favorites. You can be rich in *them* as a jellyfish at low tide with a beach full of virgin-bather-backs to clamp on to; poor is as good as rich. Getting born altogether isn't a bad thing, no matter how poor, scraggly, jealous, or disheartened (why-was-I-born) moments you have. Of course, if you start being ga-ga about just being alive and start thinking about your heart in there pumping away, sucking the blood in, swooshing it out, you can go nuts. It's like a small squirrel is in there pumping five times a minute, how did it *get* there, why does it *do* that? I wish I hadn't started thinking about my heart this *minute* . . . too weird, almost frightening! Along the same line, thinking about who you *are*, what makes you *you* needs to be avoided as much as possible or you start hallucinating.

The Feminist Movement

When people say things are going too slowly in the Feminist Movement and women are nowhere near where we ought to be, I think of something Kurt Vonnegut said to me once. Said the noted author, "We split off from the orangutan seven million years ago, but only in the past thirty years has it been generally acknowledged that women are the intellectual peers of men. I'd say your crowd is moving like a rocket ship right now." So would I.

Out-of-Fashion Names

We talk sometimes about the slipping in popularity of girls' names—Maude, Ethel, Louise, Eunice, Myra, Shirley, Grace, replaced, it seems, by Robin, Tiffany, Erica, April, Courtney, Taffy (*Taffy!*). Susan is still hanging in there. It's equal-opportunity. Wilbur, Booker, Horace, Herbert, Abner, Chester, Willard aren't showing up much either even if a man is named one of those and has a sizable estate to pass along to a namesake. My godchild is named Helen for me but has named *her* girlchild Bridget. Is my godchild still getting the jewelry? I have to think. Actually the Kathryns of this world—and Katherines, Catherines, and Cathryns—are getting to be a pain. I write lots of notes, if only to enclose with prezzies, and never know whether it's Dear Kathy, Kathie, Cathie, or Cathy. I've taken to calling them all "honeybunch" in writing. Simpler than trying to develop a computer brain *now*.

Words We Don't Use

I'm not talking about big words we don't use, like *propinquity, avuncular, meritorious, antediluvian* . . . too much work to get your mouth round them . . . but out-of-date common words like *traipsed*—she traipsed all over town—*chortle, snazzy, flustered, blustering, blaze.* Words go out of style just like eye shadow (have you really used turquoise lately?). Sometimes they come back in. I'm crazy about *tacky, cuckoo, deranged, sappy, spiffy,* and *daffy,* use them all the time. My favorite word is *pippypoo;* next favorite, *indigenous.*

Ultimate Arrogance

You think *your* smells—urine, perspiration, feces, menstrual fluid—are, if not Magie Noir, at least acceptable, but other people's are *not* . . . their smells are smelly. Actually *all* smells are okay. Smells can't help it if their DNA, especially in a hot spell, dictates sulphurous, rancid, gaseous, fetid. If smells were people and had noses, they'd probably think *we* smell funny.

Awful Women

I was guilty of man-bashing in *Cosmo* for years. Not criminal or unrelenting bashing (we mostly loved men) but enough so that the bashee could certainly tell he *had* been, having been called cheap, withholding, controlling, and mushy—men who let their children run them instead of their darling new wives—us! Bryant Gumbel took me on about this once and I confessed, pointing out that right after the bashing we always said, irritated though we were, that we couldn't get along *without* his sex for fifteen *minutes*, fifteen days, let alone longer.

What comes up and grabs me sometimes and chokes the breath way like a mongoose with its jaws around a cobra (you like that simile?), is the realization of how totally terrible *women* are. We great feminists, particularly magazine editors, forget to bash the other side. J., the eminence gris of a big publishing company—for years all editors reported to him or at least had to show him their articles and transparencies before publication so he could critique and make changes—was widowed, a semi-invalid, married to an attractive, but by all accounts, *criminally* possessive young woman. On their way to Mustique for the holidays, J. wanted to bring his nurse—a large loving black woman—along to look after him. "She's not coming and *I* will look after you," stated the bride. Bride looked after husband by showing up for every breakfast, lunch, tea, and dinner the couple was invited to, thanks to J.'s eminence and popularity, leaving her husband with a tray in his room and long tedious stretches of alone-time. Bitch.

I can offer two dozen other bitch stories if you're interested. Alicia makes her husband's life a G.I. series by declaring their older, gifted son Jason is *hers* . . . "he's Dad and Uncle Owen all in one package," allotting to her mate the limited younger one who doesn't know a modem from a CD-ROM and prefers his baseball cards to conversation. "Look what your son is doing *now*!" Alicia hisses as Junior scoops up most of the cracked crab meat for dinner for six and "her" son takes off for a Mensa meeting.

Men are victimized by bad women as women are by bad men, would you agree, you just don't hear about it, I'm convinced, because men's magazines deal with sex, not the emotional lives, of their readers, whereas women's magazines deal with both. Is it time for *Esquire, GQ, Playboy* to get busy and girl-bash a little? I know so many deserving candidates.

Truths

Everyone has a book in him, but no publisher is waiting to get it out of him nor a ghostwriter perishing to ghost, you have to get the book out of yourself.

There is no better treasure than a husband who cherishes you. Cherishing includes encouraging you to use your gifts.

When you climb trees (literally) after you are grown up, the joy of childhood does *not* come up and smack you.

Trying to appreciate deeply something good you have done is tough; to you, you are the same old so-so person.

Nothing tastes as good as dessert when you're dieting except brie and sourdough bread, industrial-strength chili, and nearly everything else not on your diet.

Ice cream is craved wantonly by others than serious nutcases.

Not having a good mother is one of life's tragedies. The price of *having* one is that she is often just as aggravating as the other kind.

There is no free lunch except those cadged by people who denigrate *your* working your tail off but are happy to have you pick up every tab.

A best girlfriend is like Mentholatum . . . inexpensive . . . nobody is trying to get it (her) away from you, soothing on nearly all occasions.

A best girlfriend is somebody you never have to lie to except about her husband or her boyfriend.

There is nothing like the welcome you get in a great European hotel when you have overtipped the last time, (mercifully, many employees stay put in their jobs).

A dentist who has never screwed up in your mouth is worth never having a date on New Year's Eve again.

You can't rekindle the honeymoon flame again when married unless you have been apart for several weeks. As soon as you get together again, are cozy and comfortable, the flame will start flickering.

For some of us there are no good hair days. We don't have the hair for it.

You can't find the fountain of youth with a face-lift, but you may run into a tiny gurgle.

Love pain is not just different from others but possibly the worst.

People who never acknowledge being jealous are just asking to go home and get sick.

When you live totally for somebody else, that person usually wants somebody else.

Sneezing and rice pudding are two of the best things there are.

Trying to get a woman out of her panty hose is about as sexy as trying to remove the skin of a sausage.

Marriage is an arrangement in which two people will argue forever about whether the air conditioner should be on or off. It will not be an equal-opportunity situation. The *on*'s will always win.

People who don't suffer from depression haven't a clue what it's like and should stop being so patronizing. People who suffer should go get help before they bore, irritate, and aggravate their loved ones into a criminal act.

Asking which is better, a strong masculine man who doesn't talk much or seem to feel much but is great in life's crises, or a sensitive, perceptive one who understands the real you but caves in a crunch is like comparing a pine tree with a chocolate chip cookie. They don't compare.

In any good restaurant there is a Siberia you may be taken to. Pique is not appropriate. If you were the restaurant owner, *you* would give the best location to *your* regular customers.

The greatest inconsistency in the human condition is how a woman feels about her looks. One day she hates them . . . really seriously hates them, next day she thinks she looks okay. Nothing has changed except maybe he finally called and she got a good night's sleep.

Never sleep with anybody who has less money or more trouble than you (old Hollywood adage).

Don't expect anything good from a male person who addresses you as Madam.

The minute a love object starts cherishing you less, you will cherish him more, possibly to the point of mania and obsession. A loved one who is loving you less and causing you pain will eventually get tiresome, however, i.e., you can't take it anymore and will leave. Eventually you will be pain free and he may even become the one who loves more.

Avignon has the best soft summer sexy air there is . . . air that won't let you be unhappy in it, air that says I am here to smooth out your brain, rest your soul, caress and love you.

The longest day is the sixth day of your diet.

If a man is cheating on you, the best thing to do is cheat on him but don't tell him. Gives life a whole new perspective.

Never assume when you come out of a building and see a taxi cruising by that there will be another one soon. The one you let glide by will be the last one for twenty minutes.

The worst thing a man can say to a woman is I'll call you and he doesn't.

What Texans say (good) about Texas is almost true.

Black

A good-looking black man told me once how much he resented his blackness . . . "big turn-off to women," he said. "It isn't fair!" As I often suggest to people who get handed something they don't need, ask for, or deserve, "We aren't dealing with fair." If all prejudice is ugly, this one seems somehow special for being based on something as banal and simplistic as color. In Little Rock, where I grew up, in the late twenties, black people got lynched. A black man who lifted his eyes from the ground to look straight at or into the eyes of a white woman could get arrested—and that was just the beginning. Raised like every other child in my town and in my time to consider "darkies" as some kind of lesser beings, I came around pretty well. At integrated John H. Francis Polytechnic High School in Los Angeles (where we moved), I actually danced with black boys and we got to be friends. Not bad for a carefully taught, mildly brainwashed seventeen-year-old twit! In New York for my last thirteen years as *Cosmo* editor one of my two personal assistants was black, and I like to think Ramona and I are sisters—I hope she feels the same way. I believe we should continue affirmative action even if we are occasionally into reverse discrimination. We've got a lot to make up for. You do remember that, unlike the Irish, Chinese, Italians—other transplants who may have had a rough time in their new country—blacks never asked to come here. Manacled in the holds of slave ships, they were plopped ashore without consultation. I'd say the woods are still dark and deep. Educational help for young and not-young black children is crucial and reasonable; education for *anybody* is a good investment. In my lifetime I'm certain black isn't going to look black, as in "you're a different color from me." On greeting such a person, he or she won't seem any more different than somebody whose skin is brown, sallow, rosy-pink from booze, pale, sunburned, etc. You won't immediately think "aha—black!" And that will be "aha—*good!*"

The Art of Seduction

Dictionary definition: to lead astray, persuade to do something disloyal, disobedient, offer a bribe, tempt to evil or wrongdoing, persuade to engage in unlawful sexual intercourse, induce to give up chastity. I don't think seduction is that. I think it's simply what you do when you squizzle into somebody's brain and untie his defenses to get him to do a specific thing you need or possibly just get him to like you and be your friend. I seduce all day long on the telephone, with head waiters, salespeople, the super, employees. To say he or she is seductive just means to me that person has charm, can talk you *into* things—a form of salesmanship. *Everybody* ought to be good at it. You seduce unconsciously, because of your *need*, with compliments, hard-core listening, appreciation of what has just been told you . . . with your whole *being*. Entertainers, actresses, singers all seduce. Sherry Lansing, the head of production at Paramount, and *60 Minutes* star Mike Wallace are the two most seductive people I know . . . deadly vicious *good* at it.

Cheating Low Grade

How much would you cheat if you got a real great cheating opportunity? Don't go sanctimonious on me, we all have a threshold. Okay, you don't want to talk about *yours* so we'll talk about mine . . . it's low. When I was handling petty cash for my boss, Don Belding, at his ad

agency, Foote, Cone & Belding, at age twenty-six I charged him twice
for a dry-cleaning pickup. "I thought we paid for that suit," he said.
"No," I said, "we didn't." He gave me the money a second time but that
was too close a call so I didn't cheat anymore with Mr. Belding's petty
cash, though I don't remember his giving me very much after that. He
knew the truth I think, though he never let knowing get in the way of
his and Alice treating me like a daughter. Maybe he figured a daughter
would have cheated worse. In that same period I collected $17 from a
business sorority sister for lunch at Scandia and never turned her
money in to the club treasurer; Yvonne must have been so swamped
with who had and hadn't paid—I had for *me* but not the sister—she
simply adjusted her bookkeeping. Not now but in olden days, before
Cosmo, I cheated . . . low grade . . . on expense accounts, substituted
the name of somebody I should have taken to lunch—client, model's
representative—for somebody I *did*—personal friend, visitor from Arkansas—or claimed some lunch person was helpful to the ad agency
who wasn't. Sheer awfulness for somebody who made as much money
as I and wasn't a poor girl anymore. I moved bond paper and paper
clips from office to home, not that I didn't use them for work going
back to the office but still, how can you have such a cheating heart
when the need isn't there?

I think cheating is kind of *in* you, born perhaps of perceived need
at a particular time, utterly inappropriate now. David hasn't got any
cheating *in* him, no cheating threshold whatever. He returns restaurant check-room stubs, hostesses' cocktail napkins carried off in his
pocket, doesn't take business deductions for nonbusiness lunches
though it would be easy. All those years at Twentieth Century Fox,
he never filled up his Chrysler 300 *once* with gas from the pump on
the back lot.

Roberta Ashley, *Cosmo's* executive editor, was another one. For
years she turned in *accurate* expense accounts—$11.65, $6.20,
$15.27, exactly what she spent for taxis, magazines—she gave the rest
of us a bad name. I guess you think it's the principle that counts . . .
that the first little dishonest dabble is as bad as *big* dabbles. I don't.
Not cheating at all would be best, of course—like David and Bobbie—
but I don't think a *little* cheating is so terrible. Big-time is something
else. A *Cosmo* art director stole a vicuña coat from a photography session for his lover. Didn't help . . . romance busted anyway. I would
consider that big-time. I'm glad I gave up the dabbles. I've got about
all the paper clips and bond paper at home I can use. Our beloved,

now gone, accountant, Red Meyer, who was *almost* as cheap as I, always said, "When you get red in the face, *stop!*" Excellent advice. Any cheater knows just what he means and does the cutoff on time.

I Don't Like

Being handed one snapshot at a time with explanation of each by "photographer." Just give me the pack and I'll go through it, thank you.

People who can't give the captain the order because they're still *deciding* (is this their last meal *ever* in a restaurant or what?).

Weather reports for the whole country. Even for your section you can't tell what it is till the local newsman finally comes on and tells you about *your* neighborhood, thanks.

Snippy secretaries—actually snippy *anything*. Any snip is a person of low self-esteem who is taking it out on *you*.

People who don't like people to say have a nice (happy) day . . . What are you supposed to say . . . I hope you fall into a manhole? Get stuck between floors in the elevator?

Pants. It's personal. I don't look nice in them. Shorts are okay. Skirts are best.

Phone menus. I never know my party's extension to punch in, can't spell his last name—is it W-E-I or W-I-E?—if that's how you're supposed to locate him. Lincoln Center will let you stay on the line twenty minutes registering options, none of which will be Lost and Found so you can learn whether they came up with your sapphire earring left under the table at a gala in Avery Fisher Hall the night before. Oh, to bring back real live people answerers.

Waiting in doctors' offices. I don't do it much anymore—have everybody pretty well trained—but recently a new doctor kept me waiting thirty minutes. When she finally got her beautiful ass out to collect me—she hadn't been doing surgery or anything dramatic—I said, "Doctor, I have an hourly rate. If you want me to wait in your reception room thirty minutes, fine, let me know and I'll be happy to send you a bill."

Everything in Moderation

Everything in moderation, including moderation, is that a good idea? I don't think so. Overdoing it . . . going till you're cuckoo . . . is my idea of good. You have to pick your arenas. Loving a man, babying friends, plowing "too much" into work are my arenas. No matter how late or how exhausted he is, Woody Allen practices his clarinet every day. In a hotel room where he can't make any noise, he's under the covers practicing. Sounds sensible to *me*. Moderation is for people who think you don't have to exercise Thursday through Friday because you did it Saturday and Sunday, who don't write love notes more than once a year lest the loved one get the idea you're stuck on them, who never screamed at a New York cab driver or ate a tray of fresh oatmeal cookies all alone. Boring, these people!

Lunch-Confirming Cheer

I've decided it's okay to call the person you've made a lunch date with two or three weeks ago the day *before* the lunch to confirm without feeling you are registering anxious, insecure, the lesser of the lunchers. What you are registering is organized . . . one of the thrillingest qualities one person can run into in another. You might have preferred your date call *you* a day early to confirm but you can live with your jumpiness for this okay cause.

Guardian Angels

You hear a lot about angels these days, the notoriety helped along by the durable CBS television show *Touched by an Angel*. I've always thought of angels as charming child-brained creatures tooling around heaven with their floaty gowns—if you believe in things like heaven or even if you don't. A facsimile of one, in its little gossamer dress, wings all fluffed out, may perch atop the Christmas tree of even a nonbeliever, but plenty of people actually think angels exist right here among us or can easily be summoned from wherever they hang out if help is needed with special situations.

My friend Clarissa summons her angel, "she's my best friend," all the time. Best friend recently helped Clarissa lift a solid oak table a few inches off the floor, Clarissa flat on her back under it, so her ten-year-old son could scooch the new rug underneath. Angel, Clarissa said, kept her from throwing out her back or kid from screwing up . . . everybody performed. I think people believe in angels perhaps because they've got to believe in something bigger than themselves and can't go all the way to God. I also observe angel-believing frequently accompanies astrology-believing, another "unfathomable" for me. I surely could use a G. Angel sometimes but have no doubt she would be ineffectual or not get her heavenly ass to the scene on time, just like the air conditioner repair people don't show when the A.C. has blimped and it's 106, or you break one of your capped teeth on an ear of corn and it's Sunday. I guess I'll just keep hacking away at life's nuisances on my own.

Slightly Mad—Them

David and I were talking about our friend Laura (not her real name) last night, an elegant, tiny Chinese lady we've known for many years. Out of the old blue David said, "Do you think Laura is just slightly mad?" "Yes, oh yes!" I cry. "Of *course* she is," grateful to the core that my husband has, with one simple question, finally explained Laura to me. "She is not totally bonkers, just a tiny fringe case," I add. David agrees. Laura believes her ancestors speak to her from heaven and direct her life, that a lack of personal cleanliness is next in badness to ripping wings off butterflies or to a deranged person toting an assault weapon to McDonald's and wiping out fifteen people, possibly worse.

Laura says the capitalist system mercilessly exploits workers (unlike in Beijing, Laura?), that milk is dangerous, cats are psychically advantaged (I might have known there'd be cats in there somewhere).

Having got Laura safely tucked into her minimadness niche, I tossed a few others in there with her without even asking David. There is Cory in my office who chatters like a cheetah (thank you,

Doctor Dolittle). "Cory, cut to the chase," you are always saying, and Cory gives you the fifteen-minute instead of the twenty-minute version. Office mates have said Cory cannot *think* unless her mouth is open (even then there is doubt). Mildly mad. Stewart, a seventy-five-year-old shamelessly-rich-from-derivatives Wall Street player seriously believes his twenty-nine-year-old ballerina girlfriend loves him for himself alone, the floor-length Crown Russian sable and BMW that came on her birthday have nothing to do with the girl's ardor . . . "she *loves* me, she *loves* me!" Dear Stu. There is the movie executive who got 100 million cashing in his stock when the company was sold and is waiting to be tapped again as a CEO. Bert is seventy. Bettina says they haven't made a really tasteful movie since 1950. *Sense and Sensibility*, Bettina? "Pretentious." *Age of Innocence*? "Not true to Wharton." Bettina has seen *The Secret Garden* 275 times. Listen, once you realize some of your friends are just a *little* around the bend . . . say, rounding the clubhouse turn . . . it gets so much easier to accept their annoying statements. You are almost doing them a favor to get them classified, so you can get on with your life. I can participate, too. This weekend I'm planning to coat all the glass fruit in an urn in the dining room with colorless nail polish . . . shouldn't take more than two hours and will make them easier to dust. After that I'm alphabetizing the spice rack.

Who Eats What or Whom

Wolves eat live buffalo. With great persistence a wolf pack manages to isolate one buffalo, get him rolled over, horns tucked out of the way, and start nibbling. I've heard some horrifying nature stuff before (wild dogs with zebra are monstrous) but this is the horrifyingest I can remember . . . eating something while it's still living. PBS nature commentator, knowing I was going to feel this way, said don't be too hard on the wolf, it doesn't have any claws to actually rip open its prey, all it can do is push it down and start gnawing, well-endowed in the tooth department (as in fangs). When the buffalo is weak enough, a lot of him no longer there, he will cooperate and die.

In my dating years, aggressive men were called wolves. I think that was too strong an appellation even for the worst, and I'm glad we've stopped calling them that. In the lion world females kill, males show up at chow time. How did the girls get themselves into such a silly position? Perhaps a little matter of otherwise they would starve. Though I think human males and females are very much alike in capabilities and accomplishments as well as emotional twins, I've often noticed woman *work* harder, at least in offices. Maybe it's that way with lions. For wolves it's equal opportunity.

Staying out of Siberia or Getting the Table at All

Headwaiters in great restaurants are not susceptible to girlish charm accompanied by dire need . . . you've got to have the table for your boyfriend's birthday or, please, not this table out by the kitchen . . . my client will *sneer*! Headwaiters are susceptible to money, usually proffered by (male) patrons who have been there (often) previously. Female money brings susceptibility also, but we tend not to deal with much of that when young, it doesn't arrive, if at all, until older. I still feel uneasy with a headwaiter in places I've never been. I *know* I'm going to be seated outside the good area and there *is* a good area in every restaurant, don't give me that old democracy bit.

Somebody once told me any part of the restaurant *he* was in automatically became the good area. Bullshit! Even if Michael Eisner and Alan Greenspan feel that way—and I don't know whether they do or not—every restaurant has a Siberia and I know when I'm *in* it. Headwaiters are metal pipes—unmoved, unshakable by needy young females who don't know the score or older dumb ones who also don't. If your livelihood depends on tips, are you going to succumb to sob stories from nymphs or take care of your good patrons? I forgive them but I only got philosophical when I started giving advertising lunches, company paid for, and gained a little clout. If I were doing my own tipping, I'd probably be back in Siberia but David could send care packages from the front. We *know* about his tipping.

Not in the Top Ten, but Satisfying

Doesn't have to be a big item. Finding almost anything lost—scissors, aubergine panty hose, alarm clock—will do. The finding joy is almost worth the pain of loss. Last week I searched house, office, car—even went back to the office at midnight after I'd come home— looking for Tiffany gold link bracelet . . . semibiggie loss. You look places you haven't *been*—behind shoe boxes in the closet, between cushions of a couch you haven't sat on, under the sink. The bracelet turned up caught in a heavy gold chain belt I'd already tucked back into its flannel bag and returned to closet. The two got caught together when I'd removed both in downstairs hall and thrown them into my Vuitton tote to take upstairs. More joy: Donna Karan fringed shawl left in a restaurant booth came home thanks to a super captain. Captain, shawl, and I all hugged when I went for retrieval. Same week: sable lipstick brush (expensive!) Susie thought she'd returned still in her desk, black cashmere beret, worn on snowy day, surfaced when we cleaned under the couch. I don't *think* I lose the stuff for a cheap thrill when we reunite, but possible.

I think *all* the things we've lost are out there somewhere waiting to be reunited with us, don't you? Some day we'll all be together. I remember and mourn each dear one no matter how long gone . . . the exquisite (and insanely expensive) David Webb brooch I left in a taxi in San Francisco, the cuff links made from antique French bath fixtures that said *froid* and *chaud* on either side that somehow fell out of their cuffs, *six* eighteen-karat gold charms that one by one escaped a charm bracelet, the Patek Phillipe wristwatch that went bye-bye in the elevator of Bullock's Wilshire, at least six *good* writing pens, including two from Cartier, that now write for new owners, and on it goes. I believe the lost ones are in a little velvet-lined case up in heaven telling each other, "Mommy is going to be up here one day, who knows how soon, and we'll have a lovely celebration." It could be a reason to *believe* in heaven.

P.S. The amount of time you spend looking for and anguishing over something lost has only 6 percent relationship with the intrinsic value of whatever you lost . . . losing is *everything*.

Virginity

Losing things . . . what about virginity? Virginity was a very big deal when I was a girl. Simple: You kept it till you got married. Simple *idea* perhaps, but the keeping wasn't so simple. I've written elsewhere of the breathtaking escapes from auto, couch, hammock, front porch, back bedroom, tent pitched on the beach. Having begun to date at sixteen, I "surrendered" at twenty—quite a long time in there to experience the steamy, delicious, satisfying struggles one shamelessly "endured." I was never close to rape *or* caving voluntarily. At that time, young men knew the rules and frequently played by them. The nice young man with whom I finally committed "the act"—then an employee at a shipbuilding plant, later a second lieutenant in the Air Force in World War II—had been my beau for over two years, putting up graciously with Never Getting There (I didn't know what a penis looked like, had never seen one, was easily brought to orgasm by somebody not doing a great deal—let's don't elaborate).

The denouement came one Sunday afternoon when we had been at the beach all day and were back at his apartment taking showers. I'd been there a hundred times before but, for whatever reason, this was *it!* Deflowering didn't hurt, I didn't bleed, I had an orgasm. The next day this thoughtful person brought me gold earrings from Brock and Company, a spiffy Los Angeles jewelry store. Sweet. After he went in the service, I visited him at basic training at March Field, saw him in Los Angeles on leave—he eventually flew over one hundred missions—but we drifted. When the war ended, he married a Chicago girl, hurting Cleo deeply not only because this might be her daughter's (an aged twenty-two) Very Last Chance, but the man was a prince—we all knew that.

When he brought my sister Danny Kaye records, he would sing, at her request, "I'm Anatole of Paris" along with Danny. One year he created Helen's Day so I could have prezzies just like a mother on Mother's Day—baby blue cashmere sweater, Chanel No. 5 cologne, eighteen-karat-gold ankle bracelet (engraved R to H), framed photograph of himself he said I should look at the back of someday. "Dearest Helen Marie, you are my beloved forever," it said. Alas, I was never in love with him—loved being adored.

One year we saw each other in Chicago for a couple of hours when I was on my way from Los Angeles to New York as a member of *Glamour* magazine's career council. His wife, a perfectly nice girl he seemed proud of, joined us. I felt nothing; nor, I'm sure, did he. After *my* marriage we talked just once on the phone. Was he really the first, he wanted to know? Yes, dear. Did my husband really make all that money from *Jaws*? Yes again, dear . . . sorry (not what he wanted to hear, I'm sure). I couldn't have had a lovelier friend with whom to lose the priceless—considered so at the time, at least—possession. I can't get a number for him from the Chicago operator but I hope he's well . . . don't need him going bye-bye.

Loaded

Want to meet someone who has everything? Me! The reason I have everything is because I never use anything up, wear it out, throw it away . . . we're talking mounds, baskets, bags, cascades, jumbles, junk piles of lipstick, shampoo, thread, elastic, paper clips, paper written only on one side, and all those shoes; bathroom soap dish is a mess of slivers that still have some good in them. Of course, except for the soap, I can't *find* anything when it's needed though I know it's in there somewhere. In an emergency I may even have to go to the store; you can spend just so many hours and days looking for an emery board. Hoarding makes me feel good like the Thing in Franz Kafka's novel, *The Castle*, who stockpiled *everything*. I hope not to wind up destroyed like the Thing who was protecting his turf when a predator crushed him *and* the castle. Every so often I give something away though it doesn't always bring cheers from the receiver. Half-used lipsticks aren't big life lighter-uppers.

Helen's Laws

The later you are starting out for a lunch or dinner date the more snarled the traffic will be.

A straight pin lost in a shag carpet will be found by somebody's foot (probably yours) sans shoes or socks.

Two weeks into your diet a restaurant that never gave you a free potato chip before will send over chocolate banana cream pie swimming in raspberry sauce, chef's compliments.

The nearer the center of the row you are seated at the theater before curtain, the more likely you are to develop a need to go to the bathroom.

After buying an umbrella on the street corner (and you have five at home), the rain will stop.

The rose you decide to pluck unobtrusively from the banquet-table bouquet will be anchored in the bowl like a palm tree in the desert.

When somebody you don't want to have lunch with in the first place cancels, you will feel hurt and annoyed rather than grateful.

Lunch is generally cancelled by the person you were dying to lunch with, not by the one with whom you hoped it wouldn't happen.

By the time you figure out that exercise won't actually flatten your stomach, only serious dieting will, you have already exercised your brains out *and* heavy-dieted and are so old that your stomach is indeed flat but your face now looks like a Weimaraner.

Like diamonds and rhinestones, sometimes you can't tell real friends from false. They look alike and perform many of the same functions. Rhinestones sparkle and dazzle just fine . . . fake friends lunch with you, laugh with you, even listen to you talk (really listen) but take rhinestones to the jeweler and you can't get money. Take faux friends to a crisis and you can't get help.

Taking Back Stuff

Although I've done my share of resisting what never should have been said yes to (the chartreuse feather boa, doormat shaped like an armadillo, twelve criminally priced salad forks) in the first place, I've also given in too much, and back the indulgence had to go. The very prospect of facing the salesclerk with the cassette player, suede skirt, peach cashmere twinset (no, you don't want to exchange, you've changed your mind *altogether*) can mess up your sleep. Why the "dreads"? Dreading returning is deep in the warp and woof of me, settling there after many an unpleasant take-back early in life.

   In young skimpy days I returned often and mercilessly, usually having *worn* the merchandise first. There was the silver fox stole foisted back on J. W. Robinson after going to a party with me the night

before. "Don't you want to pick out something else?" icy Mr. Kleinschmidt inquired (he'd had my kind before). "No," I said, "I've decided
against fur." This was long before the "people in fur have to be *creepy*"
era. The store took Wolfgang back and Mr. Kleinschmidt couldn't
have felt *much* worse than I did. Wolfgang and I had bonded, I was
just over the moon a bit with impulse buying—Wolfie had to go.

In the same era was the taffeta and velvet cloche to resettle at
the Broadway Department Store. Darling little Lily Daché lookalike
had even got caught in the rain Easter Sunday on its maiden (and
only) voyage but back it went—you can't have *shame* in these situations. Saleslady made Mr. Kleinschmidt look *friendly*, but she took
back the hat, smoothing its little feathers and muttering as she wrote
the return slip. Broadway Department Store later went broke (too
many take-backs?), Robinson's still there.

Returns and replacements can still use up happiness, though easier than in olden days if you're willing to pay $5.00 pickup charge
after telephoning. Catalogs are required by law to give refunds and
honorable, but one can still get into trouble. Right this minute
there's this miserable plant—it cost $389.00—I'm trying to give back
to the Almizurian Nursery in Brooklyn and they aren't responding
well. All its leaves have turned crispy brown in just two months due
to nothing we did or didn't do to it. Nursery "having trouble finding
a replacement"—I can imagine. I took pictures of the plant, sent
with several crispy-brown leaves to Almizurian. Things may move
along a little faster now that I've agreed to pay $100.00 for delivery
of a new plant. Of *course* I shouldn't have to but do I want a new
green plant or *what?* This send-back has ruined several days.

All during plant-exchange I have also been trying to get Mr. J. of the
Carpet Company to come pick up the goddamn Pakistani rug in my
front hall they were supposed to refringe in the carpet's native land
and I paid the delivery people $2,321.00 when it was returned *without*
fringe—sealed-up carpet hadn't been opened when check was given
out. History: rather than go for domestic-fringe replacement that
would have looked a little chalky-white, Mr. J. had convinced me to go
all the way with proper fringing in Karachi, so the carpet got on a boat
and went back "home." Two months later, "fixed" carpet returned, delivered when I'm not home, housekeeper gives delivery man our
check, carpet *then* unfurled and the bare unfringed places still as bare
as Daddy Warbucks' forehead, old fringe in the *not*-bare places carefully cleaned and tied together in proper tufts. Mr. J. and I have been

"missing each other" for the same length of time nursery hasn't been able to find replacement plant.

Finally, having explained Karachi position to me, i.e., since this is antique carpet that never had much fringe to begin with, workmen left it that way, and I have explained client's position to Mr. J., i.e., that he could have told me in the first place I was paying $2,321.00 for cleaning and reorganizing present skimpy fringe, Daddy Warbucks forehead condition would remain after rug came back from homeland and mon Dieu, I would have skipped the whole *thing*, Mr. J. has said he will pick up the carpet again and go for refringing. He did. Agonizing *hours* were spent on this project.

Okay, the rug and hundreds of dreaded confrontations are history but you never get *good* at returning, comfortable *with* it or stop doing it. My beloved assistant, Susie Schreibman, bears most of the brunt of mine. In the fifteen years Susie and I have been together, she has yet to say anything snippy like "Are you *sure* you want twenty-four pale blue candles two and a half inches in diameter, three inches high that smell like lavender" before setting out to try to *find* them, knowing they may be storeward bound mere days later if the lavender doesn't smell lavendery enough. Now the dread of burdening the store, the nursery, the carpet company, the whoever with the return is almost matched by the dread of telling Susie what's *up*. I'll let her leave at 4:00 P.M. Fridays this summer instead of 5:30 to get a head start on the ferry traffic to Fire Island where she and friends have a house. Is that an okay trade-off?

Why Don't You (I've Done All of These) . . .

Sit next to a TWA pilot deadheading from Los Angeles to Memphis and go to bed with him that night.

Cut your own hair. Saves oceans of money. You can get the hang.

Bite into the small, hard cuticle growth caused by wearing too-tight shoes (not a corn) you've pried loose from your little toe. No taste whatever but somehow satisfying.

Tell a friend you've been giving more than you've been getting. (This may finish the friendship.)

Eat a pound of *very* cold not-quite-frozen dark chocolate at one sitting.

Ask a young man in a store on the Via Veneto if you can get on behind him on his motorcycle and ride around Rome for a little while. (My young man neatly leashed my packages to the bike and gave me a scrumptious city tour. Later he asked by letter if I could help him with a Thunderbird acquisition he had in mind. Alas, I couldn't.)

Have a stone oil massage.

Scrape raw veggies with a Chore Boy plastic sponge. Takes off rough spots, leaves skin and vitamins.

Dribble water on very stale bread, plop in toaster . . . freshens it right up.

Burn an evergreen-scented Rigaud candle on your desk *every* day. People will visit just to *sniff*.

Spread semen over your face, probably full of protein as sperm can eventually become babies. Makes a fine mask—and he'll be pleased.

Kneel down on the sidewalk and pet a nice doggie being walked by his owner. You have to get down all the way down there *with* him, *his* height, not just leaning over. With the pads of your fingers come up *under* his chin, stroke, stroke, then move to the top of his head. I've done this dozens of times and haven't had my arm bitten off *yet*.

Eat salad greens—or anything else—with your fingers. Tastes better from fingertips than with all that metal against your teeth.

Tell your secretary, housekeeper, hairdresser (even if you're cutting your own hair) you couldn't live without them totally . . . true in my case.

Marriages of Convenience

All marriages that last are of convenience, aren't they? More convenient to stay married than split. Lots of *kinds* of convenience. Convenient that a wife has made a lot of money and you can finally afford the beachfront property; wouldn't want to split *now*. Convenient when families are entwined like roots of a juniper . . . you'd be divorcing an *army* (it's the European way . . . marriages stay, mistresses go bye-bye). Certainly it is "convenient" to have two original parents raising the kids rather than everybody streaking around town picking up, delivering, arranging sleepovers per the custody agreement. It's convenient (and cozy) to share life with somebody who agrees with you a lot—vacation destinations, when to order in Chinese instead of barbecue on the patio, when to fire the contractor because he stiffed you. The convenience subject came up because somebody said, during the last election, Bob Dole's marriage was one of convenience. I said I certainly hoped so and I also think they love each other. When Elizabeth visited *Cosmo,* she told us you hadn't seen courage until you watched Bob Dole try to open a milk carton (with his crippled hand). You could tell she liked him—a lot—*and* their convenient marriage.

What You Find When You Shouldn't Be Looking

A friend of mine was straightening out the wadded-up bills in her husband's pockets and found a condom. Of course she shouldn't have been in his pockets but, before finding the condom, she had smoothed out $500.00 in wadded-up bills and felt justified . . . wadded up bills make pants pockets bulgy. When Carol found the condom she *says* she said to herself, "Good for you, kiddo . . . go for it!"

These people are in their seventies. I wouldn't have reacted the same way. I would have gone for the evergreen adventurer with a hatchet.

Someday I Want . . .

To understand the exact meaning of the word *hubris* and use it in a sentence.

To see more crescent moons and full moons, and remember where I was when I saw them.

To understand the electoral college and capital gains tax . . . *finally*.

To have a concave tummy. Weighing 99 pounds hasn't done it.

Not to feel intimidated by Paris.

To tell a joke really well.

Not to shiver in nearly *all* air-conditioning. My blood will get thicker.

Never to use a four-letter word with David again *or* have him get used to my using them, whichever comes first.

Can We Get Any of These *Fixed?*

Sam, You Made the Speech Too Long

When lunch and dinner planners give out instructions to dais speakers—limit your remarks to three minutes, five minutes, twenty minutes—does *anybody* but me listen? Complying is so easy. Prepare remarks, time them with a stopwatch, cut speech to your allotted time or a few seconds less to allow for laughs (you hope). Nobody (but me) ever seems to think the instructions about length are for him or her. Participants write their little talk, like it—it was a lot of work—and nobody, by God, is going to keep them from going the distance. Can't they *tell* restless and bored as it floats up from the audience? Maybe they *can* but are powerless to cut one smidge from the talk once it's roaring down the track.

David and I recently left the funeral of a beloved man that was inching into the two-hour mark. Brothers, cousins, children all had a little something—or not so little—to say. We slunk out of the Cathedral of St. John the Divine along the far-right hand periphery so nobody noticed except the people we fell over squeezing out of the pew. At a charity dinner nonpaid entertainers recently did an hour at the Waldorf, I sent three bent teaspoons—bowl to handle—down to David in a napkin, bent teaspoons being a special signal to my beloved that I am freaking and we'd better get me out of there. This night the *"help"* was even clattering dishes.

Another famous singer recently hit the hour mark at a seventieth birthday party for a friend at the Plaza Hotel. Sunday night, for Pete's sake, and the clock is ticking toward 11:00 P.M. Even if he shut up that *minute*, you've got the emcee sign-off, good-byes to say, coats to pull out of the check room, taxis to catch, Monday to get ready for, and it'll be midnight when you get home. Is it just me? I don't think so. If a banquet, dinner, awards lunch, charity fund-raiser ever got out early, I'll bet people would cheer. You could walk, work, go to the gym, call your accountant, nap, shop, do errands, get on with your life. Is time *precious*? But I know nobody is going to get speakers to write a speech one minute shorter or, once started, get stopped by anything short of a freight train steaming into the Waldorf Astoria ballroom . . . it's their *moment*. If you want to come over to my office and have me help time your speech, I'd be glad to.

You Definitely Made the Funerals Too Long

Funerals are longer than anything. They're given, I guess, for the unbusy to hang out at the church for a few hours, snuggle down in their fur coats and feel sad and cozy . . . also, of course, for the grieving family who want Uncle Bertram and Papa Pepone to have a good send-off (Uncle and Papa don't *know* about the sending off but in respect to their memory). I've thought about bringing something to read but the light is never very good. As an attendee, I give funerals a good hour and a half and then I'm out of there. To do this you have to sit far enough back in the church to escape without fuss and on the far side of the pew. In cathedrals and big churches there's often a big outside aisle you can duck into. Isn't showing up more important to the family than *staying* through the whole ordeal even though you won't see them afterwards? I think so. A few weeks ago I went to a funeral (I told you about this) that is probably still going *on*. The man had five brothers who all spoke, along with several people from state and city government—he was a politician. I hope some over-the-top time-wise funeral-givers will come to my funeral so they will know how to do it. None of the speakers gets more than six minutes—I've written it down—five speakers tops. The plan will remove the horror for my leave-behinds of trying to get a bunch of famous people to say a few words. Like for everything else, celebrity participators are desired at funerals but my "helpers" won't have to scrounge for many—limited time allotment will cut the number needed.

Go Wash Up

Asians have a way of making me feel not sparkly clean. At the Grecian swimming pool on the twenty-fourth floor of the Mandarin Hotel in Hong Kong I start to slip into the pool, and attendant, politely but firmly, suggests "take shower before enter pool"; showers are right there at poolside. "I did that in my room," I explain. "Must take shower before going swimming pool," I am explained back. Oh well, you're going to get wet anyway but you wonder if you look smudgy or scaly or something to cause this man concern. Next morning, no attendant in sight, I start to enter the pool, am up to my waist when a Chinese gentleman already there interrupts his backstroke long enough to inform me, "Must shower before swim." Now I *know* I look smudgy.

Gosh, would the take-shower suggesters ever be busy at the Holiday Inns and Hiltons of North America if the shower edict were in place, not to mention the millions of gallons of water that would be pouring down. I remove myself from swimming pool and shower at the Mandarin . . . don't want to be thought ugly *dirty* American. Am I the only person anywhere who thinks maybe we take too *many* showers? They make your skin all puckery, hair coif squashed under shower cap. I'm for bidets, antiperspirant, cologne, and no extra shower to go swimming.

It's the Thought That Counts? Don't Be Ridiculous!

When they say that in their thank-you note, you've bombed. It is *never* the thought that counts, otherwise you could just ring up occasionally and say "thinking about you, darling, thinking about you" and skip the present or send a warm little *note* on present-day. The present *always* counts and what makes up for a poorly-picked-out present is having it come from a decent store so they can take it back and having it cost enough so taking back is worthwhile. I never do any of this myself, of course, so during the year I receive numerous "so wonderful you were thinking about me" notes. At least I know the score.

As for gifts given *me* through the years, editors are lavishly gifted because people want their wares featured in your magazine . . . sensible. I'm grateful for all the offerings—anal is anal—including the size 2 panties I couldn't get over my 36-inch hips, oceans of hair conditioner (not good for skimpy hair—bogs it down), three dozen or so visored caps, smashing on Steven Spielberg and Julia Roberts, but unflattering to *some* senior faces. I wasn't too thrilled with the cheesecake somebody sent up to my Radisson Hotel room in Minneapolis after hearing me say on television I love cheesecake. What to do but sit down right that minute and eat half of it . . . 2000 cals! I could have lived without a crate or two of books sent by both known and unknown senders, loving appreciation and excerpting in *Cosmo* clearly in mind. The book department took care of books for excerpting and, though I barely get through the main section of the *New York Times* every day (slow reader) I had to read at least the jacket copy to be able to write my "most interesting, thank you so much for thinking of me" letter. Lack of appreciation for the books me at my snippiest? Perhaps. I *know* what it means to get a book published—one of life's serious joys and, as they say, people *mean* well, but reading books aside from what I needed to read for work or chose to read from seeing reviewed in the *New York Times* took my time and energy. My idea of a great present? A bar of really *good* soap (always pleasant to use and better than you take home from the hotel room) or a pound of See's candy. Sold at LAX and SFO it's the best in the world. I can fearlessly do a calorie overlook for this treasure.

Lurking

Amy McCaw, makeup artist extraordinaire at CNN, threw a talent co-ordinator out of the makeup room the other day. He was lurking . . . standing in the door watching Amy work on a guest who was due on the set in six minutes. "Stop *lurking*," Amy commanded. "I can't concentrate."

Husbands lurk. You finally get them trained not to *hover* (six feet away, already in his evening clothes, the man is snapping, hissing, growling. "We're going to be late . . . Fifty-seventh Street is jammed . . . we should have left twenty minutes ago!" You aren't even into lashes, let alone a comb-out . . . you'll need another ten). The hoverer is immediate, up close, and verbal. Lurking is a little further back and quieter. I cured David of the hover, I think with trade-off: I would stop nagging him many times per weekend to throw out seven or eight pairs of scruffy shoes, ancient T-shirts, then start on the bookshelves (we have textbooks from his high school years, but "We don't throw away books in this house!") if he would quit hovering. Hover pretty much gone but replaced with the lurk. Lurk is navigated from a slightly greater distance somewhere across the room without words but you know he's there . . . leaning in the doorway . . . a malign presence you can see in the mirror. Did Picasso paint *Women of Algiers* with Jacqueline lurking? Does Wolfgang Puck bring off a grilled Cantonese duck with wild huckleberries, ginger, star anise, black pepper, and bok choy with Barbara hovering? How can you get anywhere near beautiful with a lurker lurking or a hoverer hovering? I'm sick of trying.

Just Real Good at One Thing

Sometimes people are brilliant at their specialty and total idiots about other people's world. That's basically okay . . . what I yapped about for years and years in *Cosmo* . . . do something the *best* and you will be recognized, rewarded, and that work will be your career . . . the passport to a good, even a great life. Still you could scream at even gifted people's limitations.

Somebody recently tried to explain to me the machinations of Wall Street news announcements so that I could suggest an online magazine for my company. He told me how reports come out of companies about new developments, the subsequent conference call, after the initial announcement, to banks, brokers, analysts, then information put on satellite for broader distribution, etc., etc., etc. Granted that I am close to hermetically sealed in terms of grasping financial information, the explanations to me were so confusing, convoluted, *pitiful* considering we were both speaking English I *think*. I was simply ready to kill him. I wasn't mad at *me* for being a financial Neanderthal, I was furious at *him* for being unable to communicate with me in simple terms. He was as bad at what *he* couldn't do well (explain simply) as I was at what he was explaining—finance. We *know* I would perish in his world . . . the sharks would have me for a snack. *He* would perish if required to put out a newsletter, let alone a magazine.

No Sense of Appropriateness

Everybody has his or her own celebrities . . . rock stars, movie stars, television newsmen. Lots of people would cross the street to see a Pope or President if he were over there and the police would let you near him (they mostly won't) but whatever your special category is I don't know many people who wouldn't let Paul Newman into theirs—a Good Guy in his personal life (donates millions to charity from his business enterprises), good to and still married to Joanne, splendid actor, elegant looking, never Too Big to fit into a chair at Rainbow and Stars to cheer Rosemary Clooney with the rest of us. I recently wrote him a letter praising *Twilight* plus sent him two good stories I'd heard I was pretty sure he hadn't. Tony Randall told them to me, if you don't mind a tiny name-drop, they were first rate. Paul's letter back said: Dear Helen, Thanks for the note and the encomium. I had heard the first one and will cherish the second. Thank David for his vote of confidence and especially that he took the time to write. Best, signed Paul. Then it said, "Dictated but not read." Is that secretary a sadist, an idiot, or *what*? Here I have this neat letter from my idol but they are all so pure over there they couldn't *pretend* he actually saw it and signed. I may take it with me someplace where I know he'll be and ask him for the signature.

Calling You at Work

There is no noncomprehension like the noncomprehension of a friend—usually a woman—who calls you at the office and chats chirpingly as though *you* had nothing to do because *she* has nothing to do. She isn't really mindless . . . you wouldn't have that kind of a friend. She just isn't as busy. *I've* sinned. Twice after surgery when I was home too zonky for the office, I bothered friends at work. *I* had the time, why wouldn't *they*? Busy doesn't mean you're more important than they are or more fully realized in any way but just that you have chosen to fit a lot into your life and aren't getting much of it done while they are phone-blabbing. It's the *timing*. Sometimes you can talk forever but do they ever ask is this a good time? Of course not! It's a good time for *them* and the idea it might not also be good for *you* isn't graspable. I can tell from the tone of somebody's voice, can't you, whether he is or isn't keen to chat. Oh

God, if there were just a few wonderful, intuitive, scared-shitless-to-bore-anybody people out there like you and me. As for getting free, "Could we chat later?" doesn't work for me. Later I'm going to be busier than ever . . . 5:30–7:30 P.M. are my peak work hours . . . so let's get it over with. I sacrificingly give the caller five minutes to babble, cursing and resenting every second. So when *is* this friend supposed to call? Any time she pleases with the understanding that at work she should keep it short. Funny, her calling may be the last vestige of discrimination. She wouldn't call a *man* at his office to carry on. You are woman and girlfriend, created for calling and talking to no matter when. I'm talking about women not in offices themselves, of course. Office women *get* it.

Cut-Offs for Phoners Who Won't Let Go

(COULD BE A MAN)

Saying you'll call later is fairly palatable to your caller but may not be what you want to do. You'll be just as busy (and he'll be just as boring) at 4:00 as at 11:00. The following cut-offs don't promise a reprise:

Jack, two people are tramping around here waiting for me to go to lunch. Guess I have to go.

Stacy, it's a little woofy around here today. I've been away for a week and they saved everything for me . . . guess I have to go.

Ginny, the air-conditioning people are finally here . . . yippee! I've waited three days. I'd better go talk to them.

The coup de grâce:

Claude, I'm so thrilled to hear from you and I'll very much look forward to our next chat (any perceptive person—not all are—will recognize this as a cut-off, conversation *over*). Variation: *Laura, you were darling to call. Don't ever stop doing that. Heaps of love. We'll talk soon.*

A woman I know tells a tiresome caller, "Excuse me, I'll be right back," puts the phone down, never returns, later hangs up. Detestable . . . she's worse than the caller! We must cushion and lie—never hurt feelings.

Avoiding a lunch date request, I'm sometimes tempted to use a cartoon caption I saw in the *New Yorker.* Man talking on phone:

"No, Thursday's out. How about never—is never good for you?" Is that seriously snotty? Yes, but I really *don't* lunch much and some people find that idea hard to get the hang of. Occasionally I get caught in a restaurant by somebody I've told I don't lunch. Well, there has to be an exception once in a while, yes? A good way not to make a date is to say "Hildy, I'll be in and out of the city a lot in the next few weeks, so let's don't plan anything now. We'll talk soon." Sometimes I wonder why anybody would want to have lunch with such a slippery person.

Gratitude and Revenge

Tony Bennett plays the Blue Note in New York, a small Greenwich Village nightclub that gives *unpretentious* new meaning. The Blue Note gave Tony his first chance to perform in New York and he never forgot. I feel Cindy Crawford could have kept gratitude in mind in turning *Cosmo* down for an and interview. She had been on the cover of *Cosmo* eight times, first as an unknown. Francesco Scavullo discovered her as he had other potential stars—Brooke Shields, Claudia Schiffer, Paulina, Carol Alt, Renee Russo—continuing to use her as she got more prominent. *Cosmo* also featured two of Cindy's exercise tapes in major photo layouts. Sold some tapes, didn't hurt us. During the time we wanted to talk to her, she gave interviews to several other magazines. I guess I don't get it with people who don't remember who was there for them first. After me boucoup-hassling her press agent . . . don't get me started on *them* . . . we finally got the interview, plus Cindy gave me a lip print when we saw each other in Moscow during the filming of *The Saint*. David produced and she was there visiting Val Kilmer. Cindy doesn't wear lipstick as a civilian but accommodated me by putting some on for *Cosmo*'s Kiss-of-the-Month beauty feature. Having got the interview and the lip print, would this now constitute evening things up? You would think so, but home from Russia, I gave my gossip columnist friend, Liz Smith, an item Cindy had told me at dinner—that Princess Di had invited her to tea in London with Princes William and Harry, who'd seen her photograph and asked Mommy to send out. Cute item. I hadn't given Lizzie anything for months and owed her. Cindy was furious. This tidbit was for Di to release or not as she wished, Cindy said. Absolutely right. If I hadn't still been pissed because twelve other magazines got an interview before us maybe I wouldn't have blabbed, or maybe I would have. You pick and choose whom to blab about and how much. I haven't a *bad* track record and Lizzie I owe *everything*. She's a loyal, never-fail friend.

Dental Manners

Do you feel rejected when your dentist wears a mask? I do. I haven't given anybody hepatitis lately that I know of and the mask distances us, seems unfriendly. After all the unspeakable things I've let this man do to me—gum surgery, wax impressions, inlays, caps, root canal—he could trust a little more. Let him wear his hit-squad paraphernalia with some of his other, possibly germy, patients. I'm pure.

I Don't Want to Hear

"You're looking at the glass half empty instead of half full" . . . what a ridiculous example of optimism! I'm supposed to be happy (relax, smell the flowers) because the glass still contains half its stuff? It also *doesn't* have half of it and is going to go down still further if you drink any or some of the contents evaporate from hot weather— i.e., life provides *further* mishaps. We half-empty people *know* we can't relax or the glass will get all the *way* empty pretty soon. Our viewpoint may be a little negative . . . glass only half full . . . but the viewpoint gives us the oomph to get out there and start filling up. Half-full is no condition for a glass to be in.

Change Is Exciting, Life-Freshening, Gets You Moving

I think "they" could show a little restraint when yapping about how change is good. *Some* change is good—trees bare and lonely in January coming back gorgeously green-leafed in May. A little- or *no*-sleeper starts logging seven hours a night (I never actually heard of anybody doing that but what a good idea). Fat to skinny . . . strike up the band. But lots of change is just plain crummy, why tell ourselves otherwise? Anybody over fifty knows the joylessness of eyesight going from twenty-twenty to twenty-eighty; I have to be nearly *under* the number 10 bus on Eighth Avenue to know whether to get on it—bus number is up over windshield. Upper arm puckers collect like a mess of tripe, tummies pooch beyond holding your breath doing any good whatsoever but we don't have to delineate just bad *physical* stuff. Recent outrage: my beloved *Reader's Digest* changed the type face and layouts to make the book jazzier and you can't *read* it. Instead of simple black type on white paper, you've got squirrelly print on tinted backgrounds, red lines, arrows and circles diverting attention from words, pippypoo sketches introducing articles. Tell me, *R.D.*, when did a quarter-inch line drawing of a Dalmatian, a gorilla, or a child in pigtails invite me *in*? The subject and the writing used to do it. I reel, I wince. After thirty-eight years of devoted readership (every *Cosmo* editor was given a subscription to the *Digest* by me to show them how effectively long articles could be condensed into smaller ones and still be terrific if the editing was good . . . the *Digest* crammed a lot *in* without ever seeming crowded) how could you do this to me? Yes, I know sales had slipped and they had to do *something*. How about freshening the content, trying some younger writers, jazzing up the look a *little* without going to tchotchke hell? I could never give up my beloved magazine, but I could *kill* you!

Compliments I Can Live Without

"You look very well," one of my closest friends said to me last night at dinner. Couldn't go all the way to *good* I guess . . . "you look *good*," let alone heavy duty "wonderful," "terrific," "fabulous." Her *husband* went all the way—"you look *great*," he said, and I liked his assessment better than her probably more accurate one. Girlfriends have said, "You look very well," to me before and I wish they would quit with the faint praise. Every girlfriend-meeting doesn't have to be a looks evaluation. If mine are barely getting by, why not wait until next time? Maybe things will have improved by then and you should speak right up! Liz Smith told me she told Cynthia McFadden the other night after they'd run into me at the theater, "Helen seems chipper." This is a compliment? Sounds to me like something you'd say about a ninety-five-year-old ex-postman who has limped down from the porch to go into town to the grocery store. My beloved pal Charlotte Veal recently told me, "Helen, you have become a very handsome woman." Carlotta, handsome is for *men*! If you can't come up with anything better I'd just skip the appraisal.

Freeloading

I never did anything *but* freeload as a young person and can't fault anybody else for taking advantage of older people willing to be exploited. As a child, adequately if somewhat thriftily fed at home, I accepted nearly all food offers, particularly from the parents of wealthy girlfriends. They even *liked* being taken advantage of, I always felt. Nobody stole the silver, I was lavish with compliments ("I never *saw* a crystal wall sconce before," "Ms. Phillips, I never tasted a pork chop that wasn't burned *up*!"), and just seeing this nice little person gobble it down was probably compensation enough, don't you think? I don't have to freeload anymore, haven't for quite some time, and don't even think it's a good idea now because, as somebody brilliantly said, there is no free lunch. If you keep eating off people (what a novel idea . . . their tummies? Chests?), they are apt to want something in return that costs a lot more than the beef tenderloin they put into you, i.e., invest in their limited partnership, give their children a job, introduce them to people you know they'd like to, etc., etc. It would be almost impossible for anybody to freeload at my *house* . . . we don't entertain much. David, far more generous and tolerant than I of the never-pay-backs, lets them do it in restaurants, never acknowledging they *are*, but he has to do it alone . . . I can't *stand* to sit there watching them wolf and reorder. I might take somebody to lunch I don't owe because I'm after an article from an in-demand writer but mostly the I'll-eat-you-pay crowd would find greener grass elsewhere. I don't think wanting reciprocity is a bad creed.

Some actors and others in show business are master-class free-loaders. They perform, light up our lives on stage, movie, and TV screens, why should they *pay*? An actor took David to dinner one night and ordered half a carafe of wine for the two of them, a salad with two forks. We've taken lots of show-business people to dinner and them I don't mind as *much*. A famous Broadway star suggested David and I have dinner with her and her husband, she asked *us*. We said fine. Nice girl . . . warm, amusing. At "21" we all ate every-thing that wasn't moving . . . drinks, three courses, wine, coffee. Nobody asked for the check so David finally did. There wasn't the slightest movement, let alone a scuffle on the part of our hosts to get the check away from him. Couple did send flowers. Funny. Flowers didn't cost as much as dinner but they were nice flowers and lots *of* them. I think it simply was their code . . . actors, performers do not *pay* for food, certainly not yours, but they will acknowledge you've done something nice for them—the ones with good manners at least.

There are of course nonfamous spongers also. The wife of a West Los Angeles friend of David's asked David's secretary for *years* to get Broadway theater tickets for her. Grace did. Wife had to pay for the tickets—there are no free theater tickets except for Tony voters and invited opening-night guests. Show producers and cast members are allotted a certain number of tickets to their shows—called house seats—but whoever uses them has to pay. After about five years of theater-ticket procuring, I once asked the wife if she ever did anything for Grace. "You mean get her a *present*?" my horrified friend wanted to know. "Yes," I said, "get her a present." Does anybody *know* what a service this is to have somebody whose office has influence fill all your theater requests, including for sold-out shows? Westwood lady did *not*. She was of the old that's-what-secretaries-*do*—help wealthy friend of their bosses get theater tickets—school.

There's also a crowd that is just as silly the other way—you can't pick up a check even if they have to pawn the silverware. I had lunch with one of those the other day. Forcibly retired from his job, he barely has money to pay maintenance for the flat, country house, and hourly perks for the family. He would *not* let me take the check even though I asked *him* to lunch. I explained that I could go right back to the office and put it on my expense account if I wanted to but, if I didn't, I was quite able to take a man, or an anybody, to lunch and was he crazy or something? We literally—arm-wrestling kind of thing—fought for the check. I asked a shrink about him later—she knows him. Why can't people be sensible? How can there *be* such silly pride at this stage of our lives . . . why not take me to lunch when he has another *job*, blah, blah, blah. Janet said, "They do that because they are fools." I liked that nice simple explanation so we didn't have to use up *my* forty-five-minute shrink hour trying to sort *him* out!

Advice—

Just a Tiny Touch

Just Do It

I don't know any way to get there except do it. The baby steps. The drudgery. Trying to get it right even if you're trying for people who may not know it when they see it and, if they see it and know it, won't necessarily thank you for it. At an early stage in life if they are bosses—and even later—I think you never tell them no if the request isn't something dishonorable. These are things I did when young that somebody asked and they didn't work out but at least I *tried*.

Age eighteen I went to the Los Angeles Public Library four Saturday afternoons in a row to research the years 1919, 1929, and 1935 for my boss, Stu Wilson, an announcer at radio station KHJ, who wanted to do a little preamble before playing songs from those years. He regularly paid me $5.00 a week to work two hours a day after school plus Saturday mornings, but for this special assignment I would get $5.00—a fortune! What the man needed were brief notes about a particular year—people jumping out of Wall Street windows in despair after the 1929 crash, bankers selling apples on street corners, a fashion trend or two, bootleg gin. What he got were pages of market news, the precipitous fall of rails and commodities, excerpts from Herbert Hoover speeches, a biography of Will Rogers, the material painstakingly recorded in my notebook, then typed back at the office. For the year 1919 Mr. Wilson was given enough World War I to start his own encyclopedia, which is where the information came from. In 1935 we were beginning to recover from the Depression. Instead of snippets, Mr. Wilson got sludge. So, though I had no idea how to research and condense, I was a big respecter of authority, especially authority with my paycheck; hiding wasn't an option. My boss resisted doing his own condensing, never could do his little preambles. I offered to return the $5.00. He gallantly refused.

A few years later I wrote a talk for my boss, Don Belding's, wife, Alice, to deliver at her garden club when she handed out prizes. At twenty-five I'd never written anything except letters, let alone a speech, and hardly knew a hollyhock from a hibiscus despite my small-town background—though flower expertise wasn't the point. Alice needed a friendly little intro . . . I gave her a self-conscious essay. She didn't say thank you. Maybe she felt I was lucky she didn't kill me.

Hemingway said, "Embrace what you fear." How could I have known to do that as a baby worker? I guess I feared getting fired or displeasing a boss or boss's wife more than embracing. These assignments in their way were creative, not running errands or baby-sitting, and I wasn't being agreeable, eager, kissypoo for *them*. Helping me, in whatever roundabout way, by helping *them* seems to have been in my bones. It's too soon to talk about saying no . . . "I'm crazed, swamped, dying, or I just don't want to do it." Have to learn to say yes a lot before you get to say no.

It's up to You

"We're all we've got," Tony Brown, the superb black radio-television host, told a large lecture hall audience of black *and* white people recently. He was explaining what his people had to get into their heads. "Ain't nobody going to do it *for* you, you've only got yourselves." We . . . you and I . . . are all *we've* got. I learned that early— would have adored having a little help with the old inadequate self grappling with problems, but basically it's *your* deal—or more accurately your responsibility—to play the cards you were dealt if we're using the old card-game analogy . . . I would add this amplification to Tony's advice. Don't expect a rich husband, talent-scout, Lotto jackpot win to fix up your life. They don't, but *you* gradually *can*. Oh, God, I'm so intense and sanctimonious . . . and so right!

Exquisite Listening

Do you want to be the beloved, precious-darling-pampered-adored one of a man and hold him forever? *Listen* to him. Of course, he has to be in your life for you to do all that listening. You can't bring him to your side by being a great little compulsive listener if Cindy Crawford is at the same party and you haven't met him yet. Never mind what men say about looks—not even in their top five in surveys when asked what they value most in a woman—looks *matter*, they just don't say so publicly. Okay, whether you're a smasher, a runner-up, or only B-list, let's say you've now got somebody in your life you would like to have like you above all others. Listen. Listen savagely. Yes, a plain girl with charm who likes men and sex can do this better than anybody. Are you paying attention? This is something I know something about.

Haven't you ever heard that serious listening is a major attraction of mistresses, even temporary paid companions, in a married man's life? "It isn't the sex so much," says Buster of the attractive woman he sees daily who isn't his wife. "The sex is good but she *listens* . . . I can talk my brains out. Sometimes we don't even *have* sex, we just talk" (i.e., Buster talks). Talking by men is said to go on a lot in traditional Japanese geisha houses or places where the man pays for sex—part of the prix fixe—and the lady of the evening happily complies if asked but often isn't asked . . . he just wants deep listening like a deep soak in one of those shoulder-high wooden tubs in a lovely Japanese inn.

Whatever the man (yours) wants to talk about is fine but could one suggest his earlier life, especially military service if he's been there? You cannot *not* endear yourself to a participator in World War II, Korea, or Vietnam by asking "Were you in charge of anything? Who was the commanding officer? What did you *do* all day?" Some of your male companions will be too young to have participated in war but, like you, they have had early-life experiences to probe. "You fell out of a canoe at Camp Wanahatchie?" "You caddied for rich Uncle Bart?" "What did you people do at Christmas?" In terms of *now*, if the subject is his business and it probably will be, you don't have to understand every word he utters, just grasp enough to keep asking questions; read newspapers and other source material so you can ask more the next time. Voluptuous, rich-chocolate fudge, "I never heard anything so wonderful as what you're telling me" attentiveness is what we're after here—seamless raptness. Important: do *not* match his stories with your own no matter how tempting. We're not talking equal rights, we're talking total surrender (his). Your stories can be heard by girlfriends, office mates, a shrink. This is "There isn't anybody in the world like my baby, she finds me *fascinating!*" time. P.S. Don't bother with accusing me of manipulation. We're listening because good men are scarce and we want a lovely one to adore *you*.

Attention Attracter

To be heard, you lower your voice. Takes concentration to do that and your mind can't be swamped thinking about important things you plan to say or you'll never remember pitch, but with a friend or in not-serious dialogue you can try. I've been pitching lower lately and find it works. Getting good results. I don't mean lowering an octave as Lauren Bacall was said to have done for her initial screen role with Humphrey Bogart in *To Have or Have Not* but just coming down a little from your usual pitch. The effort sort of starts from your chest . . . you can tell from people's reaction you're easier to hear.

You Know So-And-So . . . He Was on
Meet the Press

When people ask if you're familiar with somebody—*anybody*—heart surgeon, crooked city official, stand-up comic, nuclear physicist, tennis pro, deposed CEO—I think even if you haven't a clue you still nod or say yes so inquirer can get on with his story. Somehow a flat-out "I *don't* know this person" closes the talker down, makes him feel less interesting. Fortunately, if you say or nod yes, you *are* familiar with whom they're talking about, they usually never come back for details. I did get caught recently when somebody said, "You know blank" and mentioned an obscure opera star. I said, "Sure," and they *said*, "What operas have you seen her in?" Betrayed! Somebody with more chutzpah would have said, "Too many to mention." I took the cowardly way out and said, "Tell me *your* favorites." Usually you aren't asked. Conversation moves right along to another place and you're home free.

Take My Expert, Please

Everybody wants credit for *his* recommendation of dermatologist, hairdresser, trainer, travel agent, veterinarian, caterer. After you've gone to the trouble to scare up the name and address, you want them *used*. Mary Kelly and I are going to have a face-off one of these days when Charlotte Veal makes up her mind about an acupuncturist. She asked both Mary and me for a recommendation. Mary says *hers* does all the ankles of the ballerinas at American Ballet Theater and knees of the New York Jets. Pardon me, but acupuncturist is an *Asian* art and *mine* does Japanese and Taiwanese diplomats at the U.N., an occasional visiting head of state. Charlotte will be choosing pretty soon and *one* of her connections—the rejected one—is going to be pissed. Don't ask 'em this stuff if you're just browsing. I'm about to stop doing *any* recommendations on spec.

On the other hand, I'm wildly enthusiastic about several recommendations *received*. *Vogue*'s former executive editor Ruth Manton told me about magical Norman Orentreich, the dermatologist who, among other innovations, pioneered hair transplants and who has now been fluffing, plumping, scraping, abraiding, laserbrasioning my skin for thirty years. Silicone, in case you don't know this, is inserted with a long, thin hypodermic needle (I don't look!) to erase lines between nose and mouth—mine would be deep by now. Silicone, in equally miniscule amounts, can also free lines in temple, chin, forehead; now there's also magical botox to help. I love what Norman does to my upper lip—smoother, fuller. When silicone was illegal (it's back again, thank God!) Dr. O. substituted plasma gel—blood is extracted, boiled as you waited, and inserted with a needle just like silicone—fairly effective but not *as*.

As I wrote Norman in a letter years ago, I think his cosmetic improvements are part of what enlightened medicine and doctors are all about; see him or another good dermatologist and *feel* better because you *look* better—your whole body has to cheer up. Dermabrasion—lightly abraiding the skin with steel wool; an electrical current passes through in order to remove acne scars—I had in 1976. Pleased with results. Laserbrasion I had in 1998. With this procedure you also get skinned—top layer (yes, with a general anesthetic!), in the doctor's office—less bleeding than with dermabrasion. Norman's son David is the laser genius. Result: fine lines not reachable by silicone went bye-bye. I looked better for five minutes but my skin is so fragile I was never the best prospect for laser help; waxy skin is better. I see Norman four or five times a year; use his soap, moisturizer, makeup with sunscreen, rehabilitation creme. We've excised skin cancer—California sun-baked girls tend to have that. Dear Norman. As I often tell him, I would throw myself under a train if he told me to.

More friend recommendations. At age forty because officemate/friend Marilyn Hart's new nose job looked sensational, I went right off to her Beverly Hills surgeon, Dr. Michael Gurdin, and had rhinoplasty (nose job). During the procedure, under local anasthesia, I sobbed so incessantly—not always the brave, intrepid little lamb—Dr. Gurdin said if I didn't quiet down, he would send me back to my room. I quieted. You don't want to have to get up the courage *twice*. A bump was removed, nose made smaller, very pretty. Nineteen years later during blephorplasty (eyes) with Dr. Michael Hogan—recommended by a male coworker who looked twenty years younger after surgery—I hummed so incessantly, again under local anesthesia, Dr. H. said I was interfering with his concentration—could I maybe internalize the hums? I could. Two-hours-for-the-upper-and-two-hours-for-lower later, we have removed puffs, folds, other surplus—I'm happy again, procedure still holding.

My first rhytidectomy (facelift) at age sixty, was again with Dr. Hogan. Because of having been treated with X rays for acne as a teenager several Saturdays in a row in five-minute sessions—those crazy people *did* that then, now a dental technician covers your body with a metal blanket and scrams out of the room while doing mouth X rays that last two seconds each—my skin was permanently damaged, made thin and fragile. Norman says it's a wonder I *have* any chin. Because of skin fragility Dr. Hogan was super-conservative. I'm sure we have to bless him for that, though, my after was not too different from my before. Seven years later I had another lift with Dr. Hogan, again not dramatic but some improvement. In 1995 when I was having breast augmentation (I told you about that) with Dr. Sherrell Aston, recommended by an off-lifted beautiful friend as the ultimate for *any* cosmetic procedure (Dr. Hogan had retired), I had another tiny lift. We hope the little rascal holds for awhile, it's already been five years. What about the pain endured with these procedures? Sorry, I can't remember any. I'm sure there *was* some—not during surgery, you're dead—but during healing. After all, you've been cut and sutured for several hours but physical pain is hard to call up again, thanks goodness—emotional pain "easier."

Am I glad I had all these procedures? Would I tell you if I weren't? Yes to both questions. Pricey, very pricey, but hardly any cosmetic surgeon isn't booked into the millenium—other applicants as enthusiastic as I. Catty but reasonable question: With all that stuff that's been done, why don't I look better? I don't *know* why I don't! The surgeons did the best they could with what they had to work with, I'm sure, and I *am* seventy-eight. Isn't it possible that without the surgery I would look even worse? I think so. I don't understand people unwilling to acknowledge a single thing having been done to their countenances. You don't have to take out an ad, but what's so shameful about medical science being invoked to help you look not quite as old as you are? Cosmetic surgery isn't natural? Neither is cancer surgery (cancer *itself* is natural). Boulder Dam storing up all that water to make electricity, *not* picking up a brick to bash somebody who is being dumb and mean . . . these occurrences—or nonoccurrences—are unnatural, while sweat, smallpox, dandruff, and a raging temper are natural as rain. Maybe "unnatural" doesn't deserve such a bad rap.

Dr. Aston says, "For the majority of individuals the thought of growing old is not a pleasant one. For the aging individual cosmetic surgery helps make the transition from a more youthful stage of life to an older one more graceful and acceptable, but these procedures aren't *just* for vain older ladies. For the younger person who has not been blessed with the best of features (large nose, receding chin, small breasts), cosmetic surgery can change not only appearance but give the individual a new self-image and confidence that can't be obtained in any other way. Rhinoplasty is often performed on girls at age fifteen or sixteen . . . as soon as the hormones have settled in; boys have to wait a bit longer to get rid of a major nose bump as *their* hormones don't arrive or settle as fast." Says Dr. Aston, "Cosmetic surgery has really become an art form of the late twentieth century and will no doubt continue. Plastic surgeons have truly become sculptors of the living flesh . . . a medium that is nonforgiving . . . i.e., you can't make a mistake and do it over." I don't want *any* of mine done over! I'm glad I got such good doctor recommendations from friends.

Include Them In

When saying something heavily complimentary about a member of the same sex as the one you are talking to, you'd better remember to say every so often "Aside from *you*, or except for *you*, of course," as in, "I never saw anybody handle a meeting better or be more charming, more beautiful, smarter, wittier, funnier—except for *you*, of course." People don't like to hear you rave and rave if the compliments are in an area where the talked-to-person might possibly fit.

Writing Letters to Writers

Why am I telling you this? Because I'm crazy, that's why. Usually stuff I tell you there's plenty to go around but, in this case, if you're doing what I recommend all over the place, my doing it won't be as effective. I can't resist.

Suggestion: In writing to an author or columnist or whoever writes that you want to compliment, quote back some of his words in your letter—not whole paragraphs or blocks of text but selected laces. "Adored your book. When you said (blah, blah, blah), the rice boiled over, the phone went unanswered, I didn't breathe for an hour." He'll love reading his words back—you don't have to say a great deal else in your letter except you also loved his last book but this is *better*. The plan never misses for me—I get a fan letter *back*. "Dear Henry . . . I'm so knocked out . . . you made me *feel* 'that night at the end of the United States' ordeal.' You said 'When the cease-fire was signed even the pessimists did not foresee that final, ghastly tableau two years later when the last American helicopter took off from the roof of the U.S. embassy in Saigon with Vietnamese desperately hanging on to the craft as it lifted slowly away from the scene of America's worst defeat.'" I *know* I'll be hearing from this man.

I've written elsewhere that nothing is more welcome by anyone at any *time* than a playful, loving, appreciative handwritten note. Bryant Gumbel, host of CBS's *Early Show*, a passionate note-writer, seals the envelope, dribbles on warm wax, pushes one of his personalized seals into the wax so you get both something warm (the note . . . wax is now cold) and colorful (the seal). Nice. I type everything but instructions for the cab driver but plan to try this handwritten note, wax, and seal proposition soon.

Good Gifts

Want to be in somebody's thoughts a lot? Give him or her, if he reads—and all good people read—a great bookmark. I've been given lots through the years. My favorite is a small 2½" × 2" filigreed gold marker from the Metropolitan Museum shop that slips down on the page you're reading. If somebody reads every day, the bookmark makes you think of the person who gave it to you at least *once* a day and happily. It has to be a *super* marker because bookmarks aren't expensive to produce and tacky ones abound. Another good gift to get yourself thought about is a backrest pillow you can lean against while reading. This present-giver will be thought about every time you lie back to read your book (with the bookmark in it). ABC News correspondent Cynthia McFadden gave me a backrest pillow for my birthday two years ago. Though I adore her and we are friends, I only *see* her about four times a year. I *think* about her every night. My friend Tony says don't give his mother (89) anything she can't eat or sleep with. Sounds sensible.

Gifts for Sick People

When somebody is in the hospital, home from, or having a bad time health-wise, I don't think you should ask if there's anything you can do, anything you can send over. The answer to the first question is no, he is dying. If you could ease the pain, lower the fever, make him frisky, he'd be grateful but, since you can't, forget asking. Regarding what to send over, this sick person is not going to say, "Oh, yes, a tub of Häagen-Dazs, a six-pack of Miller's, dinner from the Four Seasons, two dozen Greenberg's brownies." His or her weak pitiful voice is going to say, "No, nothing . . . thanks for asking" and, unsaid, "Asshole!" The classy thing to do—the *only* thing to do—is go ahead and send *something*.

A sick or recovering person cannot *have* too much attention paid even if he can hardly smile at the deliverer. All flowers and plants gratefully accepted. Though the room may be looking a bit like Frank Campbell already, the sick person laid out *in* it, somebody cared, attention was paid. Most people in hospitals or home from them are not on a liquid, squishy diet so food offerings are suitable. If they can't eat the food this minute, cookies and candy can be saved or offered to visitors. You might lie low with liquor or send with a card that says "For when you get all the way well." What we are pushing here for the sick is a little more action, commitment, and nonwimpiness, fewer fake offers.

Sleepless

Somebody smart told me no matter how many hours or days you've been without sleep, trying to make yourself sleep because it's *time* is as dumb as trying to force an erection. The penis either will or won't as it sees fit, *possibly* if you, with or without a penis, just lie there, sleep will come. Why am I bringing up sleeplessness? I can sleep standing up . . . with mosquitoes under the net *with* me. I'm grateful. In case *you* have trouble dropping off, here's a word game so boring you'll sleep just to quit *playing*. Go down the alphabet and think of a three-syllable word for every letter (I cheat and leave out Q, X, Y, Z). After you've done three syllables a night or two, move on to four syllables or even five syllables. Not thinking about anything serious *is* soporific. Second game, a little more complex. Go down the alphabet and for each letter, think of something that happened to you that day. A—anxiety attack; B—bus, bridgework came out, banana; C—chocolate chip cookies; D—dance class; E—exercise; F—Florence visited, etc., etc. I usually use first names of people in my life that day rather than last, but whatever you wish. Happy snoozing.

Investing

Want some financial advice? A rich girlfriend—doesn't want her name mentioned—has given me her excellent guidelines for selecting stocks. I was astonished to know she "*ran* her own money," as they say. Arriving at marriage with a lot of it, she became a traditional wife and mother, never held a paying job (worked for charity). Her husband, a financial genius others consult, was never asked the first question about money by his bride. These are the commonsense rules by which she has done really well. One picked stock after her first visit to the store a few years ago was the Gap.

Rules

1. Try to understand what the company or product is and does.
2. Product must be needed and useful . . . a necessity in people's lives.
3. If possible, product should be something that didn't exist before so that now it can fill a need.
4. Product can't be seasonal . . . must be as wanted in July as in December.
5. Product and company should be important ten years from now, not a fad item or company.

Senior Citizen Compassion

Don't send anybody over fifty a picture of himself or herself that isn't flattering even if it's the only picture he or she will ever have of himself on your Lake Minnetonka vacation. Unlike a tactless remark or migraine, you can't get over a bad picture. Use discipline. Throw the pic in the trash.

TV Guest Alert

Asked a question by host or commentator, you shouldn't respond "Well . . ." then into your story. Starting the sentence, and many after that, with "Well" means you're an amateur. "Well" takes just a split second to say but a pro dives right in. Once you start noticing, you'll see nearly *everybody* starts his or her story with "Well." Don't you do that.

Other clean-up-your-TV-act ideas for a guest:

Come out and *say* what you want to say—brisk, meaty, concise. Talk *crisply*. Rehearse ahead of time the beginning, middle, and end to each of your thoughts . . . add a little later in the show if appropriate.

Don't plop in "you know" every two sentences—young people do that.

No *giggling*.

Yes, you *must* interrupt if another guest on the panel is usurping all the time and you can't get on. I've been usurped lots and never got to be a skillful interrupter, but TV-guesting is not for sissies. Anybody could well practice with Dr. Ruth Westheimer, the dearest, smartest, and most articulate of them all—but you have to jump *in*!

Not to Say to a Celebrity

Barbara Walters told me somebody stopped her on the street the other day when she was getting into a cab and said, "Oh, Miss Walters, you look so much more beautiful in person!" "This is supposed to be a compliment?" asks the interviewer. "I make my living in television, we work hard to get me to look good on camera. Have we failed?" Of course not. She looks divine on *The View* and 20/20. (I'd kill to have the makeup and hair help proffered Ms. Walters daily at ABC but she started *out* good.) Commenting on a civilian's looks, I think it's better to tell them, "Madonna looks like you," than "You look like Madonna." Make the star *your* person.

Straightening Up

To clean out a drawer, you have to dump everything—stockings, handkerchiefs, lingerie, knives, can openers, spatulas, pencils, clips, plastic spoons—out on the floor, no halfmeasures will do. If you start reaching in selectively—"I'll toss this metal cork that never keeps opened wine fresh anyway, this Yves St. Laurent scarf I've hated fifteen years," you might as well skip the straightening. To be organized like a crack surgical team and decide what you're really going to need to sustain life, you have to get it all out on the floor at one time.

Okay, I seem to have got everything out on the floor from my life and my brain for this book, have you found it messy? I do so hope not. Do you think I'll ever be able to get it all back in the drawer again? Maybe I won't even try.

Letter to My Daughter

Dear Anna Marie,

That isn't your real name, of course, because there isn't a real you. I don't have a daughter *or* a son, never wanted either and have no regrets this *minute* about not having one. Truth: why should I start lying *now*?

Once in a while I sort of wish I had someone to leave the family photo albums to. Dishes, silver, furniture, outsiders will be happy to cart away. Smith College has my manuscripts, papers, letters in the Sophia Smith Library, but who wants those thirty-five photo albums my invalid sister, Mary (presumably your aunt), and I put together through the years? Perhaps because of starting at age fifteen to help my mother with Mary—not a nurse but a dedicated helper—later needing to make money *always* to support them, I didn't want the responsibility of children. Whatever, I haven't a scrap of regret about kidlessness . . . maybe next lifetime. I do occasionally think about what I would *tell* a daughter if I had one and she were sitting on the hassock, me on the floor or the other way around, and we were talking. What could I say to her to keep her off drugs, make her reach *way* out for life, get her to accept herself totally, *have* a *wonderful* life? Whatever I told her wouldn't be so she could have a *better* life than *me*. Some parents get themselves all worked up about giving the kids money, position, college educations, tennis courts, things *they* never had. Except for the college education—kids often need help there—I would say forget it! I would want you to have as *good* as life as mine, better it doesn't need to be. So I'm going to fantasize that I *have* a daughter (I've named you Anna Marie), that we are visiting here in our apartment and these are few things I would say to you as we are sitting side by side.

Ready?

TOPIC ONE: LIKING YOURSELF

It's important to like, respect, even love yourself. You hear a lot about self-esteem these days, or lack of. When I was little, the subject wasn't yet in vogue so I didn't hear a *thing*, certainly not from my mother, but now self-esteem is *hot* and a *very* good idea. How do you get it? In books that I write I always emphasize *work* as the big esteem-bringer . . . undoubtedly why your mother (me) is such a workaholic. Do something good, better than others, and the esteem—*theirs* for you and *yours* for you—comes pouring in. Of course, you're also supposed to like yourself just for *being*, all God's children are equal, etc. Your mother doesn't believe in God (you'll decide this matter for yourself) but I do believe in the okayness of everybody here on earth; we *are* equal. Screw it up later yourself and you may not *be* equal any longer but basic you starts out just fine . . . *everybody* does. I don't think you need to recite a nightly mantra . . . I'm okay, I'm *okay*, you bastards! (Mother's language is frequently colorful) to keep self-esteem firmly planted, it's just *there*.

When you were a little girl, I would have told you you were pretty, smart, gifted, funny, I wouldn't have let *up* whether these things were true or not . . . I think parents should lay it on with a trowel! I would have encouraged you to follow your heart and instincts toward what interested you, some of which wouldn't amount to much—making mud pies, making *real* cookies with Mommy with extra pecans—some of which might *lead* somewhere. From a serious commitment to bugs, you might become a famous entomologist with the world making a fuss over you and paying you well. Got it? Basic you is okay and then you find other stuff to enhance the okayness.

BEAUTY

You are beautiful *enough*. Your grandmother (my mother) pretty much convinced me I *wasn't* (beautiful enough) and would need to use whatever brain I had to attract life's blessings. I wish she hadn't done that . . . you spend years trying to be more smashing without ever feeling you've smashed! Of course, a few careless words from others than mothers can corroborate a poor evaluation of one's looks. The boy next to you in botany class can rave about the class beauty, Eloise, a few seats away . . . wow, is she sensational, wow, would every guy in class like to date her . . . men can be idiots at a tiny age. In my own life later, looking at pictures of myself during those warning-from-mom years, I gleaned that I actually looked perfectly okay and didn't need to be so looks-worried but her assessment sunk in and never really left town. Studies reveal that beautiful male *and* female people do get hired more quickly, are considered more trustworthy, paid better, can secure seats on a sold-out flight to the Bahamas, etc. Let's be real. What's inside counts *most* but what's outside gets *noticed* first and if it's a little dismal, you may not make it to the get-acquainted stage. Anna Marie, if you had bad skin, nose with a big bump, protruding teeth, receding chin, really obvious facial flaws, we'd get them fixed, of course (while I *still* emphasized to you that you were otherwise *pretty!*).

When a woman gets to be thirty or so—not your age group yet—I think she should consider having a dermatologist in her life so together they can start fighting age marks. Some say these marks are character indicators. I say bullshit! (That language problem again!) Your mommy has been accused of being a little "superficial," even antinature by preaching not letting flab creep up on you, not letting sex disappear when you're older. If those things are antinature and superficial I'm Saran Wrap! Getting older *isn't* a disgrace or millions of us fortunate enough to *get* older (a little soon for you to contemplate) would have to be considered disgraceful! Not *looking* older than you need to seems sensible to me. Okay, I want you to like yourself (a) just for *being*, and (b) guiltlessly try to look as good as you can all your life by consulting doctors, dermatologists, dentists, specialists, applying all the great beauty and hair products—some are sensational—out there with your own talented hands and frisky ten fingers several days a week.

POSTURE

Something my mother (your grandmother) never told *me* and I wish she *had* . . . sit up straight, stand up straight, posture, posture, *posture!* I'm trying to get the lousy posture fixed this very *minute* and it's tough. Why would I bother so *late*? Because good posture can make more difference in how you look than virtually anything else you can do at *any* age—shoulders back, pelvis tucked in, don't bother with stomach, the pelvis-tuck will flatten it. If back and buttocks are positioned correctly, your head will do the right thing too—can't droop forward. Right this minute a rubber band is around my wrist to remind me to remember . . . sit up straight, posture, posture! You, little pushkin, have been told *now*, and earlier in this book, soon *enough*, that posture is worth every boring moment you spend remembering. I'm not going to mention other beauty procedures. You'll create your own but none, except maybe washing your face every night, is more important than this one.

FASHION

Fashion is silly. Unequivocally, unconditionally *silly* . . . always was and always will be. Fashion is putting new stuff on your body and feet every year, even every season, based on what "they"—people who make a lot of money telling you to do it and you *do* it—suggest. Well, as silly as fashion is—toes are pointy, no toes are straight *across* this season, hems must touch ankles or calves, no hems are up to the crotch, turquoise is a laugh, kelly is schlock, magenta is disgusting, black is the only acceptable "color" for all occasions. Anybody under forty wearing black when *I* was a girl was thought to be trying to look like her grandmother, a sixteen-year-old wouldn't wear black even to a funeral, a grown woman might have *one* "little black dress,"—see how silly fashion is! As I write this, the only acceptable "colors" this summer are white, ivory, beige, sand, off-white, maybe one pink dress for a daring fashion fling—is that ridiculous? Yet, Anna Marie, your mother thinks fashion is to be taken seriously, even if it is often ludicrous. Why? Because it's fun! Draping or shoeing yourself in different designs and colors every so often makes you feel frisky and new. Picking the outfits is enjoyable . . . follow or don't follow trends though you may have trouble finding anything in the stores that isn't "current." Paying for the purchase isn't such a pleasure—cashmere sweater set is *edging* toward the down payment on a BMW. Nevertheless, I want you to enjoy, indulge, go too far, have too much, never never *never* be sensible. If you have a favorite color even if it's "passe," cocoon yourself if it pleases you. Mine happens to be pink . . . aren't I the lucky one, pink right this moment is *hot*!

BAD STUFF

Grief and sorrow are sometimes our companions, go along with *being* here. Poet Robert Frost said, "Life is a painted piece of trouble." That bad? Well, anybody who didn't experience grief and sorrow sometimes would be brain-dead. If someone acts as though he or she *doesn't* feel it—denial, denial, denial—that person is asking for depression or other unpleasant consequences. I have no scintillating thoughts about getting through sorrow except to hope the big grief isn't something you brought on *yourself* like doing drugs. No, you wouldn't do that, Anna Marie, you couldn't possibly be a daughter of mine and do drugs! We'd have a little infanticide around here before I'd let addiction happen.

For consolation I've never found that remembering "This, too, shall pass"—next week, next month, next *year* present trouble will be missing in action—does a bit of good. If pain persists too long, happiness highway all clogged (you like that metaphor? Okay, I didn't think you would), I am big on shrink help—hope there are shrinks around should you need one. They don't solve problems but they *listen* and ask enough questions to start you changing—and healing.

BAD STUFF—SPECIAL DIVISION

Some not-*serious* bad stuff we do to ourselves, not on purpose, of course, but just ditzy or tired. First thing you know you've dropped a major piece of Chinese export china on the tiled kitchen floor, stepped off the curb into an icy patch of street and fractured your knee. Yes, you will be real mad at yourself but you mustn't be forever. My dearly beloved accountant, Red Meyer, used to tell David, my husband (probably your father), and me that in life there is *breakage* . . . write it off. In high school I broke two front teeth coming down a hill on a borrowed sled, plowed right into a bench at the bottom. Replacing teeth took weeks of after-school root canal work on the remaining teeth which were hit hard, casting and fitting caps with money we didn't have. If only, if *only* I hadn't borrowed that sled, I kept crying into my pillow though dentist said sleep on my *back*.

Grown up, I lose real jewelry. I left a multifaceted sapphire, ruby, emerald David Webb brooch in a taxi in San Francisco, never recovered, next year left diamond and emerald earrings in Kleenex (they hurt my ears and I took them off and put them in Kleenex) in the ladies' room of the Plaza Hotel, later retrieved but reward could have bought a Ford Taurus. Pain. Pain. Pain.

Listen, little tootsie, I want you to be a little more self-forgiving than me, less anguished about the breakage you yourself cause as well as that caused by others. Maybe you'll be a better sledder than I was and won't have accidents or you'll have more real jewelry sooner than I did and won't ache so much when it disappears. I don't know that it's realistic to expect *not* to be distressed about losses. Red Meyer didn't say *not* to be, he said just don't hang on to the pain too long after the breakage has happened.

ALL THAT GOOD STUFF OF *THEIRS*

Later in your life—you won't know these people yet—some of the most successful people in the world may be your friends or at least in your field. They are going to have bad things happen to them like you couldn't have *invented* and you know what? These tragedies *still* won't obliterate your aggravation about their success . . . that unpleasant twinge when you see one more smash television show of theirs, read one more profile in *Vanity Fair*. Not to feel put down a *little* by the sparkly, fabulous glitteriness of friends would be unnatural, not a *possibility* for us, particularly if they are doing something like us in the way of a job. Anna Marie, you will treat them with affection, brag about knowing them, but the oh-shit feeling possibly will continue. Others may envy *you*, of course. Pretty and bright and, as of this moment, *young*; older people (our sex) could *kill* you for these things but their envy doesn't help either. Occasionally schaddenfreud, that unmistakable feeling of pleasure on hearing about the misfortune of a friend will bring a smile. Are you a monster? No, you're my daughter and human. Prediction: Your own success will frequently make you happy, yes, *happy*, screw their goddamn success!

P.S. Frank McCourt, brilliant author of *Angela's Ashes*, says envy is like taking poison and waiting for the other person to die. How accurate!

LOVE

Cats and doggies, shiny early-April mornings, Picasso and Puccini, melted cheese on a toasted crumpet and, yes of course, the man you're all squidgy about and a few you aren't squidgy about but love very much just the same . . . so many different *things* to love. Anna Marie, you mustn't ever be too stingy (or careful) about love. It's okay to get it up (naughty expression having to do with a man creating a serious-enough erection to make love but appropriate here) for many objects, and often. Some of your loves will be *passions*; no matter how inappropriate others think they are, pay no attention whatever. As for the big love for a man and the big man to bestow it on, I would wish you more than one and guess what? One of these Big Ones might be married, not to you; he wants the marriage *and* you . . . *yikes!* Crazytime to get involved? Not necessarily. Him a selfish beast? Again, not necessarily. His adoration may be massive as it gets, your sex together a miracle. At some point, of course, he will have to be moved away from . . . you deserve exclusivity . . . I'm just saying although love, even *big* love, may not always be "appropriate," I don't think that makes you a murderess *or* an exploited kitten.

All through the tremendous furor about Monica Lewinsky's affair with President Clinton people asked me if Monica was a *Cosmo* girl. Yes, I said, she could have been. *Cosmo* women get involved with married men and sometimes, regrettably, fall in love with them. I think wives are responsible for keeping their husbands home—if possible. They may not be keepable and I personally never faulted Monica for what she did. Many young women in her place would have done the same thing if they could have. Where I said she couldn't be a *Cosmo* girl was having a creepy girlfriend like Linda Tripp. A bona fide *Cosmo* girl is too bright to fool around with such treacherous jerks. After the hullabaloo was over and Monica's book was a success, I wished she had gone for a lower profile. She got more un-*Cosmo* by the minute as I watched her still hankering for the limelight. Limelight is sweeter when you do something admirable to deserve it.

Now back to *your* love life, child. There may be crazy lush love for a man *not* wife-encumbered, but there's something the matter with *him* (or even *them* if you don't marry early). He makes you doubt your beauty and self-worth . . . doesn't give *all* of himself. There may even be other women . . . "mulitples" are ego-shatterers.

My darling child, magical sex does not always show up attached to the right man. When this person and his magical sex get too "expensive"—too many tears, blues, lonesomeness, too often feeling angry and taken for granted, the pain outweighing the pleasure, the *single* magic man will have to go, too, just like the married one. I do want to suggest that every sexual encounter in your life doesn't have to be a major one and I actually hope, after you know he isn't HIV positive, you are not *too* choosy (downright finicky) about sex partners. As a young person nobody would want you to be pushed, pressured, or intimidated into sex. You need to get your sexual bearings but later, all grown up, it may occur to you as it did to me that men are *not* villains because they want us "that way." Some of us actually think of being wanted "that way" as a compliment! Sex is so intimate, do we really suppose *all* men want *all* women just because we have that place between our legs? Men have to give *more* in sexual intercourse, exert the big energy, give *all* (men can't fake) possibly have you *judge* them by performance—embarrassing! I just can't think a man is a villain because he has the hots for you, the feeling reciprocated or not.

You prefer not to be horizontal unless "it's Big Time and he's Perfect"? Come, come, my darling. A little disappointing sex—nice person but you aren't making it together—won't blemish your life or exacerbate your sinus condition. Whomever you are having sex with on a regular basis and you aren't quite in the mood, I suggest you have sex anyway. Do *you* like rejection? Yes, you may fake an orgasm. Pretty obvious I guess that your mother (me) was always boy-crazy, starting at age six, and I think that's just fine. At some point along will come Mr. Right—cliché designation but appropriate. He will be a *good* man, delicious in bed but also kind, gentle, smart, mad about *you*. Grab him. You'll need to read Mommy's books to find out how to do that.

Marry only for love? Some people think marrying for *wealth* isn't a bad idea, after all, wealthy people can also be *attractive*. As a wide-eyed little person, twenty-four years old, working at Loeb and Loeb, a prestigious law firm in Los Angeles, I was one who thought such a thing and one day asked my boss, Paul Ziffren, one of the powerful attorneys in the firm, if he could help. Marrying rich, I explained, might be a good way to solve a lot of problems for my wheelchair-bound sister and not-too-far-from-penniless mother. Many of the firm's clients were fat cats, I pointed out. Perhaps he could select one for me. Mr. Z. looked searchingly at me, though he didn't need to search that hard, we saw each other all day long and he knew exactly what I looked like: scrawny and cute, not pretty. "Helen," he said, "the kind of man you are thinking of, seriously rich, can marry anybody he wants to—a movie star, famous fashion model, heiress, somebody from a great family, her father a financial or political star—he isn't necessarily going to want to marry *you*, whatever your inclinations!" I was hurt but not massively, always pretty good at dealing with reality. I let Los Angeles tycoon Joe Drown, one of our clients who had just bought the Bel-Air Hotel, and one or two other "possibles" out of my sight and began (excerpt for a short period as a keptive) the "normal" romantic adventures that would finally lead me, twenty-two years later, to the terrific, *not* wealthy, man I would marry. To sum up, I wish you a rich *full* romantic life, even with its occasional pain and anguish. I don't want you going for safe and skimpy.

Anna Marie, I should point out the man you marry, when the time comes, will have a serious flaw, at least one. If the flaw were a tarpaulin, it would stretch all the way from the roof of the World Trade Center 110 floors down to the parking lot. If it were a ribbon, the flaw would wrap all the way around Eastern Europe. Nothing to worry about. You've got one or more big ones yourself—we all do. We don't know what yours are yet—you're too young to ascertain—but I don't think you need to obsess about them, nobody can improve herself to perfection. Let's just say if there isn't enough spiffy stuff about the man you plan to marry to make up for *his* flaw or flaws, then you'd best look for somebody else. If his spiffy stuff is pretty outstanding, you will live with his flaws as you both live with *yours*, okay?

MONEY

Money matters. Only a silly goose thinks it doesn't. Money will be your friend when other friends have left town, will help you keep your dignity and have fun when you're old. Yet some youngish people (you?) don't think money matters . . . it's going to be the days of wine and roses forever. Woody Allen and I were chatting about this the other night, he appalled, as I am, by young people who just float about refusing to get real about money—acquiring or growing it. "They don't think their pure beautiful souls should trifle with anything so crass," said the director. Though you shouldn't care *only* about money to the exclusion of joy and creativity. Don't be one of those sillies, Anna Marie. From a fairly early age, I hope you will put aside something from every paycheck. You do not have to have every life's indulgence this minute. Though I said fashion is okay to enjoy, fashion can be done on the cheap with imagination. So can decorating the flat, a used car is fine, St. Croix can wait till *next* year. I want you to read the business section of the paper. Study the stock market. Though I saved money, I never could get the hang of making money *make* money. If I hadn't married a smart (if penniless at the time, later good investor) person I'd be cooked and wouldn't have a sou to leave to *you*. We don't get snippy about money or it will get snippy about *us*.

To Keep from Going Nuts

With my genes, you may find yourself terminally bored with speeches, sermons, meetings when people go on too long, no sense whatever of their own nonfascinatingness. This is what you do: In your head pick a pair of letters—could be C and T, M and N, P and L, whatever. Go down the alphabet and find a word that contains *both* the letters you've picked. Let's say C and T. Okay, it's AttraCT, BaCTeria, CaT, DuCT, ExaCT, FaCT, GoTCha, HaTCh, etc. You don't have to pick two new letters each time you're bored, just use the old ones; I use the same ones over and over; making words also helps me go to sleep. Like this word game any better? See how many famous people, dead or alive, you can think of whose initials are M. M.—start with Marilyn Monroe. During boredom, you can also do your pelvic exercises (good for vaginal muscle tone). Retract your sphincter muscle, pull it up into your vagina, hold a moment, and let go. Repeat at least fifty times. You may still be bored but you won't be so fidgety and irritated . . . also good for love-making.

Okay, let's close down the conversation (though I'm doing most of the talking!) Rather early in your life I would hope you could start "getting it," receiving the *truth* of a scene or spoken words. With sensitive antennae—just like an insect, crab, lobster—you register what you've heard or seen, take it down to a secret compartment of yourself where hunches and intuition hang out, file what you've heard or seen, or possibly take action. "Getting it" is knowing when someone is talking bullshit or truth. Example: "Your screenplay is terrific—several people here like it—but we aren't making Civil War movies just now." Truth: "Nobody read your screenplay, or we read it and think it's terrible."

Man/woman example: "You're the most fascinating person I've ever met but I think we should take our time searching each other out, finding all the truths about each other. Let's move quietly, deliberately." Truth: He doesn't want to see you as often as you want to see *him*. "Getting it" can mean sizing up an *occasion* . . . determining whether the party is really to honor an illustrious guest or collect spiffy people the host can hit later for his charity. Anna Marie, these are rather sophisticated examples for somebody young and tender. "Getting it" in your case now would simply mean listening carefully, letting your instincts tell you what's really going on. Eventually the talent can apply to one's personal capabilities. David's longtime associate Pamela Hedley says our capacity for self-delusion is infinite but people who "get it" don't self-delude. You can be realistic about your shortcomings, however, "get it," and still fly to the moon.

What other qualities do I wish for you? Empathy . . . knowing what it's like for *them*. It isn't enough just to listen, give pats and hugs but think they are nuts. They may *be* nuts, and if pats and hugs are all you can offer, fine, but *feeling* what he or she feels is what makes you beloved or at least not perceived as a fathead. Want somebody to do something—we are all selling all the time. Send in the empathy! How is your pitch registering? Why would they want to do what you ask? Your need isn't sufficient to get a yes answer, their selfish interest may *be*. If there is no reason for a yes *except* your need, better say that, too. "I need you to do this. You've got a million other things on your mind but I'm hoping you will blah, blah, blah, blah." You are empathizing with how they will perceive your request. Do be succinct, practice ahead of time if necessary . . . empathize with their capacity for *boredom*!

Emotional empathy: always be careful about telling somebody something that will hurt. "You missed a great party!" Was he even invited? Watch it with happy news about a rival's success . . . how is he going to feel when you announce Marv just got a three-book contract with Random House and a large advance? Maybe he should hear the news from somebody *else*. Can you *get* empathy if you haven't any? I think you can if you practice, practice . . . how is this coming across to *them*? What are they feeling? Empathy is different from sympathy which doesn't require your feeling a *thing*. Empathy means you're inside there *with* them. Famous oil painting of a woman in low-cut ball gown, a man's hand plunged down her dress, titled *Empathy*. Artist, asked to explain title says, "Simple. Fellow feeling in the bosom of a friend." Oh Anna Marie, you don't deserve this foolishness!!

Speaking of getting people to do things, they actually love to do things for you, they really do. The doing brings *them* more pleasure, it sometimes seems, than it does *us*. Why is that? Maybe the act shows how smart they are, how resourceful and enterprising or maybe they just plain love us and want to see us happy. The doing can come not from intimates, however, but just people. Whatever causes folks to get such pleasure from giving I'm frequently overwhelmed by it. So will you be.

What else do I want for you or want to tell you? I would hope that you have a well-furnished mind; start creating one now. Just keep pouring stuff in from good books, good conversations (you might not even take part but just listen to the smart ones), newspaper reading, television viewing. You can't be interested in and absorb *everything* (A GONORRHEA VACCINE IS TESTED IN MICE, REVIVING THE QUEST TO TAME THE ENERGY OF STARS) but I don't want you ever to stop stoking.

Another big want of any mother for her child . . . can there *be* a bigger want? Health! You can surely contribute with exercise. I ought to let you wait until later if you wish—I was forty before getting seized—but hope you'll sign up sooner. Truest of truths: you *can* mould your own body, it has to do what you tell it to. If I could wish you one physical accomplishment (I don't have it) that would be tennis . . . dashing out there in your tennis whites meeting such nice people, but if you aren't a tennis whiz, maybe you'll get mother's ability to dance; crowd is less natty but you can show off Charlestoning just as well as acing and we're talking *serious* fun. Of course, once you start exercising, you'll do something on a regular basis . . . regular and *relentless*. Whatever exercise speaks to you, speak right back! Oh dear, nobody has yet said a word about caring for the human race, being good to other people, particularly those less fortunate. Philanthropy is part of liking yourself, Anna Marie; you'll find the cause to which you want to dedicate your zeal and money—I trust you. Last thing I want you to know, pussycat. Calories count . . . every baby one of the little bastards, in chicken salad and carrot juice as in crème brulee and dark chocolate mints. Don't ever rationalize that *any* of them missed the boat!

Sleepy? You've been a great listener. I love you.